Bible White Papers

A Collection of Topical Theological Essays

Charlie Edwards, PhD, ThD

BIBLE WHITE PAPERS
Published by Edwards Ministries, Inc., Chattanooga, TN

Copyright © 2013 Charlie Edwards
All rights reserved.
ISBN: 978-0-9914146-1-1

Other books by Charlie Edwards:
Caribbean Sentinel (novel) Tate Publishing, Inc.
Church PA System Handbook, Edwards Ministries, Inc.
Published in the United States of America.

DEDICATION

This book is dedicated to the ministries of two preachers who made a significant impact early in my Christian experience. Both of these men stood tall in the area of Bible exegesis. Their sermons and books were a great encouragement and challenge for me to read, meditate on, and seek to understand the word of God. These men were not perfect, but in spite of their weaknesses they bore much fruit. Paul wrote, **"Therefore I take pleasure in infirmities, in reproaches, in necessities, in persecutions, in distresses for Christ's sake: for when I am weak, then am I strong"** (2 Cor. 12:10). Just as these men were imperfect, this writer claims no measure of perfection for this collection of Theological papers. It is, however, my desire to see the Holy Spirit use these white papers to challenge the reader to go beyond the place in their walk with God where reading the Bible is a duty or a chore. There is a point where it becomes a delight. It can become something that you look forward to! What does God have for me today – hidden in these passages? Psm. 119:24, **"Thy testimonies also *are* my delight *and* my counsellers."** Psm. 119:103, **"How sweet are thy words unto my taste! *yea, sweeter* than honey to my mouth!"** Psm. 119:163, **"I hate and abhor lying: *but* thy law do I love."** Psm. 119:174, **"I have longed for thy salvation, O LORD; and thy law *is* my delight."**

I would also like to dedicate this book to Gloria, who is my best friend, lover, spouse, proof reader, encourager, and co-laborer in ministry. Thank you for understanding the Melancholy in the area of Inclusion. I love you!

CONTENTS

Cover design by Charlie Edwards.

All Scripture references are from the Authorized Version.

INTRODUCTION

The word of God is the most fascinating book in existence. It was written by men, **"…holy men of God spake *as they were* moved by the Holy Ghost."** (2 Pet. 1:21). In other words, the Bible was written by God, but He used mortal men to actually pen the words. The word of God is the final authority for everything, including science, philosophy, all the "isms," and all the "ologies." It is infallible and God-breathed. It is eternal and infinite. It could not have possibly been authored by man. It says, "…**verily every man at his best state *is* altogether vanity"** (Psm. 39:5). No mortal man would write that. The same God that wrote it promised to preserve it for all generations (Psm. 12:7). Would God allow errors (by men) into His word? Of course not. If there were errors contained therein, it would cease to be His word. His preservation and perfection demand inerrancy. It contains the answers to all the real issues of life: Why do the righteous suffer? What is the meaning of life? Why would God allow such a horrible thing to happen? Why me? Why now? How do I deal with my pain? Is there a heaven? Is there a hell? How do I get to heaven and how do I avoid hell? How do I raise my children?

How do I get along in this world?

It is not the purpose of this book to answer all these questions. This book is an anthology (or collection) of various subjects that have their explanation and meaning in the word of God. This collection of white papers is a demonstration of what was said in the previous paragraph. Each section presents a subject or question that is answered and settled from God's word. Some of the topics will be familiar to the average Christian. Some of the topics of discussion may be new to you. There are several subjects discussed in this book (again with its origin found in Scripture) that this author has never seen discussed anywhere, verbally or in written form. Other subjects covered herein can easily be found in other writings. There are some subjects discussed about which the reader may question the need or rationale for such a deliberation. Our position on the validity of the subject matter is as follows: If it is mentioned in the word of God, it is worth our discussion regardless of its seeming importance or lack thereof.

We are admonished by the Apostle Paul to study the Scripture to show ourselves approved unto God (2 Tim. 2:15). It is a basic need in the life of the child of God. But sadly, for many of the saints it is a neglected chore. But once a Christian "discovers his Bible" and taps into the "the depth of the riches both of wisdom and knowledge of God" (Rom. 11:33) his walk with Christ will be even richer. It is our prayer that the reader will be edified and challenged to spend even more time reading the most fascinating book in the world as a result of these Bible studies.

CHAPTER ONE

GOOD FRIDAY OR GOOD WEDNESDAY

Preface

THERE ARE THOSE WHO MIGHT THINK
the of this paper is irrelevant, divisive, and undeserving of any
appreciable time on the part of the twenty-first century
Christian. On the contrary, the topic of discussion is of
utmost importance. It has to do with the most important
event in the lives of sinful men. It has to do with the once-
and-for-all payment of the sin debt of the world. Since Adam
and Eve partook of the forbidden fruit, the Adamic sin
nature has been passed down to all men (Rom. 5:12). Since
the wages of sin is an eternal lake of fire (Rom. 6:23, Rev.
20:15) and the only reprieve is Jesus Christ (John 10:9), any
information having to do with the details of Calvary and
understanding what the Holy Spirit has to say about it,
irrespective of its seeming insignificance, should be
investigated by the student of Scripture with all due gravity.

One of the many things with which God concerns Himself is the passage of time. He formed the heavens and the earth in six twenty-four hour days (Gen. 1:5). He allowed the sojourning of the children of Israel, who dwelt in Egypt for a period of four hundred thirty years before they were allowed to leave (Ex. 12:40-41). The Holy Spirit, in certain locations in Scripture, carefully listed the number of years certain people lived before bearing children, then listed the number of years they lived afterward (Gen. 5 and 11). He also indexed all the kings that ruled over Israel and Judah, giving their age when they became king as well as the number of years they reigned (1 and 2 Chron.). The Scripture declared the coming of the Messiah (Gen. 3:15, Deut. 18:15, 18, Isa. 53, et al). No one knew exactly when, but He came, right on time, after a certain period of time elapsed, and no sooner.

What are we saying? We are saying that God is zealous about time and its precise passage. When He gives us a definite period of time regarding a certain event, then we can count on that happening just as God said. Case in point: if Jesus Christ said **"...three days and three nights..."** (Mat. 12:40), He meant three days and three nights and *not* one day and two nights. **"...Jesus answered, Are there not twelve hours in the day?"** (John 11:9). If it is listed in the word of God, then it is worth our time to study it, learn it, and teach it to others. The Scripture says, **"Every word of God *is* pure:"** (Prov. 30:5).

Introduction

Every year in the United States and around the globe, people of all faiths observe "Good Friday" as a sacred day in the history of Christianity. It is also generally understood that Jesus Christ, after being crucified, was placed in a tomb, and remained there three days and three nights. The age-old puzzle is, how does one get three days and three nights between 6 PM Friday and early Sunday morning? Moreover, where would one expect to find an answer to this enigma? There are many sources of information on this subject. Many people might ask their minister, priest, pastor, elder, etc. for understanding on this topic, while others might Google it. Some look to tradition and the "church fathers" for light on the mysterious theme. However, there is only one real source for any truth regarding the Lord Jesus Christ and that is, of course, the word of God.

When the reader approaches the word of God for light on a subject such as this, there are certain prerequisites that must be met if he expects to come away with any real understanding. First of all, he must truly be born again. The Apostle Paul said, **"But the natural man receiveth not the things of the Spirit of God: for they are foolishness unto him: neither can he know *them*, because they are spiritually discerned."** (1 Cor. 2:14). In plainer words, if you have not received Christ as your Savior, much of what the word of God says will be taken as myth or fairy-tales. It means an unsaved man will be unable to "receive" understanding of the Scripture. It is the Holy Spirit, residing in us (1 Cor. 3:16) that illuminates the Scripture (not a knowledge of Greek and Hebrew syntax). Granted, the unregenerate reader can get the surface truths, as evidenced by the world's general understanding of Bible stories. However, when we come to the subjects of doctrine, prophecy, typology, and eschatology, the unsaved reader is "up the creek without a paddle."

The second thing the reader needs is a humble heart. The Psalmist said, **"LORD, thou hast heard the desire of the humble: thou wilt prepare their heart, thou wilt cause thine ear to hear:"** (Psm. 10:17). **"...God resisteth the proud, but giveth grace unto the humble."** (James 4:6).

The third thing needed to understand the word of

God is a believing mind. Paul said in 1 Thes. 2:13, **"For this cause also thank we God without ceasing, because, when ye received the word of God which ye heard of us, ye received *it* not *as* the word of men, but as it is in truth, the word of God, which effectually worketh also in you that believe."**

With respect to interpretation of the Scripture, a simple rule-of-thumb for the Bible student is as follows: If it is possible to take the verse literally; interpret it literally. If it is impossible to interpret it literally; take if figuratively. For example: Christ said, **"I am the door: by me if any man enter in, he shall be saved, and shall go in and out, and find pasture."** (John 10:9). He did not mean that He was a literal door hanging on hinges with latch and key. He meant what He said, He is the only entrance into eternal life. If one expects to escape hell, he cannot do so by faithful attendance to church, taking the Eucharist, baptism, living a good life, doing good deeds, etc. As Christ told Nicodemus, **"Ye must be born again."** Again, James said, **"And the tongue *is* a fire, a world of iniquity: so is the tongue among our members, that it defileth the whole body, and setteth on fire the course of nature; and it is set on fire of hell."** (James 3:6). It is impossible for one's tongue to be a literal fire; therefore it is taken figuratively.

Jesus said in Mat. 12:40, **"For as Jonas was three days and three nights in the whale's belly; so shall the Son of man be three days and three nights in the heart of the earth."** This passage will be our starting point to show the reader that Jesus Christ spent three days and three nights in the tomb. We will provide all the Scriptures to prove this truth. It will be up to the individual reader of this paper to account for his own position on this topic after being exposed to the information that follows. We will make it apparent with a clear presentation of Scripture that all four Gospels show the exact day on which Christ was crucified and placed in the tomb. That day was not "Good Friday," but Wednesday.

The First Passover (Exodus 12)

The crucifixion of the Lord Jesus Christ took place at the time of the Feast of the Passover in Jerusalem. In order to get the facts we must go back to the origin of this Jewish Feast. The word "festival," as some refer to the Jewish feasts, is not found in Scripture nor does it mean the same thing. Moses and the children of Israel observed the first Passover just prior to their exodus from Egypt. Pharaoh did not want the Jews to leave. God called Moses to lead the Children of Israel out of Egypt into the land originally promised to Abraham and his descendents (through Isaac). The final in the series of judgments God brought upon Pharaoh and the Egyptians was the most severe of all. At midnight the firstborn in every family (including animals) was to be slain by the destroyer (Ex. 12:23). To protect the Children of Israel from this catastrophic incident, God instructed Moses to take certain precautions. Each family was to kill a lamb at a certain time of the day. The blood of this lamb was to be placed in a basin. Hyssop was used to dip into the blood and strike the lintel and side-posts of the door of their home. That evening they were to roast this lamb and eat it with unleavened bread. They were to pack their bags and be ready to leave as they ate the Passover lamb. That night at midnight the destroyer came and killed all the firstborn in Egypt, including Pharaoh's firstborn son. This was the final straw for Pharaoh. He sent for Moses and ordered the Jews to get out of Egypt.

The Jews were to eat unleavened bread for seven days following the Passover. Since the Jewish day begins at sundown, the lamb was eaten on the first of the seven days of unleavened bread (in the evening). The Passover came on the 14th of Abib (Lev. 23:5). The 15th was the Feast of

Unleavened Bread. **"In the fourteenth *day* of the first month at even *is* the LORD'S passover.** And on the fifteenth day of the same month *is* the feast of unleavened bread unto the LORD: seven days ye must eat unleavened bread."** (Lev. 23:5-6). The Passover day or the 14th day later became known as the "Day of Preparation" in the New Testament (Mat. 27:62, Mark 15:42, Luke 23:54, John 19:14, 31, 42).

The Sabbath and Holy Convocations

In Lev. 23 we read of the seven Feasts given to Israel. **"And the LORD spake unto Moses, saying, Speak unto the children of Israel, and say unto them, *Concerning* the feasts of the LORD, which ye shall proclaim *to be* holy convocations, *even* these *are* my feasts."** (Lev. 23:1-2). This verse tells us the feasts were also known as "holy convocations." The verse to follow (vs. 3) points out that the regular, weekly Saturday Sabbath was also a Holy Convocation. **"Six days shall work be done: but the seventh day *is* the sabbath of rest, an holy convocation; ye shall do no work *therein*: it *is* the sabbath of the LORD in all your dwellings."**

The student of Scripture needs to understand that it is possible to have more than one Sabbath in one week. A Sabbath is a Holy Convocation and a Holy Convocation is a Sabbath. Any one of the seven feast days given to the Jew is considered to be a Sabbath in Scripture. In Lev. 23:24 the Scripture says, **"Speak unto the children of Israel, saying, In the seventh month, in the first *day* of the month, shall ye have a sabbath, a memorial of blowing of trumpets, an holy convocation."** Here we see that the Feast of the Trumpets is considered a Sabbath. The Day of Atonement is a Sabbath according to Lev. 23:32, which reads, **"It *shall be*** unto you a sabbath of rest, and ye shall afflict your souls: in the ninth *day* of the month at even, from even unto even, shall ye celebrate your sabbath." Lev. 23:39 is instructive in two ways: first it shows that the Feast of Tabernacles is a Sabbath, second it indicates that eight days later another Sabbath will occur regardless of what day of the week it is. "**Also in the fifteenth day of the seventh month, when ye have gathered in the fruit of the land, ye shall keep a feast unto the LORD seven days: on the first day *shall be* a sabbath, and on the eighth day *shall be* a sabbath"** (Lev. 23:39). This is all very significant when we determine what day of the week Christ was crucified later in this paper.

All rules applying to Saturday Sabbath apply also to Feast Days. In Exodus 35:3 we read, "**Ye shall kindle no fire throughout your habitations upon the sabbath day."** In Lev. 23:3 we read, "**Six days shall work be done: but the seventh day *is* the sabbath of rest, an holy convocation; ye shall do no work *therein*: it *is* the sabbath of the LORD in all your dwellings."** The Jew was not to kindle a fire or do any work on a Sabbath. The penalty was death by stoning (Num. 15:33-36). Since a Holy Convocation was considered a Sabbath, the same commands were applicable.

The Lamb of God

John the Baptist saw Jesus Christ and said, "... **Behold the Lamb of God, which taketh away the sin of the world"** (John 1:29). John understood that Christ was the Lamb of God and recognized Him even before he was born (Luke 1:44). The Apostle Paul said, "**Purge out therefore the old leaven, that ye may be a new lump, as ye are unleavened. For even Christ our passover is sacrificed for us:"** (1 Cor. 5:7). As the Passover Lamb, Christ had to be killed on the fourteenth of the first month of the Jewish year, which is April (spoken of in Scripture as Abib or Nisan). He was to be kept up all night before the day of his death (Ex. 12:6) and was to be killed during the afternoon.

In order to determine the exact day, in which Jesus was crucified, we need a fixed point in time. One of those fixed points is resurrection day or the first day of the week. Because of the passage in Gen. 2:2-3, we know that Sunday is the first day of the week. **"And on the seventh day God ended his work which he had made; and he rested on the seventh day from all his work which he had made. And God blessed the seventh day, and sanctified it: because that in it he had rested from all his work which God created and made."**

The Jews had to remove Christ's body from the cross before evening, or sunset. This comes from a passage in Deut., which says, **"And if a man have committed a sin worthy of death, and he be to be put to death, and thou hang him on a tree: His body shall not remain all night upon the tree, but thou shalt in any wise bury him that day; (for he that is hanged *is* accursed of God;) that thy land be not defiled, which the LORD thy God giveth thee *for* an inheritance"** (Deut. 21:22-23). Christ was, of course NOT worthy of death, but nevertheless this was the rationale for taking Him down from the cross before sundown.

We know from the creation narrative that the Jewish day begins in the evening because God used the phrase, **"and the evening and the morning were the first day."** Therefore, Christ was placed in the tomb just before the beginning of the Jewish day. **"When the even was come, there came a rich man of Arimathaea, named Joseph, who also himself was Jesus' disciple"** (Mat. 27:57). **"And now when the even was come, because it was the preparation, that is, the day before the sabbath,"** (Mark

15:42). **"And that day was the preparation, and the sabbath drew on"** (Luke 23:54). **"There laid they Jesus therefore because of the Jews' preparation *day*; for the sepulchre was nigh at hand"** (John 19:42).

Since the period began in the evening, we will count three evenings and mornings for the necessary three days and three nights. Our starting point will be Wednesday evening at sundown. This takes us to sundown Saturday evening for the completion of Christ's three-day/night period. If you make it Thursday sundown, then Christ came up early since He was seen by witnesses early Sunday morning. If you make it Friday sundown, then He only spent a day and a half in the tomb. Again, we should quote our Lord when He said, **"For as Jonas was three days and three nights in the whale's belly; so shall the Son of man be three days and three nights in the heart of the earth."** (Mat. 12:40). If Christ only spent two nights and a single day in the tomb, then He lied when He made the statement found in Matthew 12:40. The writer of Hebrews says, **"That by two immutable things, in which *it was* impossible for God to lie, we might have a strong consolation, who have fled for refuge to lay hold upon the hope set before us"** (Heb. 6:18). Moreover, if Christ did not complete the necessary three days and three nights in the tomb, then our atonement is incomplete. Let me say emphatically, that Christ *did not lie* in Matthew 12:40 (or anywhere else) and since He did complete the three-day and three-night period of time, our atonement is complete!

The resurrection of Christ took place at approximately sundown Saturday evening (not sunrise on Sunday morning). This completed His three-day and three-night period in the tomb. He was not seen until early Sunday morning as the following passages indicate: **"And very early in the morning the first *day* of the week, they came unto the sepulchre at the rising of the sun"** (Mark 16:2). **"Now** upon the first *day* of the week, very early in the morning, they came unto the sepulchre, bringing the spices which they had prepared, and certain *others* with them" (Luke 24:1). "The first *day* of the week cometh Mary Magdalene early, when it was yet dark, unto the sepulchre, and seeth the stone taken away from the sepulchre" (John 20:1).

Where was Jesus between Saturday sunset and early Sunday morning? We don't know. There is nothing in the Scripture (that anyone has found) that indicates where He was and what He did during that time.

Explanations

This is not an easy study by any means. There are some things in the word of God that must be prayed about after hours of study. The Lord does not put everything within easy reach. Paul knew this when he said, **"Study to shew thyself approved unto God, a workman that needeth not to be ashamed, rightly dividing the word of truth"** (2 Tim. 2:15). There are certain things in Scripture that are very difficult to understand. That does not mean that they are beyond understanding. Isaiah wrote, **"Whom shall he teach knowledge? and whom shall he make to understand doctrine?** *them that are* **weaned from the milk,** *and* **drawn from the breasts. For precept** *must be* **upon precept, precept upon precept; line upon line, line upon line; here a little,** *and* **there a little"** (Isa. 28:9-10).

There are no errors in the word of God. The Bible says, **"Who can understand** *his* **errors? cleanse thou me from secret** *faults*" (Psm. 19:12). If there were mistakes in the Bible, no mortal man could figure them out. The Scripture says, **"Every word of God** *is* **pure: he** *is* **a shield unto them that put their trust in him. Add thou not unto** his words, lest he reprove thee, and thou be found a liar" (Prov. 30:5-6). In Rev. 22:18-19, we find a curse on anyone that adds to or takes away from the word of God. When we come to a passage that appears to be a problem, then we must study a little harder and ask God to **"open thou mine eyes"** (Psm. 119:18).

The reason some believe Christ was crucified on Friday comes from a misunderstanding of three passages in the New Testament. These passages are found in Mark 15:42, Luke 23:54-56, and John 19:31. For example: **"The Jews therefore, because it was the preparation, that the bodies should not remain upon the cross on the sabbath day, (for that sabbath day was an high day,) besought Pilate that their legs might be broken, and *that* they might be taken away"** (John 19:31). It is commonly misunderstood that "the Sabbath day" as mentioned referred to Saturday. The Sabbath spoken of was not Saturday, but the day after the Preparation Day, which was the Feast of Unleavened Bread. The passage refers to this special Sabbath as an "high day." We showed in the passages above how a Feast Day is also a Sabbath Day for the Jew. If you are still in doubt, go back and study Lev. 23. There was more than one Sabbath during the week that Christ was crucified.

The Last Supper

There are those who say that the Disciples ate the last Passover with Christ the night before He was crucified. This was not possible. Let us go back and read Lev. 23:5 again: **"In the fourteenth *day* of the first month at even is the LORD'S passover."** The fourteenth day was considered the preparation day for the feast of Unleavened Bread, which was eaten after sundown. After sunset meant it was the 15th of the month ("at even") when it was actually eaten. A careful reading of Lev. 23:18 will show that the seven days of unleavened bread began on the 15th and ended on the 21st. If the Passover was eaten on the 14th (proper), the last day being the 21st would make it eight days of unleavened bread. Now let's read the passage. **"In the first** *month*, **on the fourteenth day of the month at even, ye shall eat unleavened bread, until the one and twentieth day of the month at even"** (Ex. 12:18). The Israelites in Egypt killed the Passover Lamb and put the blood on the door posts and lintel of their home on the 14th. They packed their bags and *prepared* to leave that night (it was a preparation day). They didn't actually eat the lamb until that evening (after sunset, making it the 15th).

On Tuesday evening, after sunset, making it the first part of Preparation Day (the Jewish day begins at sunset) Christ had the Last Supper with His disciples. It was during this meeting that Christ spoke to them about the New Covenant in His blood. This was to be His final meeting with the twelve disciples before the crucifixion. There are certain passages given in Matthew, Mark, and Luke, which, appear to indicate that this final meal was the Passover. A closer inspection of these verses, the context, and other passages show that this was NOT the Passover feast. Let us now list these passages:

"And he said, Go into the city to such a man, and say unto him, The Master saith, My time is at hand; I will keep the passover at thy house with my disciples. And the disciples did as Jesus had appointed them; and they made ready the passover" (Mat. 26:18-19).

"And the first day of unleavened bread, when they killed the passover, his disciples said unto him, Where wilt thou that we go and prepare that thou mayest eat the passover?" (Mark 14:12).

"And wheresoever he shall go in, say ye to the goodman of the house, The Master saith, Where is the guestchamber, where I shall eat the passover with my

disciples?" (Mark 14:14).

"And his disciples went forth, and came into the city, and found as he had said unto them: and they made ready the passover" (Mark 14:16).

"Then came the day of unleavened bread, when the passover must be killed. And he sent Peter and John, saying, Go and prepare us the passover, that we may eat" (Luke 22:7-8).

"And ye shall say unto the goodman of the house, The Master saith unto thee, Where is the guestchamber, where I shall eat the passover with my disciples?" (Luke 22:11).

"And they went, and found as he had said unto them: and they made ready the passover" (Luke 22:13).

"And he said unto them, With desire I have desired to eat this passover with you before I suffer" (Luke 22:15).

Each one of these verses, upon first reading could possibly indicate that the Last Supper was actually the Passover Feast. The Scripture admonishes us in 2 Timothy 2:15, **"Study to shew thyself approved unto God, a workman that needeth not to be ashamed, rightly dividing the word of truth."** Luke 22:7 indicates that it was Tuesday after sunset, or Preparation Day. Each of the passages listed above could be interpreted to mean the disciples were to have a meal in the upper room that night during the preparation for the feast the following day. In reality, these verses could go either way. That is, they could mean they would have a meal the evening before the Passover Feast, or they could actually eat the Passover Feast.

In rightly dividing the word of God we will examine the context as well as other passages in order to arrive at the proper understanding. The Gospel of John clears it all up for us in chapter 13. John wrote, **"Now before the feast of the passover, when Jesus knew that his hour was come that he should depart out of this world unto the Father, having loved his own which were in the world, he loved them unto the end. And supper being ended, the devil having now put into the heart of Judas Iscariot, Simon's *son*, to betray him; Jesus knowing that the Father had given all things into his hands, and that he was come from God, and went to God; He riseth from supper, and laid aside his garments; and took a towel, and girded himself"** (John 13:1-4). This passage clearly indicates that the preceding meal (the Last Supper) took place *before* the Passover Feast.

Moreover, in the same chapter after Christ washed the feet of the disciples and after He instructed them that one of them would betray Him, John wrote, **"Jesus answered He it is, to whom I shall give a sop, when I have dipped *it*. And when he had dipped the sop, he gave *it* to Judas Iscariot, *the son* of Simon. And after the sop Satan entered into him. Then said Jesus unto him, That thou doest, do quickly"** (John 13:26-27). The two verses that follow also indicate that the Last Supper *was not* the Passover Feast. **"Now no man at the table knew for what intent he spake this unto him. For some *of them* thought, because Judas had the bag, that Jesus had said unto him, Buy *those things* that we have need of against the feast; or, that he should give something to the poor"** (John 13:28-29). Everyone present thought that Christ instructed Judas to purchase what was necessary for the Passover Feast, which was still in the future.

There is yet another passage in John, which makes clear the fact that Christ was killed before the Feast of Unleavened Bread (Passover). This is found in John 18:28 as follows, **"Then led they Jesus from Caiaphas unto the hall of judgment: and it was early; and they themselves** went not into the judgment hall, lest they should be defiled; but that they might eat the passover."

Christ was the Passover Lamb, which was to be killed on the fourteenth of the month of Abib (Ex. 12:6). He was crucified at 9 AM Wednesday and remained on the cross until approximately 3 PM. Mark 15:25 says, **"And it was the third hour, and they crucified him."** The Jewish evening begins at sunset or approximately 6 PM and the Jewish day begins at sunrise or approximately 6 AM. This was the third hour of the day, or about 9 AM. From noon until 3 PM darkness covered the earth. Matthew, Mark, and Luke recorded, **"Now from the sixth hour there was darkness over all the land unto the ninth hour"** (Mat. 27:45). **"And when the sixth hour was come, there was darkness over the whole land until the ninth hour"** (Mark 15:33). **"And it was about the sixth hour, and there was a darkness over all the earth until the ninth hour"** (Luke 23:44). In the ninth hour Christ died. **"And when Jesus had cried with a loud voice, he said, Father, into thy hands I commend my spirit: and having said thus, he gave up the ghost"** (Luke 23:46). Between 3 and 6 PM His body was removed from the cross and placed in the tomb (Mat. 27:57-61, Mark 15:42-47, John 19:38-42). After sunset (making it the fifteenth), the Passover lamb was to be eaten in the Feast of Unleavened Bread (Lev. 23:5-6).

Sunset on our Saturday marked the completion of the three-day and three-night period Christ spoke of in Mat. 12:40. Therefore, the resurrection of Christ took place after sunset (our) Saturday night: Mat. 28:1-10; Mark 16:1-18; Luke 24:1-49; John 20:1-23.

The traditional Easter Sunday sunrise service takes place approximately twelve hours *after* the resurrection of our Lord. Perhaps a more appropriate time to honor the resurrection of Jesus Christ would be Saturday evening at sundown.

Conclusion

When Christ said He would be three days and three nights in the heart of the earth, He meant it literally and not figuratively. The phrase "three days" is used nine times in the New Testament in reference to the amount of time Christ would be in the tomb. The phrase "third day" is used fourteen times in reference to the same event. Between Friday sunset and Sunday morning sunrise is only one and one-half days. The reason for some who believe that Christ was crucified on Friday has to do with a misunderstanding of the Sabbath mentioned in Mark 15:42, Luke 23:54-56, and John 19:31. This error is understandable without a clear understanding of the Jewish Sabbaths. However, when we learn that a Feast Day, such as the Feast of Unleavened Bread is also a Sabbath, we understand that it was not the weekly Saturday Sabbath spoken of in the three passages above. Therefore, with more than one Sabbath occurring during Christ's crucifixion week, we can allow the proper period of time (three days and three nights) for Christ in the tomb, just as He prophesied. The other area of confusion centers on the difference between the beginning and ending of the Gentile and Jewish twenty-four hour day. It is our prayer that this treatise provides a better understanding of this often-misunderstood issue as well as challenges the reader to spend time reading the Scripture on a daily basis.

CHAPTER TWO

THE JUDGMENT SEAT OF CHRIST

Introduction

THERE ARE FUTURE EVENTS ON GOD'S calendar to which all Christians should look forward. The next great event will be the calling out of the Church of Jesus Christ. This is commonly referred to as the *Rapture* of the Church. The Apostle Paul said in 1 Thes. 4:16-17, **"For the Lord himself shall descend from heaven with a shout, with the voice of the archangel, and with the trump of God: and the dead in Christ shall rise first: Then we which are alive *and* remain shall be caught up together with them in the clouds, to meet the Lord in the air: and so shall we ever be with the Lord."**

Another future event in the lives of all Christians will be the receipt of a "glorified body." The Scripture says in 1 John 3:2, **"Beloved, now are we the sons of God, and it doth not yet appear what we shall be: but we know that,**

when he shall appear, we shall be like him; for we shall see him as he is." John tells us, "we shall be like him." The Apostle Paul said in 1 Cor. 15:52 **"In a moment, in the twinkling of an eye, at the last trump: for the trumpet shall sound, and the dead shall be raised incorruptible, and we shall be changed."** "**We shall be changed,**" indicates our present frail, mortal bodies will be different from what we have always known. We will have a resurrection body like that of Christ after His resurrection. Christ had the ability to vanish before people's eyes in Luke 24:31. He was able to make Himself invisible, walk through doors and walls in John 20:19, and appear in the midst of brethren. In Luke 24:16 and John 20:14 He was able to change His appearance so that He would not be recognized by those who knew Him well. In Acts 1:9 Christ stood on the ground and defied gravity and ascended up into the heavens before the eyes of the disciples. The Christian can actually look forward to having a glorified body like Jesus Christ.

The Marriage Supper of the Lamb will be a great gathering of all the saints following the Judgment Seat of Christ. John said in Rev. 19:9, **"And he saith unto me, Write, Blessed *are* they which are called unto the marriage supper of the Lamb."** It's always an enjoyable occasion when Christians gather together and work their way through tables full of delicious foods of every description and sit around tables to enjoy a meal together. But one day we will be gathered around a very special banquet table. At the head of this table will be seated none other than the Lord Jesus Christ Himself. What a great occasion that will be.

Another future event will be our position with Jesus Christ. That is, we will be *with Him* forever. The verse quoted above from 1 Thes. 4:17 says, **"and so shall we ever be with the Lord."** We will actually be in the presence of Jesus Christ! We will "know Him as we are known," as Paul said in 1 Cor. 13:12, **"For now we see through a glass, darkly; but then face to face: now I know in part; but then shall**

I know even as also I am known." What a great experience that will be!

There are other great events that we can look forward to: Seeing our loved ones who have long since gone to Glory. We will have the ability to understand that which is impossible for a finite mind. That is to say, the things that break our hearts in this life will all make sense when we have "the mind of Christ," (2 Cor. 2:16). We will get to meet the people in the Scripture we've read about so many times: Moses, Samuel, David, Micaiah, Jeremiah, Isaiah, Paul, Simon Peter, Joshua, Elijah, and many others. We will have the privilege to witness the national revival of Israel. The joy of serving the King of Kings and Lord of Lords in the Millennium and for all eternity will be ours forever!

However, when we come to the subject of the Judgment Seat of Christ, we should understand that for many Christians, this will not be a happy and joyous occasion. Let us study this ominous event in our future and see why.

The Judgment Seat of Christ

The Judgment Seat of Christ is a future event on God's calendar, which will be attended by Christians of all the ages. It should be noted that this judgment *is not* to determine whether the person will go to heaven or hell, since only the saved will be present. It is, rather to judge the quality of the works of each individual Christian during his or her life after salvation.

Paul said in 2 Cor. 5:10, **"For we must all appear before the judgment seat of Christ; that every one may receive the things *done* in *his* body, according to that he hath done, whether *it be* good or bad."** Every Christian will face his Savior in a one-on-one meeting and give account of his life. Paul understood the gravity of this occasion as illustrated in verse 11, **"Knowing therefore the terror of the Lord, we persuade men;"** Paul's epistles to the Corinthian church were just that. They were addressed to Christians, not the unsaved. In plainer words, he was not warning unsaved people about the "terror" of God sending someone to hell for eternity. He was emphasizing the seriousness and severity of the Judgment Seat of Christ.

The Apostle Paul had insights into eternal things that the rest of us do not have. The reason for this is the fact that he had a supernatural experience. The Lord allowed him to witness and see things that no mortal man had ever seen (2 Cor. 12:1-4). Paul knew the Judgment Seat of Christ was a serious occasion for every Christian. His writings are filled with the idea of "living right." Over and over again he admonishes the Christian to do right, fight temptation, don't give in to the flesh, serve God, etc. Onesiphorus helped Paul when he was in a Roman prison. In 2 Tim. 1:18 Paul prayed that God would show his friend mercy at the Judgment Seat of Christ.

After Simon Peter denied Christ three times and the cock crew, the Bible says in Luke 22:61-62, **"And the Lord turned, and looked upon Peter. And Peter remembered the word of the Lord, how he had said unto him, Before the cock crow, thou shalt deny me thrice. And Peter went out, and wept bitterly."** Just for an instant, Simon Peter looked into the eyes of the Lord Jesus and saw how he had miserably failed his Savior in his actions. He immediately understood his wasted opportunity to bear the reproach of Christ rather than deny Him, but it was too late. Though this is not the Judgment Seat of Christ, it is a similitude of what will take place.

Millions of Christians will stand before Jesus Christ and be confronted with their Christian lives. They will see all the opportunities they had to serve God and witness for Jesus Christ. The time they wasted on meaningless pastimes, mindless television programs, and pointless pursuits will go up in a blaze before their eyes. God gives us time and abilities. These are opportunities to serve the Lord. We can use them for self and the world or we can use them for God. What has God given you that you can put to use for Him?

Who When Where

"For we must all appear before the judgment seat of Christ; that every one may receive the things *done* in *his* body, according to that he hath done, whether *it be* good or bad" (2 Cor. 5:10). Let's take a closer look at the Judgment Seat of Christ and learn from the Scripture. Let us also remember what Paul said in 2 Tim. 3:16, "All scripture *is* given by inspiration of God, and *is* profitable for doctrine, for reproof, for correction, for instruction in righteousness." It is to our benefit to listen to what Paul says and take heed, since it is profitable for doctrine, for reproof, for correction, and for instruction in righteousness.

First, who is it that Paul is addressing in the context? The word, "we" is used twenty-six times in the chapter. Each use is for Christians. The epistle was written to the *Christians* at Corinth. Therefore, all of us who name the name of Christ can count on appearing before the Judgment Seat of Christ, as Paul warns the Corinthians.

Secondly, *when* will this judgment take place? The Scripture says in 1 Cor. 4:5, "Therefore judge nothing before the time, until the Lord come, who both will bring to light the hidden things of darkness, and will make manifest the counsels of the hearts: and then shall every man have praise of God." He said, "until the Lord come…" This indicates this judgment will take place when He comes.

The student of Scripture understands that the Second

Coming of Christ takes place in two parts. The first part is when He descends from heaven in 1 Thes. 4:16-17, **"For the Lord himself shall descend from heaven with a shout, with the voice of the archangel, and with the trump of God: and the dead in Christ shall rise first: Then we which are alive *and* remain shall be caught up together with them in the clouds, to meet the Lord in the air: and so shall we ever be with the Lord."** We will meet Jesus Christ in the air. At the second part of His return, His feet actually touch the earth during the Second Advent proper (Zech. 14:4, Rev. 19, et al). The first and second "parts" of the Second Advent are separated with a period of time known as Jacob's Time of Trouble (Dan. 12:1), Daniel's Seventieth Week (Dan. 9:24), or more commonly referred to as the Tribulation (Mat. 24:21, Rev. 2:22, 7:14). Therefore, the Judgment Seat of Christ will actually take place during this seven-year period.

Third, *where* will this judgment take place? Paul wrote in 1 Thes. 4:17, **"Then we which are alive *and* remain shall be caught up together with them in the clouds, to meet the Lord in the air: and so shall we ever be with the Lord."** Let me emphasize the words, "caught up together with them in the clouds, to meet the Lord in the air…" To be precise, when the Rapture of the Church takes place, we will be miraculously taken up into the air to this meeting with the Lord. We have already seen (above) that this judgment will take place when the Lord comes.

Running a Race

Paul says in 1 Cor. 9:24-27, **"Know ye not that they which run in a race run all, but one receiveth the prize? So run, that ye may obtain. And every man that striveth for the mastery is temperate in all things. Now they *do it* to obtain a corruptible crown; but we an incorruptible. I** therefore so run, not as uncertainly; so fight I, not as one that beateth the air: But I keep under my body, and bring *it* into subjection: lest that by any means, when I have preached to others, I myself should be a castaway."

In this passage, Paul compares our life in Christ to, "they which run in a race." Again, we will emphasize the eternal security of the believer (1 John 5:13) and point out that Paul's "runners" represent Christians. At the end of this race, crowns will be given to the winners. Since Jesus Christ lost none of His sheep (John 17:12) all that run this race, though they may not receive a crown, they will not be lost.

Paul says, "So run that ye may obtain" the prize. The prize he spoke of is an incorruptible crown. He compares it to the corruptible crown, or in many cases a laurel wreath given to ancient Olympic runners. This is the origin of the term "Bema Seat." The Greek word for "seat," or Bema (where the judge sat to determine who came in first, second, and so forth), is used to describe this great event. Some of the runners will receive a crown, others will not. So, is the Judgment Seat of Christ. We (Christians) are all runners. Some will receive incorruptible crowns and others will not.

Crowns or Bonfires

We have shown that all who are saved or born again, we are runners in the race that Paul mentions, we will finish this race, we will stand before the Bema Seat, and we will have their "race" or Christian life examined by the One who sits upon the throne, none other than the Lord Jesus Christ.

Paul wrote about the Judgment Seat of Christ, **"For other foundation can no man lay than that is laid, which is Jesus Christ. Now if any man build upon this foundation gold, silver, precious stones, wood, hay, stubble; Every man's work shall be made manifest: for**

the day shall declare it, because it shall be revealed by fire; and the fire shall try every man's work of what sort it is. If any man's work abide which he hath built thereupon, he shall receive a reward. If any man's work shall be burned, he shall suffer loss: but he himself shall be saved; yet so as by fire" (1 Cor. 3:11-15).

Some things evident from this passage are first of all the fact that there is a foundation laid that only Christ could have completed. It is upon this foundation that every Christian's works are "built." There are two categories of Christian works: Incorruptible (gold, silver, precious stones) and corruptible (wood, hay, stubble). Every Christian's works will be made manifest (examined before all). These works will be revealed or tried by fire. The true motive behind the works will come out and be made manifest. Incorruptible works will abide or remain. Incorruptible works will earn a reward. Corruptible works will not abide or remain. Corruptible works will be burned. The runner, though his works were corruptible will be saved in spite of his lack of incorruptible works. Every Christian has opportunity to build upon Christ's foundation. Every Christian can choose which category he or she desires. Only incorruptible works earn a reward.

This passage indicates there is a foundation upon which every Christian builds a structure. This foundation is Jesus Christ and His finished work on Calvary. It should be noted here that we are not saved from our sin by works. The Judgment Seat of Christ (as we have stated) is for those who have received Christ as Savior. We do not work to get saved; we work because we are saved. The Bible says in Titus 3:5, **"Not by works of righteousness which we have done, but according to his mercy he saved us, by the washing of regeneration, and renewing of the Holy Ghost;"**

Our works for Jesus Christ will be judged as either corruptible or incorruptible. If they are determined to be "wood, hay, stubble," they will be burned and the Christian receives no rewards. If they are judged as incorruptible, rewards are given. Jesus Christ will look at the motives behind our service for Him. Did we serve Him for our own glory and popularity? Did we speak up for Christ when we had opportunity?

There is a certain reproach about identifying ourselves with Jesus Christ. The writer of Hebrews mentions this in Heb. 11:26, **"Esteeming the reproach of Christ greater riches than the treasures in Egypt: for he had respect unto the recompence of the reward."** The context in this passage is Moses choosing to identify himself with the Hebrews (reproach of Christ) rather than enjoying the easy life of Pharaoh's son. We are encouraged to apply this principle to our own lives in Heb 13:13, **"Let us go forth therefore unto him without the camp, bearing his reproach."** Paul wasn't afraid to speak up for Jesus Christ outside the camp. It ultimately got him beheaded. It is easy for us to give a word of testimony in our local church. When we have the opportunity to mention Jesus Christ in public or at work is it as easy as it is in church? This is a situation that counts as reproach in this world, but at the Judgment Seat of Christ it will count as gold, silver, and precious stones.

Crowns

Every Christian will stand before Jesus Christ at the Judgment Seat of Christ. Their works will be reviewed and judged. We must realize that this life is the only opportunity we have to earn rewards. All corruptible works will be burned. *Now is the time to earn rewards or crowns.*

What will be done with these crowns? We are shown the answer in Rev. 4:10-11: **"The four and twenty elders fall down before him that sat on the throne, and worship him that liveth for ever and ever, and cast their crowns before the throne, saying, Thou art worthy, O Lord, to**

receive glory and honour and power: for thou hast
created all things, and for thy pleasure they are and were
created.**" If there are any crowns earned by the Christian, he
will take them and cast them before the throne of Jesus
Christ because He is worthy.

What type of works must be done in order to earn a
crown? The answer to this is found in the New Testament.
There are five different crowns spoken of in Scripture.

Crown of Life

The Crown of Life is the Martyr's Crown. This crown
is mentioned twice in Scripture. The Bible says in James 1:12,
**"Blessed *is* the man that endureth temptation: for when
he is tried, he shall receive the crown of life, which the
Lord hath promised to them that love him."** It is also
mentioned in Rev. 2:10, **"Fear none of those things which
thou shalt suffer: behold, the devil shall cast *some* of you
into prison, that ye may be tried; and ye shall have
tribulation ten days: be thou faithful unto death, and I
will give thee a crown of life."**

Since Calvary there have been many who were killed
for the cause of Christ. They remained faithful to Christ unto
a horrible and untimely death. To name a few who were
martyred for Jesus Christ: Simon Peter, Matthew, Paul, James
Zebedee, Phillip, James the Just, Stephen, Matthias, Andrew,
Mark, Jude, Bartholomew, Luke, Thomas, and others. These
and many more were killed for their testimony of Jesus Christ
and no doubt earned their Crowns of Life.

Crown of Glory

The Crown of Glory is known as the Shepherd's
Crown. Three times Christ asked Simon Peter, **"Lovest thou**

me?" in John 21. Each time Peter answered Him, Christ said *either* **"feed my lambs"** or **"feed my sheep."** John wrote, **"He saith unto him the third time, Simon, *son* of Jonas, lovest thou me? Peter was grieved because he said unto him the third time, Lovest thou me? And he said unto him, Lord, thou knowest all things; thou knowest that I love thee. Jesus saith unto him, Feed my sheep"** (John 21:17). Simon Peter, later in his ministry understood the significance of his Savior's words when he wrote, **"Feed the flock of God which is among you, taking the oversight *thereof*, not by constraint, but willingly; not for filthy lucre, but of a ready mind; Neither as being lords over *God's* heritage, but being ensamples to the flock. And when the chief Shepherd shall appear, ye shall receive a crown of glory that fadeth not away"** (1 Pet 5:2-4). The Crown of Glory that Peter wrote about is the reward for those faithful pastors who feed the Lord's flock with the word of God.

Crown of Rejoicing

The Crown of Rejoicing is the Soul Winner's crown. It is mentioned twice in the word of God. Paul wrote in 1 Thes. 2:19, **"For what *is* our hope, or joy, or crown of rejoicing? *Are* not even ye in the presence of our Lord Jesus Christ at his coming?"** He also said in Phil. 4:1, **"Therefore, my brethren dearly beloved and longed for, my joy and crown, so stand fast in the Lord, *my* dearly beloved."** In both passages, he wrote to his converts and spoke of them as his "crown of rejoicing (Thessalonians) and "crown" (Philippians).

The Scripture says in Prov. 11:30, **"The fruit of the righteous *is* a tree of life; and he that winneth souls *is* wise."** The Crown of Rejoicing will be rewarded to **"he that winneth souls"** at the Judgment Seat of Christ.

Crown of Righteousness

The Crown of Righteousness will be given to those who look forward to the Second Coming of Jesus Christ. The Bible says in 2 Tim. 4:8, **"Henceforth there is laid up for me a crown of righteousness, which the Lord, the righteous judge, shall give me at that day: and not to me only, but unto all them also that love his appearing."**

Maybe you will never be a pastor and have opportunity to earn the Crown of Glory. Perhaps you've never led a soul to Christ. In our country it is doubtful that many will be martyred. However, here is an opportunity to earn a crown to cast at the feet of our Lord. This crown is rewarded to the one who longs for Christ to return, those who "love his appearing." Every Christian should pray every day and ask the Lord Jesus to return today. The final verse in the word of God is John's earnest plea for the Lord to return. **"He which testifieth these things saith, Surely I come quickly. Amen. Even so, come, Lord Jesus"** (Rev. 22:20).

It is referred to as a crown of righteousness because no one wants the Lord to come back if they are living in sin. Looking and praying for the return of the Lord Jesus can only be done by someone who is walking in fellowship with the Savior. Though they are far from perfect, those who long for Christ's return are ever conscious of their failures and look to the word of God and prayer for daily cleansing. Every day we should pray, Even so come Lord Jesus.

Crown Incorruptible

The Crown Incorruptible is the Victor's Crown spoken of by Paul. In his own words, **"And every man that striveth for the mastery is temperate in all things. Now they *do it* to obtain a corruptible crown; but we an** incorruptible. I therefore so run, not as uncertainly; so fight I, not as one that beateth the air: But I keep under my body, and bring *it* into subjection: lest that by any means, when I have preached to others, I myself should be a castaway." (1 Cor. 9:25-27).

In this passage Paul wrote of the daily battle with the flesh. Like Paul, we all have to bring our flesh or "our body" into subjection (vs. 27). We must battle the flesh every day. We live in a world that is ruled by the Prince of the power of the air. There are temptations almost everywhere you look. It is popular to give in to the lust of the flesh.

Paul speaks of the armor that must be worn by Christians in order to get the victory. He wrote, **"Wherefore take unto you the whole armour of God, that ye may be able to withstand in the evil day, and having done all, to stand. Stand therefore, having your loins girt about with truth, and having on the breastplate of righteousness; And your feet shod with the preparation of the gospel of peace; Above all, taking the shield of faith, wherewith ye shall be able to quench all the fiery darts of the wicked. And take the helmet of salvation, and the sword of the Spirit, which is the word of God:"** (Eph. 6:13-17).

In this passage Paul tells us we can have the victory over the flesh and stand in the evil day if we take unto us the whole armor of God, if we girt our loins with Truth. Put on the breastplate of Righteousness, if we shod our feet with the preparation of the Gospel of Peace if we use the shield of Faith, if we don the helmet of Salvation, and if we use the sword of the Spirit.

Paul goes on to tell us more about the enemy we face daily. In Ephesians 6:12 he wrote, **"For we wrestle not against flesh and blood, but against principalities, against powers, against the rulers of the darkness of this world, against spiritual wickedness in high *places*."** The only way we can hope to gain any victory over these enemies is with the supernatural suit of armor listed above and a supernatural book.

Conclusion

The Judgment Seat of Christ will not be a happy and joyous occasion for most of us. I have failed the Savior so many times I feel like I've worn out 1 John 1:9 **(If we confess our sins, he is faithful and just to forgive us *our* sins, and to cleanse us from all unrighteousness).** But no one can wear out the Scripture. The Holy Spirit emphasizes this great truth by repeating the following verse three times, **"Heaven and earth shall pass away, but my words shall not pass away"** (Mat. 24:35, Mark 13:31, Luke 21:33).

Simon Peter asked Christ about how many times forgiveness should be granted in Mat. 18:21-22. We read, **"Then came Peter to him, and said, Lord, how oft shall my brother sin against me, and I forgive him? till seven times? Jesus saith unto him, I say not unto thee, Until seven times: but, Until seventy times seven."** The point here is you can't wear out a verse by repeatedly claiming it in honest confession of sin.

There will be many tears shed at the Judgment Seat of Christ. We will see the souls we could have won to Christ. We will see all the opportunities of service for Christ that were wasted. Lost chances to speak up for Jesus Christ will be realized. We will see all the work we could have done but didn't do. We'll see the pointless work we did go up in a bonfire. Many of the things that were so important to us amounted to wood, hay, and stubble. We will realize lost rewards, lost loved ones, lost children, and lost parents. But most of all we will understand the fact that it is too late to serve God.

Perhaps there is someone who says, "There won't be

any tears in heaven." You are correct. The Bible says in Rev. 21:4, **"And God shall wipe away all tears from their eyes; and there shall be no more death, neither sorrow, nor crying, neither shall there be any more pain: for the former things are passed away."** But wait, this verse doesn't come until after the White Throne Judgment which is over a thousand years *after* the Judgment Seat of Christ. From what we read about the Judgment Seat of Christ there will be much sorrow and crying on the part of Christians at this ominous future event. Yet there are those who confidently look at this event without apprehension. They are evidently confident that they have arrived at a plane of righteousness, a level of spiritual achievement, or confidence in their good works that even the Apostle Paul never reached. Remember it was Paul that said, **"Knowing therefore the terror of the Lord, we persuade men; but we are made manifest unto God"** (2 Cor. 5:11). The great Bema Seat is nothing to take lightly. We will stand before our Savior and give an account of our lives. We will look into the same eyes that looked at Simon Peter just before he went out and wept bitterly. There won't be any pretense, only truth. There are things we can get away with in this life, but not at the Judgment Seat of Christ.

The Good News

The good news is it is not too late. We still have time to serve Jesus Christ. There are still opportunities to earn rewards and crowns to cast at His feet. We don't have to come to Christ empty-handed. What greater gift is there to present to the Savior than the crowns we earned in service to Him? Is there something you can do for Jesus Christ? You can pass out Gospel tracts. You can pray for the salvation of loved ones and friends and enemies too. You can take an active part in your local church and support missions. You can spend time reading the word of God as well as time in prayer. You can visit someone in the hospital or the rest home. You can brag about Jesus Christ and mention Him often at work and bear the reproach of Jesus Christ. You can pray for and look forward to His soon coming. You can fight the good fight of faith and be victorious over temptation.

But this treatise was written to Christians. If you have read this and you are not certain about your personal relationship with Christ, then this should be dealt with first. Or perhaps you are certain that you do not have a relationship with Jesus Christ. First, understand that without Christ, you have no hope of escaping condemnation and the lake of fire. The Bible says in John 14:6, **"Jesus saith unto him, I am the way, the truth, and the life: no man cometh unto the Father, but by me."** Second, you must receive Him as savior. **"But as many as received him, to them gave he power to become the sons of God,** *even* **to them that believe on his name:"** (John 1:12). Third, you receive Him by calling upon Him. **"For whosoever shall call upon the name of the Lord shall be saved"** (Rom. 10:13). **"All that the Father giveth me shall come to me; and him that cometh to me I will in no wise cast out"** (John 6:37).

CHAPTER THREE

EAT HIS FLESH AND DRINK HIS BLOOD: WHAT DID CHRIST MEAN?

An Exposition of John 6:53-56

Introduction

THIS PASSAGE IS ONE OF THE MOST peculiar readings in the New Testament. It is also one of the most misunderstood passages of the Bible. Yet, the words came directly from the Lord Jesus Christ Himself. What did the Savior mean? If I am to have eternal life does that mean I am supposed to literally eat His flesh and drink His blood? Are you baffled by what you read? Don't be alarmed; many Christians are in the same quandary. The Bible says, **"Study to shew thyself approved unto God, a workman that needeth not to be ashamed, rightly dividing the word of truth"** (2 Tim. 2:15). The Apostle Paul tells us to study the word of God in order that we "rightly divide" it or, to correctly understand and interpret it. It is the purpose of this paper to do just that, with respect to the passage quoted.

The word of God is a miraculous book. It is a supernatural book. It is a perfect book. It is a one-of-a-kind book that contains the answer to this passage as well as countless others. When we come to the Bible for answers, we must first make sure that our attitude is correct. Heb. 4:12 says, **"For the word of God *is* quick, and powerful, and sharper than any twoedged sword, piercing even to the dividing asunder of soul and spirit, and of the joints and marrow, and *is* a discerner of the thoughts and intents of the heart."** This verse indicates the word of God discerns the thoughts and intents of our heart. The Lord is very zealous about His word. Jer. 23:29 - ***"Is* not my word like as a fire? saith the LORD; and like a hammer *that* breaketh the rock in pieces?"** Isa. 66:2 - **"For all those *things* hath mine hand made, and all those *things* have been, saith the LORD: but to this *man* will I look, *even* to *him that is* poor and of a contrite spirit, and trembleth at my word."** John 8:31 - **"Then said Jesus to those Jews which believed on him, If ye continue in my word, *then* are ye my disciples indeed;"** John 12:48 - **"He that rejecteth me, and receiveth not my words, hath one that judgeth him: the word that I have spoken, the same shall judge him in the last day."**

In the light of the verses listed above (and there are plenty more), we need to understand that the attitude of our heart should be right when we come to the Scripture for answers. The Lord looks into our hearts and seeks someone who is genuine and wants to know the truth. He sees our intents and motives for learning something from the Bible. The word of God is "interactive." It has been in existence long before "social media" was ever conceived. So, what will you do with something you read that you don't like? What if you find something that hits you right between the eyes? What will your reaction be if the Holy Spirit puts His finger on a "rotten spot" in your life? Will an effort be made to correct it? Let me make it clear here: if you are a human being, there will be "rotten spots." (Ecl. 7:20, **"For *there is* not a just man upon earth, that doeth good, and sinneth not."**) The Lord wants to see a humble heart and a believing mind when we come to the word of God. Let us never be guilty of saying, **"Yea hath God said"** or questioning what God said (Gen. 3:1).

In this study we will see what God has to say about this passage and take it to heart. We will not change any word of the text. We will not call on Jehudi to come and cut out what we don't like. We will take it just as the Holy Spirit wrote it and preserved it (Psm. 12:6-7).

Context

First of all let us take a look at the context of the passage. The sixth chapter of John contains: First of all, the Feeding of the Five Thousand (vs. 1-14). This event is mentioned in all four Gospel accounts. Couple this with the feeding of the four thousand mentioned in Matthew and Mark and we have six times where Christ miraculously fed hungry Jews in the wilderness. This looks back to when God miraculously fed Israel in the wilderness for forty years. It looks even farther back to when Joseph, a type of Christ, fed Israel during the great 7-year famine. It looks forward to when Israel will again be in the wilderness, fleeing from the Antichrist (this time) for three and one-half years. **"And the woman fled into the wilderness, where she hath a place prepared of God, that they should feed her there a thousand two hundred *and* threescore days"** (Rev. 12:6).

Then we come to the passage where Jesus walks on the Sea (vs. 15-21). This event is mentioned in all but Luke's Gospel and is also extremely significant. This is a picture of the Second Advent of Jesus Christ (see our booklet entitled,

"The Prophetic Significance of Christ Walking on the Sea").

The Bread of Life Discourse (vs. 22-30) follows. Here Christ uses the miraculous feeding as an illustration that He Himself is the True Bread. He contrasts this Bread of Life with Moses and the manna of Exodus 16 (vs. 31-52). Christ then comes to our text verse (vs. 53-66) and proceeds to completely baffle some of His disciples. The final portion of the chapter deals with Simon Peter and the confirmation of his faith in Christ (vs. 67-71).

From the context of the chapter, please notice *miraculous food* and the act of *eating*. This will be discussed further later. Before we get to that, let us notice the Jew's reaction to what Christ said in our text. Verse 52 says, **"The Jews therefore strove among themselves, saying, How can this man give us *his* flesh to eat?"** Their reaction was not unlike anyone else's after hearing the words. In verse 60, we read, **"Many therefore of his disciples, when they had heard *this*, said, This is an hard saying; who can hear it?"** Some considered this a hard saying, indicating their inability to accept the word of God. Finally, in verse 66, **"From that *time* many of his disciples went back, and walked no more with him."** Here we learn that some of His disciples left Him because of these words. Obviously, what Christ said in this passage was difficult for those who heard His words. Many of those who followed Him left. After that the Lord Jesus turned to His twelve disciples and asked, **"Will ye also go away?"** Notice also that Christ did not run after those that left in an attempt to encourage them to change their mind. He did not say, "What I really meant was..." They left and He watched them leave.

Misunderstood Passage

John 6:53-56 – **"Then Jesus said unto them, Verily, verily, I say unto you, Except ye eat the flesh of**

**the Son of man, and drink his blood, ye have no life in
you. Whoso eateth my flesh, and drinketh my blood,
hath eternal life; and I will raise him up at the last day.
For my flesh is meat indeed, and my blood is drink
indeed. He that eateth my flesh, and drinketh my blood,
dwelleth in me, and I in him."**

Our text is the basis for gross misinterpretation and
misunderstanding in many modern churches today. There are
two concepts that spawned from this passage, which are
practiced in most cities in our country and around the world
today.

Consubstantiation: This is a belief proposed by
Martin Luther, that the substance of the body and blood of
Jesus coexists with the substance of the bread and wine in the
Eucharist. That is, the bread and wine "spiritually" become
the actual body and blood of Christ during the "Eucharist."

Transubstantiation: The Roman Catholic belief that
the whole substance of the bread and the wine changes into
the substance of the body and blood of Christ when
consecrated in the Eucharist. To be precise, the bread and
wine "actually become" the body and blood of Christ in the
"Eucharist" when eaten.

Both of these so-called "doctrines" spawned from
John 6 and neither have any substantive Scriptural
foundation. Our text has absolutely nothing to do with the
Lord's Supper. Let me repeat that: Our text (John 6:53-56)
has nothing to do with the Lord's Supper. In these two false
doctrines, the act of crucifying the Savior is repeated each
time the act is performed. Each time the ritual of the
Eucharist is performed in the churches that believe in
consubstantiation and transubstantiation, our Lord and
Savior is crucified again. The Eucharist, in many cases, is
performed every Sunday morning. The Scripture says in
Hebrews 10:10, **"By the which will we are sanctified
through the offering of the body of Jesus Christ once *for***

all." Jesus Christ was crucified *only once*. That was all that was needed. The continuous repetition of the murder of Christ on Golgotha's hill is senseless. It happened "once for all." Now would be a good time to define the Lord's Supper.

What is the Lord's Supper?

The institution of the Lord's Supper is found four times in the New Testament. Those locations are Mat. 26:26-29, Mark 14:22-25, Luke 22:17-20, and 1 Cor. 11:23-25. Our text in John 6 is not on that list. Upon examining these four passages, the reader will learn the following: Jesus Christ Himself instituted it during the Last Supper with His disciples. **"And as they were eating, Jesus took bread, and blessed *it*, and brake *it*, and gave *it* to the disciples, and said, Take, eat; this is my body"** (Mat. 26:26). **"And as they did eat, Jesus took bread, and blessed, and brake *it*, and gave to them, and said, Take, eat: this is my body"** (Mark 14:22). **"And he took the cup, and gave thanks, and said, Take this, and divide *it* among yourselves"** (Luke 22:17). **"For I have received of the Lord that which also I delivered unto you, That the Lord Jesus the *same* night in which he was betrayed took bread..."** (1 Cor. 11:23).

The Lord's Supper is a Memorial. When we partake of it, we look back to the cross as well as look forward to the Second Advent of Christ. **"And when he had given thanks, he brake *it*, and said, Take, eat: this is my body, which is broken for you: this do in remembrance of me. After the same manner also *he took* the cup, when he had supped, saying, This cup is the new testament in my blood: this do ye, as oft as ye drink *it*, in remembrance of me"** (1 Cor. 11:24-25). **"For as often as ye eat this bread, and drink this cup, ye do shew the Lord's death till he come"** (1 Cor. 11:26).

The Lord's Supper is for those who know Christ as Savior. It is pointless for an unsaved person to memorialize the death, burial, and resurrection of Christ, as well as look forward to His Second Coming. As members of the "Body of Christ," we have a spiritual union (communion) with Jesus Christ. Paul spoke of this in 1 Cor. 10:16-17 **"The cup of blessing which we bless, is it not the communion of the blood of Christ? The bread which we break, is it not the communion of the body of Christ? For we *being* many are one bread, *and* one body: for we are all partakers of that one bread."** Paul points out that as members of the Body of Christ and partakers of "that one bread" we *are* "one bread."

Paul compares our communion with Christ as members of His Body to the Old Testament Aaronic priest which ate the sacrifice on the altar, **"Behold Israel after the flesh: are not they which eat of the sacrifices partakers of the altar?"** (1 Cor. 10:18)

The Lord's Supper is a time of spiritual self-examination. **"But let a man examine himself, and so let him eat of *that* bread, and drink of *that* cup"** (1 Cor. 11:28). This spiritual self-examination includes the act of confessing known sin and clearing up any obstructions to fellowship with Christ.

The Lord's Supper is one of two ordinances of the Local Church. The other is baptism. As a memorial, the Lord's Supper is a time of spiritual reflection for the believer. It is a time to look back at our own salvation experience and remember where we were when God found us. There was a time in our lives when we were alone and without God. **"That at that time ye were without Christ, being aliens from the commonwealth of Israel, and strangers from the covenants of promise, having no hope, and without God in the world"** (Eph. 2:12). The Holy Spirit drew us to Christ. John 6:44 says, **"No man can come to me, except** the Father which hath sent me draw him: and I will raise him up at the last day." It should be a time when the believer expresses his love to his Heavenly Father in appreciation for salvation and the abundant life in Christ. A sense of personal unworthiness should accompany this praise. We do not observe the Lords' Supper to get saved. We get saved by receiving Jesus Christ as Savior and no other way.

The Fall of Man is Associated with Eating

We read in Gen. 2:16, **"And the LORD God commanded the man, saying, Of every tree of the garden thou mayest freely eat:"** These instructions were actually given before Eve was created. Adam had the liberty of eating from **"every tree of the garden."** This, of course, included the tree of life (Gen. 2:9). For more on the tree of life see our paper on this subject. Later, Eve would be instructed in the rules of the Garden. So they could eat of any of the trees with the exception of the tree of knowledge of good and evil. Gen. 2:17, **"But of the tree of the knowledge of good and evil, thou shalt not eat of it: for in the day that thou eatest thereof thou shalt surely die."** The penalty for eating this fruit was death. They had free access to the tree of life. They were in perfect conditions with fellowship with God, eternal life, pain-free childbirth, perfect weather conditions, no work, no curse on the earth, etc. All this was contingent upon one restriction. They could look at the forbidden fruit. They could touch it, feel it, smell it, and admire it. They were not to *eat* it.

Adam and Eve did eat of the fruit and the First Adam brought death to every man (1 Cor. 15:22). The Bible says in Rom. 5:12, **"Wherefore, as by one man sin entered into the world, and death by sin; and so death passed upon all men, for that all have sinned:"** Remember, all this happened as result of *someone eating something*. Millions of souls burning in hell for all eternity are the result of the simple act of eating the forbidden fruit.

Atonement is Associated with Eating

In the book of Exodus we find the Children of Israel were held in bondage in Egypt for a period of four hundred years (Gen. 15:13, Acts 7:6). God commissioned Moses to lead them out of Egypt to the land promised to Abraham (Gen. 12:7). In order to convince the Jews to follow Moses, God gave him the power of signs and wonders. The Scripture says, **"For the Jews require a sign"** (1 Cor. 1:22). When the Children of Israel beheld the signs and wonders, they believed. The Lord did many signs and wonders (through Moses) just prior to taking the Israelites out of Egypt (Ex. 5-14). The final judgment was the first Passover. The Hebrews were instructed to take a lamb and kill it in the afternoon. The Jew was to take hyssop and dip it in the blood of the lamb and strike it on the lintel and doorposts of his house (Ex. 12). At midnight that night, the Destroyer would come and kill the firstborn in every family that did not have the blood on the doorframe.

After the lamb was slain and the blood applied, it was to be roasted on a fire. In Ex. 12:8-11 we read, **"And they shall eat the flesh in that night, roast with fire, and unleavened bread;** *and* **with bitter** *herbs* **they shall eat it. Eat not of it raw, nor sodden at all with water, but roast** *with* **fire; his head with his legs, and with the purtenance thereof. And ye shall let nothing of it remain until the morning; and that which remaineth of it until the morning ye shall burn with fire. And thus shall ye eat it;** *with* **your loins girded, your shoes on your feet, and your staff in your hand; and ye shall eat it in haste: it** *is* **the LORD'S passover."** They were required to "eat the flesh" of the lamb as part of the atonement. If they failed to eat the flesh of the lamb, it would be an incomplete atonement and their first-born would be slain.

Later, when God gave Moses the Law, specific instructions were given for burnt offerings in the Tabernacle. In Ex. 29:32-33 we read, **"And Aaron and his sons shall eat the flesh of the ram, and the bread that *is* in the basket, *by* the door of the tabernacle of the congregation. And they shall eat those things wherewith the atonement was made, to consecrate *and* to sanctify them: but a stranger shall not eat *thereof*, because they *are* holy."** When the priest sacrificed the animal for atonement, it had to be roasted and the flesh eaten by the priest. If this was not done, it was an incomplete atonement. An incomplete atonement is no atonement.

Bread in John 6

Now let us go back to John 6 and look at this group of Jews speaking to Christ. The Lord had just rebuked the people for seeking Him not for the miracles, but for a full belly (vs. 26). After that Christ said, **"Labour not for the meat which perisheth, but for that meat which endureth unto everlasting life, which the Son of man shall give unto you: for him hath God the Father sealed"** (vs. 27). These Jews are speaking in earthly, physical terms (meat that perishes) and Christ is speaking in spiritual terms (Bread of Life).

The group then spoke of the manna eaten in the wilderness. **"They said therefore unto him, What sign shewest thou then, that we may see, and believe thee? what dost thou work? Our fathers did eat manna in the desert; as it is written, He gave them bread from heaven to eat. Then Jesus said unto them, Verily, verily, I say unto you, Moses gave you not that bread from heaven;**

but my Father giveth you the true bread from heaven. For the bread of God is he which cometh down from heaven, and giveth life unto the world. Then said they unto him, Lord, evermore give us this bread.**" (John 6:30-34) Again, the people spoke of earthly bread and Christ spoke of Heavenly Bread.

Christ pointed out to this group (vs. 49) that their fathers who ate the bread in the wilderness (manna) are now dead. This bread was associated with Moses and the Law. In verse 51 Christ said, **"I am the living bread which came down from heaven; if any man eat of this bread, he shall live for ever: and the bread that I will give is my flesh, which I will give for the life of the world."** The contrast is between two different breads from heaven – one ends up in death and the other in life. The contrast is Mosaic Law and Grace in Christ. The writer of Hebrews 10:4 said, **"For *it is* not possible that the blood of bulls and of goats should take away sins."** Christ offered Himself as the Bread of Life from Heaven as the ultimate atonement for sin. This bread was to be "eaten."

Eating as an Act of Appropriation

In John 4 we find the meeting of Christ with the woman at the well. After speaking to her about water that springs up into everlasting life (vs. 14) the woman departs into the city and witnesses for Christ (vs. 28-29). Meanwhile, His disciples return with food and offer some to Jesus Christ. Verse 32 is His response, **"But he said unto them, I have meat to eat that ye know not of."** Christ referred to a heavenly "meat." Verse 34 says, **"Jesus saith unto them, My meat is to do the will of him that sent me, and to finish his work."** Again, the people around Him spoke of physical food while Christ spoke of spiritual "meat." Christ's spiritual meat was to do (appropriate) His Father's will.

In John 6:27 we read, **"Labour not for the meat which perisheth, but for that meat which endureth unto everlasting life, which the Son of man shall give unto you: for him hath God the Father sealed."** This verse admonishes us to choose the spiritual over the physical and does so in the context of eating. Therefore, when Christ told this group of Jews they must "eat His flesh," He spoke in spiritual terms as an act of appropriating Christ as Savior.

Drink My Blood

We have already pointed out our text is not the Lord's Supper. The Lord's Supper is a memorial, looking back to Christ's death, burial, and resurrection. At the time of John 6 Christ would have been approximately 32.5 years old, with about one year before His crucifixion. Jesus Christ began His ministry when He was thirty years old (Luke 3:23). In the Old Testament the priest could not begin to work in the Tabernacle until he was thirty. Joseph, a type of Christ, was thirty when he began his work for Pharaoh (Gen. 41:46). David, a type of Christ, was thirty when he began to reign as king (2 Sam. 5:4). The ministry of Jesus Christ was three and one-half years in length. We know this because there are four Passovers in the Book of John. They are: John 2:13, 5:1, 6:4, and 12:1. Simple math shows Christ's birthday six months from the Passover. That would not be in December, but about the time of the Feast of Tabernacles. This date can also be extrapolated by a study of the course of Abia (Luke 1:5 and 1 Chron. 24) during the reign of King Solomon. See our paper on "The Course of Abia" for additional details.

The main reason our text is not the Lord's Supper is the fact that Christ, in John 6, had not yet died on the cross. According to Heb. 9:16 a testament requires the death of the testator before it becomes effective. Therefore, the New

Testament is not yet officially in effect since Calvary is still in the future. Remember, the Lord's Supper is a memorial.

During this time the Jews still observed the Passover, the Sabbath, abstained from eating pork, etc. The Law of Moses was still in effect in Palestine. When Christ healed lepers (Mat. 8:2-4, Mark 1:44, and Luke 17:14), He told them to go show themselves to the priest and offer the appropriate gift as commanded in Lev. 14. Yet during His ministry He forgave the sins of many based simply on their faith in Him. This was a "transition period" between the Law of Moses and our present dispensation where people are saved by grace through faith in the finished work of Jesus Christ. By a transition period, we mean that there was overlap between the Old and New Testament periods.

Drinking blood is forbidden before the Law (Gen. 9:4), under the Law (Lev. 17:12), and after the Law (Acts 15:20). When Christ said, "drink my blood" it was an act of appropriation. It was the act of applying the blood of Christ to an individual soul. John 7:37-39 – **"In the last day, that great *day* of the feast, Jesus stood and cried, saying, If any man thirst, let him come unto me, and drink. He that believeth on me, as the scripture hath said, out of his belly shall flow rivers of living water. (But this spake he of the Spirit, which they that believe on him should receive: for the Holy Ghost was not yet *given*; because that Jesus was not yet glorified.)"** Christ spoke figuratively here, since you cannot drink a person. In Mark 10:36-39 another passage shows figurative drinking. **"And he said unto them, What would ye that I should do for you? They said unto him, Grant unto us that we may sit, one on thy right hand, and the other on thy left hand, in thy glory. But Jesus said unto them, Ye know not what ye ask: can ye drink of the cup that I drink of? and be baptized with the baptism that I am baptized with? And they said unto him, We can. And Jesus said unto them,**

Ye shall indeed drink of the cup that I drink of; and with the baptism that I am baptized withal shall ye be baptized:" The cup from which Christ drunk was the torment of becoming a personification of sin on the cross and God the Father turning His back on His beloved Son. This was spoken of as "drinking." This was the same cup Christ prayed about in Gethsemane (Mat. 26:39, Mark 14:36). Another cup is mentioned in Psm. 116:13, **"I will take the cup of salvation, and call upon the name of the LORD."** Here again, drinking is figurative.

Summary

When Jesus Christ told the Jews to eat His flesh and drink His blood, He did not mean the physical act of eating and drinking. Under these conditions, if someone wanted to get saved today where would he go to find the body and blood of Christ to consume? That person would be unable to find those two commodities and thus remain unsaved. But where is the Body of Christ? Where is the Blood of Christ?

Saved, born again believers make up the spiritual Body of Christ (1 Cor. 12:27). However, Christ's physical body is found in Heb. 12:2, **"Looking unto Jesus the author and finisher of *our* faith; who for the joy that was set before him endured the cross, despising the shame, and is set down at the right hand of the throne of God."** This verse is given in the present tense and indicates where Christ is today.

What about His blood? Where is it? According to Heb. 9:11-28, Christ took His own blood and offered it once and for all in the Heavenly Tabernacle. Verses 20-28 **"Saying, This *is* the blood of the testament which God hath enjoined unto you. Moreover he sprinkled with blood both the tabernacle, and all the vessels of the ministry. And almost all things are by the law purged** with blood; and without shedding of blood is no remission. *It was* therefore necessary that the patterns of things in the heavens should be purified with these; but the heavenly things themselves with better sacrifices than these. For Christ is not entered into the holy places made with hands, *which are* the figures of the true; but into heaven itself, now to appear in the presence of God for us: Nor yet that he should offer himself often, as the high priest entereth into the holy place every year with blood of others: For then must he often have suffered since the foundation of the world: but now once in the end of the world hath he appeared to put away sin by the sacrifice of himself. And as it is appointed unto men once to die, but after this the judgment: So Christ was once offered to bear the sins of many; and unto them that look for him shall he appear the second time without sin unto salvation."

Now let us look at the results of Christ's statement in our text. In verse 53 the result of not eating His flesh and drinking His blood is **"Ye have no life in you."** In verse 54 He says whoever eats His flesh and drinks His blood **"hath eternal life and I will raise him up at the last day."** In verse 56 He said he that eats His flesh and drinks His blood **"dwelleth in me and I in him."** Notice all three of the results of doing this in these three verses are the result of the New Birth. The entire passage is a figurative invitation by Christ to the New Birth. Jesus Christ wanted those people to come to Him in salvation. Have you been born again?

If your answer is no, you must understand that **"The wages of sin is death"** (Rom. 6:23). By the word, "death" Paul spoke of eternal damnation in hell. The only way anyone can be saved from burning in hell is through Jesus Christ and His work of atonement at Calvary. The Bible says in John 1:12, **"But as many as received him, to them gave he power to become the sons of God, *even* to them that**

believe on his name." Whoever comes to Christ with a genuine desire to be saved does not get turned down. John 6:37 – **"All that the Father giveth me shall come to me; and him that cometh to me I will in no wise cast out."** You can accept Jesus Christ's payment for your sin and receive Him today. Pray and ask Him to forgive you and save you from your sins. Do it now.

CHAPTER FOUR

THE PROPHETIC SIGNIFICANCE OF CHRIST WALKING ON THE SEA

Preface

AS LORD OVER HIS CREATION, THE Lord has the option to abide by the laws of physics that He instituted, or simply chose to ignore them. This is seen many times in Scripture. For example, Jesus Christ rode into Jerusalem upon a colt, the foal of an ass, whereupon no man had ever ridden (Zech. 9:9, Mat. 21:1-11, Luke 19:29-38, John 12:12-19). Anyone who has ever worked with this animal knows that this simply doesn't happen. An ass must first be "broken" before it will allow a rider. Not so with the Lord Jesus Christ. The animal was completely submissive to Him without going through the training process. In another situation, Jesus Christ needed to address a large crowd of people and teach them the mysteries of the Kingdom of Heaven (Mat. 13:2, Mark 4:1, Luke 5:3). This time He worked *with* the laws of physics by boarding a small boat and pushing off a short distance from the shore. He *sat down* in the boat to speak while His audience *stood* on shore (above Him) and was heard by all in attendance. When we study sound wave propagation, we can understand why He did that. Sound waves travel at 1100 feet per second and have a tendency to rise. Water always finds the lowest point in any terrain. The ancient Greek and Romans incorporated this into their theaters. The best auditoriums (acoustically) have the podium at a low point, with the majority of the seating gradually rising around and above the speaker. Here, Christ used existing laws of physics to aid Him in His goal. Again, Jesus Christ ignored the laws of gravity in Acts 1:9 and levitated Himself up into Heaven. When Christ traveled throughout Palestine, His mode of travel was mostly on foot or in a boat. He could very well have flown to His destination by faith (1 Cor. 13:2, **"…and though I have all faith, so that I could remove mountains…"**) but instead, chose to abide by the laws of physics in His personal travels.

The passage we will look at in this paper is concerned with one particular occasion when the Lord Jesus chose *not* to abide by the laws of physics, but instead, He exerted His lordship over them. Three times in the Gospels (Matthew, Mark, and John), this event was recorded. Anything mentioned thrice is very significant. The virgin birth of Christ is only mentioned twice in the gospels (Matthew and Luke). Of the four Gospels, the ascension of Christ is only mentioned twice (Mark and Luke). The passage explaining what it is to be born again is only mentioned a single time in the book of John. But, when Jesus Christ walked on the sea, He had three different writers record the event. These passages are found in Mat. 14: 22-36, Mark 6:45-56, and John 6:15-21.

What is the significance of this event? Why was it mentioned three times? What does it mean? Does it have to do with prophecy? If so, in what way was it prophetic? We will answer these and other questions in the following pages. Before we look at our text, there is one addition point to make, by way of introduction.

Water

God's use of water as an instrument by which He conducts His affairs, needs to be noted. *Water* is used throughout the Scripture in diverse applications and locations. It is also used with a variety of purposes. In fact, the subject of the significance of water in the Scripture is so voluminous, we can only briefly highlight certain points for the purpose of this paper.

It is mentioned in the second verse in Genesis. **"…and darkness *was* upon the face of the deep. And the Spirit of God moved upon the face of the waters."** From the beginning of time, water has played a part in the activities of God. The Lord used water as a tool of judgment when He drowned out an entire world with the great flood (Gen. 6-8). He used water as a platform for many miracles for the benefit of the Jews in the Exodus and wilderness wanderings. Moses turned water into blood in Exodus as a sign for the Jews (Ex. 7). God used it as judgment for Pharaoh and his armies when the Red Sea enclosed them (Ex. 14). God used it to slake the thirst of Israel when Moses smote the rock at Meribah (Ex. 17). Rain was one of the promises given to the Jews in the Palestinian Covenant. If they lived according to His law, God would make sure the early and latter rains would provide the water for good crops (Deut. 28). Again, rain served as showers of blessing in Ezk. 34. Elijah walked into Ahab's court and told the king it would not rain for three and one-half years, bringing famine to the land because of Israel's sin (Jam. 5:17). At the end of that famine a great rainstorm came (1King 18). This is a picture of the great rainstorm that will precede the Second Advent of Jesus Christ (Rev. 1:7 et al).

Jonah prayed to God out of the belly of the whale and depicted Christ's death, burial, and resurrection from the bottom of the sea. The condition to Naaman's cleansing was that he wash himself seven times in the Jordan River (2 King. 5). This typified John's baptism of Old Testament Jewish purification and repentance. It also is a type of New Testament salvation by grace and the sin-cleansing power of the Blood of Jesus Christ. The first public miracle that Christ did was to turn water into wine in John 2. The Ethiopian eunuch, after receiving Christ as Savior, said, **"See, *here is* water; what doth hinder me to be baptized?"** Philip then baptized him. There are many more passages in Scripture where the Holy Spirit uses water to convey a message.

The First Advent of Jesus Christ was one of the most important and significant events that has ever been recorded in both human history as well as the word of God. However, when we look at the main theme of Scripture, including prophecy and typology, we see that Christ's Second Advent takes the front seat in terms of magnitude, importance, and frequency of mention. From God the Father's point of view, He sent His only begotten Son to earth to resolve Israel's sin problem. While here, He did His best to invite God's Peculiar Treasure back into fellowship with the Father, but they refused. In fact they ended up murdering Him in His attempt. And it is wonderful that during this time, God allowed the lowly gentile to enjoy the benefits of fellowship with God through His Son's redemptive work on Calvary's cross. On God the Father's calendar, the day that His Son returns in Glory to take His rightful place on the Throne (in Jerusalem) to rule the earth and the rest of the universe with a rod of iron is far more important than the day sinful man crucified Him in shame.

Of the many typological pictures of the Second Advent found in the Bible, Christ walking on the sea is yet another. Here the Holy Spirit again uses water to illustrate a part of the Day of the Lord, when He returns in power, vengeance, and glory.

Water Walking

Mat. 14:22-26 – **"And straightway Jesus
constrained his disciples to get into a ship, and to go
before him unto the other side, while he sent the
multitudes away. And when he had sent the multitudes
away, he went up into a mountain apart to pray: and
when the evening was come, he was there alone.** After
Christ miraculously fed (over) five thousand people, He
told His disciples to get into a boat proceed to a certain
destination while He went up on a mountain to pray.
**But the ship was now in the midst of the sea, tossed with
waves: for the wind was contrary.** While He prayed, a
storm arose and threatened the disciples. Earlier we
mentioned the great storm that precedes the Second
Advent of Christ. This verse is one of many pictures of
that great storm. **And in the fourth watch of the night
Jesus went unto them, walking on the sea. And when the
disciples saw him walking on the sea, they were
troubled, saying, It is a spirit; and they cried out for
fear."**

During the storm, Christ appears to the men. But
instead of being happy to see their Savior, the Scripture says
they were "troubled." The word "troubled" is found in both
the Matthew and Mark passages. Why were they troubled?
Let's allow the Scripture to answer that.

Trouble

In Acts 7 Stephen preached his final sermon. During
the message he spoke about Abraham, Isaac, and Jacob and
the Hebrew lineage ultimately leading to Jesus Christ. When

he got to Joseph in vs. 13 he said, **"And at the second *time* Joseph was made known to his brethren;"** Right here is one of those many references to the Second Advent we mentioned earlier. The first time Joseph's brethren came to Egypt to get corn (Gen. 45) they did not recognize the younger brother they sold into slavery for twenty pieces of silver. Joseph recognized his brethren, but kept his identity from them. It was during their second visit that he revealed his identity. The first time Jesus Christ came, His brethren, the Jews, did not recognize Him as their Messiah. When He comes the second time, they will.

Let's look at the reunion between Joseph and his brethren a little closer in Gen. 45:1-3: **"Then Joseph could not refrain himself before all them that stood by him; and he cried, Cause every man to go out from me. And there stood no man with him, while Joseph made himself known unto his brethren. And he wept aloud: and the Egyptians and the house of Pharaoh heard. And Joseph said unto his brethren, I *am* Joseph; doth my father yet live? And his brethren could not answer him; for they were troubled at his presence."**

When the Christian reads passages like this one, he should pray and ask the Holy Spirit to open his eyes of understanding. These verses of Scripture give us a small glimpse of some of the characteristics of the actual moment when the remnant of Jews recognize Christ as the Messiah at His return. Joseph bore no malice toward his brethren for their misdeeds. When his brethren realized in whose presence they stood, the Scripture says, **"they were troubled at his presence."**

Now we can understand why the disciples were "troubled" when they saw Christ walking on the sea in the midst of the storm. It is actually a picture of the Jews at the Second Advent of Christ. The Nation of Israel will realize who it was that they crucified ages ago and then they will mourn.

"And I will pour upon the house of David, and upon the inhabitants of Jerusalem, the spirit of grace and of supplications: and they shall look upon me whom they have pierced, and they shall mourn for him, as one mourneth for *his* only *son*, and shall be in bitterness for him, as one that is in bitterness for *his* firstborn. In that day shall there be a great mourning in Jerusalem, as the mourning of Hadadrimmon in the valley of Megiddon. And the land shall mourn, every family apart; the family of the house of David apart, and their wives apart; the family of the house of Nathan apart, and their wives apart; The family of the house of Levi apart, and their wives apart; the family of Shimei apart, and their wives apart; All the families that remain, every family apart, and their wives apart. In that day there shall be a fountain opened to the house of David and to the inhabitants of Jerusalem for sin and for uncleanness" (Zech. 12:10-14 to 13:1).

There are other places in Scripture the use of the word, "trouble" appears in reference to the Jew in the Tribulation. For example, Job is a picture of the Jew in the Tribulation. Job 23:15 – **"Therefore am I troubled at his presence: when I consider, I am afraid of him."** Lamentations is also a picture of the Jew in the Tribulation. Lam. 2:11 – **"Mine eyes do fail with tears, my bowels are troubled, my liver is poured upon the earth, for the destruction of the daughter of my people; because the children and the sucklings swoon in the streets of the city."**

Daniel spoke of a great time of trouble for the Nation of Israel. Dan. 12:1 – **"And at that time shall Michael stand up, the great prince which standeth for the children of thy people: and there shall be a time of trouble, such as never was since there was a nation *even*** to that same time: and at that time thy people shall be delivered, every one that shall be found written in the book."

After the resurrection of Christ, He appeared to His disciples in Luke 24:36-40 – **"And as they thus spake, Jesus himself stood in the midst of them, and saith unto them, Peace *be* unto you. But they were terrified and affrighted, and supposed that they had seen a spirit. And he said unto them, Why are ye troubled? and why do thoughts arise in your hearts? Behold my hands and my feet, that it is I myself: handle me, and see; for a spirit hath not flesh and bones, as ye see me have. And when he had thus spoken, he shewed them his hands and his feet."** When His disciples saw Him, they were also "troubled." Then the Lord Jesus showed them the wounds in His hands and feet. A similar passage found in Zechariah, regarding Christ's nail-pierced hands and the Jewish aftermath: Zech. 13:6 – **"And *one* shall say unto him, What *are* these wounds in thine hands? Then he shall answer, *Those* with which I was wounded *in* the house of my friends."** Immediately following, we find verses 7-9 having to do with the Trouble the Jews experience during the Tribulation and the death of two-thirds (66.6%) of the Jewish population. **"Awake, O sword, against my shepherd, and against the man *that is* my fellow, saith the LORD of hosts: smite the shepherd, and the sheep shall be scattered: and I will turn mine hand upon the little ones. And it shall come to pass, *that* in all the land, saith the LORD, two parts therein shall be cut off *and* die; but the third shall be left therein. And I will bring the third part through the fire, and will refine them as silver is refined, and will try them as gold is tried: they shall call on my name, and I will hear them: I will say, It *is* my people: and they shall say, The LORD *is* my God."**

Christ Walked on the Water in the 4th Watch

When the disciples saw Christ walking on the sea, it was the fourth watch of the night. Mat. 14:25 – **"And in the fourth watch of the night Jesus went unto them, walking on the sea."** This has considerable prophetic significance when we study the four watches given in Scripture.

The prophet Isaiah warned Israel of impending judgment from God for the sins of the nation. In anticipation of the invasion of Sennacherib (2 Kings 18), Isaiah wrote, **"The burden of Dumah. He calleth to me out of Seir, Watchman, what of the night? Watchman, what of the night? The watchman said, The morning cometh, and also the night: if ye will enquire, enquire ye: return, come"** (Isa. 21:11-12). The watchman stayed up all night watching for any approaching enemy. There were four watches given in Mark 13:35 – **"Watch ye therefore: for ye know not when the master of the house cometh, at even, or at midnight, or at the cockcrowing, or in the morning:"** Those four watches were: 6 – 9 PM, the evening watch; 9 – 12 PM, the midnight watch; 12 – 3 AM, the cockcrowing; and 3 – 6 AM, the morning watch.

Verse 35 is given in the middle of a passage, which commands us to watch: **"But of that day and *that* hour knoweth no man, no, not the angels which are in heaven, neither the Son, but the Father. Take ye heed, watch and pray: for ye know not when the time is. *For the Son of man is* as a man taking a far journey, who left his house, and gave authority to his servants, and to every man his work, and commanded the porter to watch. Watch ye therefore: for ye know not when the master of the house cometh, at even, or at midnight, or at the cockcrowing, or in the morning: Lest coming suddenly he find you sleeping. And what I say unto you I say unto all, Watch"** (Mark 13:32-37).

A similar passage is given in Luke with the same admonition with a subtle addition: **"Let your loins be girded about, and *your* lights burning; And ye yourselves like unto men that wait for their lord, when he will return from the wedding; that when he cometh and knocketh, they may open unto him immediately. Blessed *are* those servants, whom the lord when he cometh shall find watching: verily I say unto you, that he shall gird himself, and make them to sit down to meat, and will come forth and serve them. And if he shall come in the second watch, or come in the third watch, and find *them* so, blessed are those servants. And this know, that if the goodman of the house had known what hour the thief would come, he would have watched, and not have suffered his house to be broken through. Be ye therefore ready also: for the Son of man cometh at an hour when ye think not"** (Luke 12:35-40).

In this passage the Holy Spirit mentions in vs. 36 that when Christ comes, He will be coming directly from a wedding. According to Rev. 19 the Marriage Supper of the Lamb takes place just prior to the Second Advent.

Verse 38 mentions the possibility of Christ coming during the second and third watch. He didn't come. We are now in the fourth watch of the night (Laodicean Church) relative to the seven churches mentioned in Rev. 2-3 and the Lord has yet to come. The Second Advent of Jesus Christ will be a time of Judgment and Glory. For example: In the morning watch judgment fell upon Sodom (Gen. 19). The judgments against Pharaoh and Egypt by Moses in Ex. 7-10 all took place in the morning. In Ex. 14:24 God's judgment falls in the fourth watch of the night (Pharaoh in the Red Sea). In Ex. 16:7 the Glory of the Lord is seen in the morning watch. In Josh. 6, it was in the morning when the priests encompassed the city of Jericho seven times and blew the trumpets, causing the walls to come down. It was in the morning that David (type of Christ) killed Goliath (type of Antichrist) in 1 Sam. 17. In Psm. 30:5, **"weeping may endure for a night, but joy *cometh* in the morning."** Jer. 21:12 – **"O house of David, thus saith the LORD; Execute judgment in the morning, and deliver *him that is* spoiled out of the hand of the oppressor, lest my fury go out like fire, and burn that none can quench *it*, because of the evil of your doings."** In Mal 4:2 Christ comes in the morning. In Mat 14, Mark 6, and John 6 Christ comes walking on the sea in the morning watch. In Rev. 22:16 Jesus Christ said, **"I am the root and the offspring of David, *and* the bright and morning star."**

According to these and other passages of Scripture, Christ will return in the morning watch. The Bible says in Mat. 25:13, **"Watch therefore, for ye know neither the day nor the hour wherein the Son of man cometh."** We don't know the day or the hour, but the Scripture is loaded with clues about when the Second Advent takes place.

Conclusion

The three records of Christ walking on the sea give us a graphic picture of the Lord Jesus overriding the laws of physics and illustrating His return. The Jewish disciples (Nation of Israel) are in the midst of a terrible storm (Tribulation), Christ returns after a short time when He was up on a high mountain praying (He's now seated at the right hand of God the Father making intercession for us – Mark 16:19, Act. 2:33, 7:55, 5:56, Rom. 8:34, Col. 3:1, Heb. 10:12, and 1 Pet. 3:22), when the disciples see Him they are troubled, Jesus Christ says, **"It is I, be not afraid,"** then the disciples receive Him into the ship (Israel's national revival) and He calms the storm. That scenario sums up what will take place in Israel's future.

We are commanded to watch: 1 Thes. 5:2 – **"For yourselves know perfectly that the day of the Lord so cometh as a thief in the night."** 2 Pet. 3:10 – **"But the day of the Lord will come as a thief in the night; in the which the heavens shall pass away with a great noise, and the elements shall melt with fervent heat, the earth also and the works that are therein shall be burned up."** Rev. 3:3 – **"Remember therefore how thou hast received and heard, and hold fast, and repent. If therefore thou shalt not watch, I will come on thee as a thief, and thou shalt not know what hour I will come upon thee."**

In this paper, we spoke of the Second Advent proper. The Rapture of the Church is the next thing to take place on God's prophetic calendar. It could happen at any time. Are you ready to meet the Lord. If you do not know Christ as your Savior, seek Him now. The Bible says in Rom. 10:13 **"For whosoever shall call upon the name of the Lord shall be saved."** Call upon Him now and ask Him to forgive you of your sins and save your soul before it's too late. May God bless you.

CHAPTER FIVE

ORNAN'S THRESHING FLOOR

Forward

WHEN THE SUBJECT OF ORNAN'S Threshing Floor is mentioned, many Christians exhibit a baffled look. Others who may remember reading about it in the historical books (of Scripture) fail to see the significance and write it off as a subject unworthy of any serious study. Let us point out first of all there is nothing in Scripture that is not worthy of our in-depth study. The Bible says, **"All Scripture *is* given by inspiration of God and *is* profitable for doctrine, for reproof, for correction, for instruction in righteousness"** (2 Tim. 3:16). In addition, we read in Proverbs 30:5, **"Every word of God *is* pure:"** Luke, the physician wrote, **"That man shall not live by bread alone, but by every word of God"** (Luke 4:4). There are many more passages on this, but we'll stop with three verses. Secondly, as we study Ornan's Threshing Floor, the reader should quickly see the significance of this study.

The Threshing Floor

A threshing floor is normally a large flat area similar to a slab of concrete. In many cases it is solid stone. When the husbandman harvested his crops, he brought them to a threshing floor. Whether corn, wheat, barley, cumin, fitches, or whatever, the stalks were spread out on the floor for threshing. Threshing took place in different fashions. Sometimes an ox trampled on them. Other times the ox pulled a cart and wheels of the cart supplemented the hooves of the ox. In many cases the farmer beat the stalks with sticks or rods. Sometimes the ox pulled a cart with sharp, iron spikes that threshed the stalks. **"Behold, I will make thee a new sharp threshing instrument having teeth: thou shalt thresh the mountains, and beat them small, and shalt make the hills as chaff" (Isa. 41:15). "For the fitches are not threshed with a threshing instrument, neither is a cart wheel turned about upon the cummin; but the fitches are beaten out with a staff, and the cummin with a rod. Bread *corn* is bruised; because he will not ever be threshing it, nor break *it with* the wheel of his cart, nor bruise it *with* his horsemen"** (Isa. 28:27-28). The idea of threshing is to separate the grain from the tare. The stalks are dried and must be beaten or ground to remove the wheat from the stalk.

Winnowing is the next step in the process. After the stalks are beaten or mashed, the results are tossed into the air with pitchforks and the wind blows the chaff away. The heavier grain falls back to the floor. The threshing floor was normally located in a windy environment, such as the top of a hill or mountain. The process is repeated until only the grain is left on the floor. It is then swept up and put into sacks. In modern farming equipment this process is done in the field and only the grain is brought back for storage in the silo.

Threshing floors are mentioned several times in Scripture. However, there are three that have been given specific names. Interestingly, all three named threshing floors have double names. The first is found in Gen. 50:10-11 and is referred to as Atad's threshing floor as well as Abelmizraim. This was the site of the 7-day mourning period of Joseph's entourage during his trip from Egypt to Canaan to bury his father Jacob. The second is known as Nachon's threshing floor, AKA Perezuzzah. This was the site where Uzzah put his hand on the ark of God to stabilize it (while it rode on a cart). God smote him as result. The subject of this paper is the third named threshing floor. We will see that it is found in 2 Sam 24 and 1 Chron. 21 and is referred to as Ornan's threshing floor as well as Araunah's threshing floor.

Before we get to the text, we should look at the time in Israel's history in which this passage occurs. This event took place approximately twenty years after David's sin with Bathsheba. He has returned to Jerusalem after fleeing the confrontation with his son Absalom, who is now dead. Joab murdered Amasa and put down Sheba's revolt (2 Sam. 20). David had just been through a three-year drought (chapter 21:1-9) because of Saul's treatment of the Gibeonites. In Judges 9 the Gibeonites presented themselves to Joshua as travelers from a far country in an effort to avoid annihilation. Joshua believed their story and made league with them only to learn they resided right there in the land. Saul broke the oath, thus the judgment of God upon Israel (Josh. 9:19-20). Since the Lord told David, **"the sword shall never depart from thine house"** (2 Sam. 12:10), the times of peace between wars was short-lived. Thus we have the background for our text.

The chronicle of Ornan's threshing floor is given twice in Scripture. This indicates the considerable significance of the site's geographic location. We will see some subtle differences in the two passages as well as annotate the seeming contradictions in the text. Our approach to Scripture is simple: there are no mistakes in the word of God. The Psalmist asks the question, **"Who can understand _his_ errors?"** (Psm. 19:12). The implied answer is nobody. With this in mind, let us turn to our text.

"And again the anger of the LORD was kindled against Israel, and he moved David against them to say, Go, number Israel and Judah" (2 Sam. 24:1). The writer says, **"again the anger of the LORD..."** because the Lord's anger was kindled in 2 Sam. 21:1-9 mentioned above. Now let's look at 1 Chron. 21:1 – **"And Satan stood up against Israel, and provoked David to number Israel."** Here we see our first supposed contradiction in the text. The first passage says the Lord moved David to number Israel and Judah and the second one says Satan is the guilty party. This should not be a contradiction to anyone who read Job 1 and 2. The order ultimately comes from God and Satan carries out the directive. Both passages are correct as they stand.

2 Sam. 24:2 – **"For the king said to Joab the captain of the host, which was with him, Go now through all the tribes of Israel, from Dan even to Beersheba, and number ye the people, that I may know the number of the people."** The idea is simple; David wants to know the number of the men of Israel and Judah (Ex. 12:36, 2 Sam. 24:9). This indicates David's lack of faith in the Lord's ability to watch over and protect his (David's) kingdom. David simply wanted to know the strength of his army.

When we read the Bible we see that the Lord is interested in numbers. There is even a book with that title. The Lord is very particular about how and what He numbers. In 1 Chron. 11-12 He numbered the mighty men. In 1 Chron. 25 He numbered the workmen. In 1 Chron. 23 He numbered the Levites. In 1 Chron. 25 He numbered the musicians. In

Psm. 147:4 He numbered the stars. In Ezk. 4 He numbered the days. In Acts 4:4 He numbered the converts. In Rev. 5:11 He numbered the heavenly host. In Acts 1:15 He numbered the church members. The idea here is that it is God who keeps the numbers and not man. The Lord knows all the numbers including the number of the hairs of our heads (Mat. 10:30 and Luke 12:7).

2 Sam. 24:3-4 – **"And Joab said unto the king, Now the LORD thy God add unto the people, how many soever they be, an hundredfold, and that the eyes of my lord the king may see it: but why doth my lord the king delight in this thing? Notwithstanding the king's word prevailed against Joab, and against the captains of the host. And Joab and the captains of the host went out from the presence of the king, to number the people of Israel."** Joab knows the Scripture and understands the significance of Exodus 30:12, which states, **"When thou takest the sum of the children of Israel after their number, then shall they give every man a ransom for his soul unto the LORD, when thou numberest them; that there be no plague among them, when *thou* numberest them."** David's Captain of the Host knew that the Lord would not be pleased with the king's command and made an attempt to dissuade David from his order. No ransom was given and the plague began just as God said.

1 Chron. 21:4 – **"Nevertheless the king's word prevailed against Joab. Wherefore Joab departed, and went throughout all Israel, and came to Jerusalem."** We jump to the 1 Chron. narrative for David's response to Joab's plea. 1 Chron. 21:7 – **"And God was displeased with this thing; therefore he smote Israel."** We have shown why God was displeased. David is given three choices from the Lord (verse 12) as result of his unauthorized numbering: 1 - Three years famine. 2 - Three months to be destroyed by his foes. 3 - Three days pestilence in the land (plague).

David's choice is the shortest in duration. 1 Chron. 21:14-15 – **"So the LORD sent pestilence upon Israel: and there fell of Israel seventy thousand men. And God sent an angel unto Jerusalem to destroy it: and as he was destroying, the LORD beheld, and he repented him of the evil, and said to the angel that destroyed, It is enough, stay now thine hand. And the angel of the LORD stood by the threshingfloor of Ornan the Jebusite."** The killing began with seventy thousand men. The word, "repent," means a change of mind about something. When the Scripture says the LORD "repented him of the evil," it means the LORD changed His mind about continuing with the slaughter. He had compassion on His people and cut it short.

1 Chon. 21:16 – **"And David lifted up his eyes, and saw the angel of the LORD stand between the earth and the heaven, having a drawn sword in his hand stretched out over Jerusalem. Then David and the elders *of Israel, who were* clothed in sackcloth, fell upon their faces."** Included among King David's entourage were the elders of Israel. Our text points out that they were clothed in sackcloth. This indicates God's judgment had been in effect for some time. Joab's efforts to number the tribes (with the exception of Levi and Benjamin - vs. 6) had to have taken a while to accomplish. The unexplained deaths had already begun in large numbers, hence the elder's attire. It is in our text that they learn of the cause. In addition, they were still in the midst of the most recent of God's judgment, which was the three years without rain mentioned in 2 Sam. 20:1.

1 Chron. 21:17 – **"And David said unto God, *Is it* not I *that* commanded the people to be numbered? even I it is that have sinned and done evil indeed; but *as for* these sheep, what have they done? let thine hand, I pray thee, O LORD my God, be on me, and on my father's house; but not on thy people, that they should be**

plagued." David was a man after God's own heart (1 Sam. 13:14 and Acts 13:22) and as such, he asked for God's judgment to be upon himself and his father's house rather than the Nation of Israel. Nowhere do we read of Saul or Solomon praying in this manner – or any subsequent king in either Israel or Judah.

1 Chron. 21:18 – **"Then the angel of the LORD commanded Gad to say to David, that David should go up, and set up an altar unto the LORD in the threshingfloor of Ornan the Jebusite."** David is given instructions (through Gad) to set up an altar unto the LORD. No command is given to offer a sacrifice, but David knows it is expected. The Lord is not prone to verbiage.

1 Chron. 21:20-21 – **"And Ornan turned back, and saw the angel; and his four sons with him hid themselves. Now Ornan was threshing wheat. And as David came to Ornan, Ornan looked and saw David, and went out of the threshingfloor, and bowed himself to David with *his* face to the ground."** Ornan (called Araunah in 2 Sam.) and his four sons were threshing wheat at his threshing floor when all this took place. Imagine Ornan and his sons threshing away and appearing over them, in mid air, the Angel of the Lord with a drawn sword stretched out over Jerusalem. Our text says they **"hid themselves."** This was the same thing Adam did in Gen. 3:10 when he heard the Lord calling him. Why did Ornan and his sons hide from the Angel of the Lord? Because they were sinners confronted with a manifestation of a Holy and Righteous God. Ornan then sees King David approaching his position and immediately falls down in obeisance.

1 Chron. 21:22-23 – **"Then David said to Ornan, Grant me the place of *this* threshingfloor, that I may build an altar therein unto the LORD: thou shalt grant it me for the full price: that the plague may be stayed from the people. And Ornan said unto David, Take *it* to thee,**

and let my lord the king do *that which is* good in his eyes: lo, I give *thee* the oxen *also* for burnt offerings, and the threshing instruments for wood, and the wheat for the meat offering; I give it all." David gets right to the point of the meeting and Ornan is only too happy to oblige. The King also makes it clear that a full and fair price will be paid for the property. Having just seen the Angel of the Lord and now in the company of the King of Israel, Ornan nervously offers to relinquish the livestock, tools, and property at no charge.

1 Chron. 21:24-25 – **"And king David said to Ornan, Nay; but I will verily buy it for the full price: for I will not take *that* which is thine for the LORD, nor offer burnt offerings without cost. So David gave to Ornan for the place six hundred shekels of gold by weight."** There are two transactions that take place at this encounter. The verse we just quoted shows the purchase of **"the place"** for a total of six hundred shekels of gold. In the 2 Sam. 24 text, we find the second transaction, **"And the king said unto Araunah, Nay; but I will surely buy *it* of thee at a price: neither will I offer burnt offerings unto the LORD my God of that which doth cost me nothing. So David bought the threshingfloor and the oxen for fifty shekels of silver"** (vs. 24). In this acquisition David bought **"the threshingfloor and the oxen for fifty shekels of silver."** We are not told how large the area surrounding the threshing floor consisted of, but "the place" obviously was more than just the floor. This was another supposed contradiction in the text. So, for a total of 100 shekels of gold and 50 shekels of silver, David received the oxen, threshing tools, the threshing floor, and a certain amount of surrounding acreage.

1 Chron. 21:26 – **"And David built there an altar unto the LORD, and offered burnt offerings and peace offerings, and called upon the LORD; and he answered him from heaven by fire upon the altar of burnt**

offering." God sent fire from heaven and consumed the offering, acknowledging David's prayer.

Threshing Floor Associated with Judgment of God

From our text we learn that Ornan's threshing floor was associated with the judgment of God. As we continue to study the Scripture we learn there is more history for this particular piece of property. In Gen. 22:2 we read, **"And he said, Take now thy son, thine only *son* Isaac, whom thou lovest, and get thee into the land of Moriah; and offer him there for a burnt offering upon one of the mountains which I will tell thee of."** Abraham's intent, in obedience to the Lord, to sacrifice his only son Isaac is a picture of God the Father offering His only Son, the Lord Jesus Christ on Calvary. Further, it is a picture of the once-and-for-all judgment of sin on the part of Jesus Christ. The offering David made on Ornan's threshing floor on Mt. Moriah was the second act of the judgment of God at this geographic position.

How did we know Ornan's threshing floor was on Mt. Moriah? 2 Chron. 3:1 – **"Then Solomon began to build the house of *the LORD* at Jerusalem in mount Moriah, where the LORD appeared unto David his father, in the place that David had prepared in the threshingfloor of Ornan the Jebusite."** This was the site God instructed David to have his son build the Temple. When we read in 1 Kings about the details of the Temple construction, we learn that the floor of the Temple consisted of planks of fir. However, the planks that covered the "floor" (threshing floor) were of cedar (1 Kings 6:15-16). This cedar floor was in the Oracle, or the Holy Place, over which, the Ark of the Covenant stood.

The Temple that Solomon built was destroyed in approximately 600 BC by Nebuchadnezzar. God sent judgment for Israel's idolatry in the form of the Babylonian Captivity. This is mentioned three times in Scripture. It is mentioned in the last chapter of 2 Kings, the last chapter of 2 Chronicles, and the last chapter of Jeremiah. It is also interesting that the Jerusalem Temple was to be built and destroyed three times. The first destruction, as we said was in 600 BC. Then approximately 70 years later Cyrus of Persia sent Ezra and a group of Israelites to begin reconstruction of Jerusalem (Ezra 1). Then shortly thereafter Nehemiah and more Hebrews came back to Jerusalem to help with the walls, Temple, and Levitical order. In approximately 20 BC Herod undertook to "remodel" this Temple and took 46 years to do so (John 2:20). He gave the Temple a face-lift and erected retaining walls around the perimeter of the Temple, filling in the area (since it was on top of a hill). Many additional porches and structures were added to the existing Temple. Herod's crews increased the level area surrounding the Temple to approximately 35 acres. This was the great Herod's Temple that stood during the days of Christ's ministry. Then in 70 AD Titus of Rome destroyed this Temple. Jews were killed and the rest were scattered in the great Jewish Diaspora.

Between 687 and 691 AD the Moslems built the Mosque of Omar on the site of the Jewish Temple. The threshing floor of Ornan is directly beneath the dome and is appropriately called "The Dome of the Rock." It should be noted that our texts (2 Sam. 24 and 1 Chron. 21) both plainly show that King David purchased this property fair and square from Ornan the Jebusite. The transaction is properly recorded showing purchase price as well. Therefore, contained in every Bible ever printed, are two title deeds to this property, which show the Nation of Israel as rightful owner.

We mentioned Herod's retaining walls erected to

enlarge the level area encompassing the Temple. The southwest retaining wall is known as the "Wailing Wall." For centuries Jews have come to this location and offered prayer to Jehovah. The Bible says in Job 34:28 **"he heareth the cry of the afflicted."** The Lord knows the property belongs to the Jews. He gave it to them and He will make certain they get it back.

During the Great Tribulation, the Temple will again be erected. We know this because of at least two passages of Scripture: First, 2 Thes. 2:4 – **"Who opposeth and exalteth himself above all that is called God, or that is worshipped; so that he as God sitteth in the temple of God, shewing himself that he is God."** Here Paul tells us that the Son of Perdition will enter into the Holy Place in the Temple and proclaim himself God (Dan.3 and 6). Second, Rev. 11:1 – **"And there was given me a reed like unto a rod: and the angel stood, saying, Rise, and measure the temple of God, and the altar, and them that worship therein."** In this passage, John writes about measuring the Temple of God in the middle of the Tribulation. It is possible that the Temple spoken of in Rev. 11 could actually be in the form of a tent or tabernacle. It took years to build the first two Temples and the time will be limited during the seven-year Tribulation. The Tabernacle that stood in Shiloh was referred to as a "temple." **"So Hannah rose up after they had eaten in Shiloh, and after they had drunk. Now Eli the priest sat upon a seat by a post of the temple of the LORD"** (1 Sam 1:9).

So, this will be the third Temple (or tabernacle) built on this same location – Ornan's Threshing Floor. This Temple will also be destroyed at the end of the Tribulation when the Lord returns (Rev. 19). There will be a final Temple built on this site. Ezekiel wrote about this in chapters 41-42. It will be the Millennial Temple during the thousand-year reign of Christ.

Threshing Floor Associated with Harvest Time

Threshing, as we have pointed out is done at the end of the farming cycle. The crops are gathered in and the final task is to separate the wheat from the tare. This is illustrated for us in the Book of Ruth. Boaz is harvesting his crop and spends time on the threshing floor. Ruth 3:2 – **"And now *is* not Boaz of our kindred, with whose maidens thou wast? Behold, he winnoweth barley to night in the threshingfloor."** The Jew was not to harvest his field completely. **"And when ye reap the harvest of your land, thou shalt not wholly reap the corners of thy field, neither shalt thou gather the gleanings of thy harvest"** (Lev. 19:9). He was to leave the corners and gleanings for the poor and the stranger. Therefore, Boaz instructed his harvesters to leave some for Ruth, as well as some "handfuls on purpose." Boaz camped out at night on the threshing floor and stayed in a booth.

Prophetic Significance of the Threshing Floor

John the Baptist said in Mat. 3:11-12 – **"I indeed baptize you with water unto repentance: but he that cometh after me is mightier than I, whose shoes I am not worthy to bear: he shall baptize you with the Holy Ghost, and *with* fire: Whose fan *is* in his hand, and he will throughly purge his floor, and gather his wheat into the garner; but he will burn up the chaff with unquenchable fire."** John is using the threshing floor as an illustration of the Second Coming of Jesus Christ. The harvest about which John speaks takes place at the end of the Tribulation. Again, in Mat. 13:30 we read, **"Let both grow together until the harvest: and in the time of harvest I will say to the reapers, Gather ye together first the tares, and bind them in bundles to burn them: but gather the**

wheat into my barn." Jesus Christ is the speaker in this passage, likening the threshing floor to the time of great judgment. Later, His disciples ask Him to explain what He meant in verses 36-40. **"Then Jesus sent the multitude away, and went into the house: and his disciples came unto him, saying, Declare unto us the parable of the tares of the field. He answered and said unto them, He that soweth the good seed is the Son of man; The field is the world; the good seed are the children of the kingdom; but the tares are the children of the wicked** *one***; The enemy that sowed them is the devil; the harvest is the end of the world; and the reapers are the angels. As therefore the tares are gathered and burned in the fire; so shall it be in the end of this world."**

The Threshing Floor is Associated with Feast of Tabernacles

The Feast of Tabernacles is a Jewish Memorial similar in nature to the ordinance of the Lord's Supper. The Old Testament Jew at the Feast of Tabernacles was to look back to when God led them out of bondage in Egypt and into the Promised Land. And he was to look forward to Kingdom Rest after regathering and restoration. Lev. 23:39 – **"Also in the fifteenth day of the seventh month, when ye have gathered in the fruit of the land, ye shall keep a feast unto the LORD seven days: on the first day** *shall be* **a sabbath, and on the eighth day** *shall be* **a sabbath."** For the Christian, the Lord's Supper is an ordinance of the Church observed to look back at our blood redemption at Calvary and look forward to Christ returning again (1 Cor. 11:24-26). The Feast of Tabernacles took place after all the harvest work was finished and the grain was swept up off the threshing floor and put in sacks. It was a time of mirth and thanksgiving to God for the harvest. It was also known as the

Feast of Ingathering (Ex. 23:16 and 34:22). The crops were all gathered in and completed. Earlier we mentioned how Boaz was camped out on the threshing floor in a tabernacle during this time. During the Feast of Tabernacles, the Jew was to stay in a booth, which was a tent-like, temporary structure.

When Christ took Peter, James, and John with Him to the Mount of Transfiguration (Mat. 17 and Mark 9), they saw Moses and Elijah standing by Jesus Christ in His Glory. Here, Christ was illustrating for them the "Kingdom of God come with Power" (Mark 9:1). Simon said, **"Master, it is good for us to be here: and let us make three tabernacles; one for thee, and one for Moses, and one for Elias"** (vs. 5). Peter associated Christ's glory and the coming of His kingdom with the Feast of Tabernacles. Albeit he was rebuked from heaven for his failure to elevate Jesus Christ to the position above Moses and Elijah, his observation is significant.

Threshing Floor is Associated with Second Advent

When Jesus Christ returns, He will come back in judgment and wrath. The Scriptural proof of this statement is simply too voluminous to list. However, let's look at two passages: Isa. 63:1-6 – **"Who *is* this that cometh from Edom, with dyed garments from Bozrah? this *that is* glorious in his apparel, travelling in the greatness of his strength? I that speak in righteousness, mighty to save. Wherefore *art thou* red in thine apparel, and thy garments like him that treadeth in the winefat? I have trodden the winepress alone; and of the people *there was* none with me: for I will tread them in mine anger, and trample them in my fury; and their blood shall be sprinkled upon my garments, and I will stain all my raiment. For the day of vengeance *is* in mine heart, and** the year of my redeemed is come. And I looked, and *there was* none to help; and I wondered that *there was* none to uphold: therefore mine own arm brought salvation unto me; and my fury, it upheld me. And I will tread down the people in mine anger, and make them drunk in my fury, and I will bring down their strength to the earth."

This passage points out a number of particulars about the Second Advent: First, Christ returns with "dyed garments." The dye turns out to be blood when we get to Rev. 19. Second, Christ returns in "Glory," which is mentioned in the text. Fourth, Christ returns in "the Greatness of His Strength." Fifth, He treads the winepress alone – again Rev. 19. Sixth, He treads people in His anger. Seventh, He tramples them in His fury. Eighth, Their blood shall be sprinkled on His garments – Rev. 19. And finally, The Day of Vengeance is in His heart.

Rev. 19:11-16 – **"And I saw heaven opened, and behold a white horse; and he that sat upon him *was* called Faithful and True, and in righteousness he doth judge and make war. His eyes *were* as a flame of fire, and on his head *were* many crowns; and he had a name written, that no man knew, but he himself. And he *was* clothed with a vesture dipped in blood: and his name is called The Word of God. And the armies *which were* in heaven followed him upon white horses, clothed in fine linen, white and clean. And out of his mouth goeth a sharp sword, that with it he should smite the nations: and he shall rule them with a rod of iron: and he treadeth the winepress of the fierceness and wrath of Almighty God. And he hath on *his* vesture and on his thigh a name written, KING OF KINGS, AND LORD OF LORDS."**

The Lord Jesus returns upon a white horse "and in righteousness he doeth judge and make war." His eyes will be as a flame of fire. He will have many crowns on His head. His vesture will be dipped in blood. His name is called The Word of God. He will be followed by the Armies, which were in heaven, also mounted on white horses. These Armies will be clothed in fine linen, white and clean. A sharp sword goeth out of His mouth, which He will use to smite the nations. He will rule them with a rod of iron. He treadeth the winepress of the fierceness and wrath of Almighty God. On his vesture and on his thigh a name written, KING OF KINGS, AND LORD OF LORDS.

The threshing floor is a place where the stalks are beaten, mashed, and ground. The same is true for the winepress. The harvested grapes are squashed in order to get the grape juice. The Scripture likens the Second Advent of Christ to the "violent" actions of harvest time. Let's look at more violent passages depicting Christ's Second Advent. Isa. 41:15-16 – **"Behold, I will make thee a new sharp threshing instrument having teeth: thou shalt thresh the mountains, and beat** *them* **small, and shalt make the hills as chaff. Thou shalt fan them, and the wind shall carry them away, and the whirlwind shall scatter them: and thou shalt rejoice in the LORD,** *and* **shalt glory in the Holy One of Israel."** Psm. 2:9 - **"Thou shalt break them with a rod of iron; thou shalt dash them in pieces like a potter's vessel."** Jer. 51:33 – **"For thus saith the LORD of hosts, the God of Israel; The daughter of Babylon** *is* **like a threshingfloor,** *it is* **time to thresh her: yet a little while, and the time of her harvest shall come."** Mic. 4:13 – **"Arise and thresh, O daughter of Zion: for I will make thine horn iron, and I will make thy hoofs brass: and thou shalt beat in pieces many people: and I will consecrate their gain unto the LORD, and their substance unto the Lord of the whole earth."** Hab. 3:12 - **"Thou didst march through the land in indignation, thou didst thresh the heathen in anger."**

These passages liken Christ's return to the Threshing Floor. These verses also show a totally different Jesus Christ than when He first came. When He returns, the Nation of Israel will recognize Him as the Messiah (Zech. 13:6 and Acts 7:13). The Jews will receive their land back, as typified in the book of Ruth. Jesus Christ will be their Kinsman Redeemer.

During the Millennium, Jesus Christ will rule and reign with a rod of iron. We made mention the Millennial Temple in Ezekiel 41 and 42. Christ's throne will be a place of judgment. We have shown how Ornan's Threshing Floor was a place of judgment. Could it be that the throne upon which the Lord Jesus will sit will be located in the Holy Place in the Millennial Temple – or, situated directly over Ornan's Threshing Floor? Solomon's throne was in the Palace (1 Kings 7:7) and not the Temple, but Solomon was not the object of Israel's worship. The Holy Place or Oracle in the Temple represented the presence of God. Since Jesus Christ will be present to rule and reign would not this be the appropriate place for His throne? The answer is yes, Christ's throne *will be* in the Holy Place or the Oracle in the Temple. There are passages of Scripture to support this view.

First, we'll look in Rev. 8:1-3 – **"And when he had opened the seventh seal, there was silence in heaven about the space of half an hour. And I saw the seven angels which stood before God; and to them were given seven trumpets. And another angel came and stood at the altar, having a golden censer; and there was given unto him much incense, that he should offer it with the prayers of all saints upon the golden altar which was before the throne."**

This passage is given during the half-hour of silence in Heaven between the seven Seal Judgments and the seven Trumpet Judgments. This scene takes place in the Heavenly Tabernacle, mentioned in Heb. 9:11 and 23, as well as Ex. 25:9 and 40. Notice the end of verse 3, where it mentions "the golden altar which was before the throne." In the Tabernacle in the wilderness, the golden altar of incense stood immediately before the veil. On the other side of the veil was the Holy Place where the Ark of the Covenant sat. Upon the Ark rested the Mercy Seat. When Jesus Christ said, *"It is finished"* and gave up the ghost, the veil was rent in twain from the top to the bottom. At this point the earthly Temple, at the same time of its decommissioning, became like unto the Heavenly Tabernacle (the pattern). That is, there would be no obstruction between the presence of God (His Throne) and the incense altar, which represents the prayer of the saints. This would also indicate the Throne upon which Jesus Christ will sit to rule and reign in Jerusalem during His 1000 year reign, will indeed be situated in the Holy Place (or Oracle) immediately above Ornan's Threshing Floor.

Secondly, when we examine the passages in Ezekiel describing the Millennial Temple, more support for this idea is provided. The Scripture speaks of the Lord's presence in several verses. In Ezk. 41:22 – **"The altar of wood *was* three cubits high, and the length thereof two cubits; and the corners thereof, and the length thereof, and the walls thereof, *were* of wood: and he said unto me, This *is* the table that *is* before the LORD." In Ezk. 42:13 – "Then said he unto me, The north chambers *and* the south chambers, which *are* before the separate place, they *be* holy chambers, where the priests that approach unto the LORD shall eat the most holy things: there shall they lay the most holy things, and the meat offering, and the sin offering, and the trespass offering; for the place *is* holy."** In Ezk. 43:7 – **"And he said unto me, Son of man, the place of my throne, and the place of the soles of my feet, where I will dwell in the midst of the children of Israel for ever, and my holy name, shall the house of Israel no more defile, *neither* they, nor their kings, by their whoredom, nor by the carcases of their kings in their** high places." In Ezk. 48:35 – *"It* **was round about eighteen thousand** *measures*: **and the name of the city from** *that* **day** *shall be*, **The LORD** *is* **there."**

There is a third proof for our thesis that the Millennial Throne of Jesus Christ will be situated in the Oracle of the Temple, directly over Ornan's Threshing Floor. This final evidence is found in 2 Thes. 2:4 – **"Who opposeth and exalteth himself above all that is called God, or that is worshipped; so that he as God sitteth in the temple of God, shewing himself that he is God."** This passage describes a time in the middle of the Great Tribulation when Satan enters the Holy Place in the Temple and sits down on the Mercy Seat, demanding the worship of all humanity. The reason for this action is that he knows the Lord will occupy this position (in person) in just three and a half years. The Devil is and has been the greatest imitator of Christ (Isa. 14:14, 2 Cor. 11:14).

It is our prayer that this study will encourage the Christian to appreciate his Bible and study it to show himself approved unto God. It is also our desire for these studies to edify the Body of Christ. May the Lord bless the reader as he lives for Christ and explores the depths of the riches of the word of God.

CHAPTER SIX

PRE-TRIBULATION RAPTURE

Preface

THE CHURCH WILL NOT GO THROUGH the Tribulation. When we say "Church," we include any single member of the Body of Christ. When we say "Tribulation," we speak of the 7-year period of trouble just prior to Christ's Second Advent. It also means any and all parts of the Tribulation. In this paper, we will explain why this is a fact and give the Scripture proof for this position. Christians should know what they believe and why they believe it. The word of God is the final authority for all matters of faith and practice. There is a right way and a wrong way to divide Scripture. There are those who believe the Church or a part of the Church will go through the Tribulation or a part of the Tribulation. They have Scripture to prove their position. The problem is the verses given as proof *are for a different dispensation.* The context of the passage determines this. The Apostle Paul said, **"Study to shew** thyself approved unto God, a workman that needeth not to be ashamed, rightly dividing the word of truth" (2 Tim. 2:15).

Definition of Terms

Church - When we use the term, "Church," we mean the Body of Christ, or the collective body of all who have received Jesus Christ as Savior. The Church is not a building. The Church *assembles in the building.* The Church is a "called-out assembly." The Church you attend is a local group of believers. If you are born-again in Christ you are in "The Church."

Tribulation – The Tribulation is a period of seven years, which serves as a time of great trouble for the Nation of Israel preceding the Second Coming of Jesus Christ. This period of time begins *after* the Body of Christ (Church) has been removed from the earth. The purpose of the Tribulation is to bring judgment upon the Jews (Israel) for their sin, followed by reconciliation to God, followed by everlasting righteousness (Dan.9:24). The Scripture uses a furnace as an analogy. Prov. 17:3 – **"The fining pot *is* for silver, and the furnace for gold: but the LORD trieth the hearts."** Isa. 48:10 – **"Behold, I have refined thee, but not with silver; I have chosen thee in the furnace of affliction."** Ezk. 22:18 – **"Son of man, the house of Israel is to me become dross: all they *are* brass, and tin, and iron, and lead, in the midst of the furnace; they are *even* the dross of silver."** Ezk. 22:20 – **"As they gather silver, and brass, and iron, and lead, and tin, into the midst of the furnace, to blow the fire upon it, to melt *it*; so will I gather *you* in mine anger and in my fury, and I will leave *you there*, and melt you."** Ezk. 22:22 – **"As silver is melted in the midst of the furnace, so shall ye be melted in the midst thereof; and ye shall know that I the LORD have poured**

out my fury upon you." After the sin is dealt with, then comes reconciliation and everlasting righteousness. **"Seventy weeks are determined upon thy people and upon thy holy city, to finish the transgression, and to make an end of sins, and to make reconciliation for iniquity, and to bring in everlasting righteousness, and to seal up the vision and prophecy, and to anoint the most Holy** (Dan. 9:24).

During this Time of Trouble and subsequent reconciliation for the Nation of Israel comes a national recognition of Jesus Christ as the Jewish Messiah. There will only be a remnant of the Nation left at the time of the Second Advent of Christ. (For more complete information on the Tribulation see our booklet, "The Great Tribulation."

Rapture – The term, "Rapture" speaks of the time when "The Church" will be caught up to be with Christ. 1 Thes. 4:16-17 – **"For the Lord himself shall descend from heaven with a shout, with the voice of the archangel, and with the trump of God: and the dead in Christ shall rise first: Then we which are alive *and* remain shall be caught up together with them in the clouds, to meet the Lord in the air: and so shall we ever be with the Lord."** This is a time when saved people all over the world will simply disappear from earth. It is the next thing that will take place on God's prophetic calendar of events.

Pre-Tribulation Rapture – This is simply the understanding that the Church will be Raptured out of this world *before* the Great Tribulation begins. It is the purpose of this paper to explain the truth and reality of this term.

Differences

There are numerous types and divisions of churches around the world. When the Rapture takes place, people who know Jesus Christ as Savior will be taken out of the world irrespective of "church membership" or denominational attachment. There will be Lutherans, Catholics, Methodists, Presbyterians, and others caught up in the Rapture. The common characteristic among all will be conversion to Jesus Christ as Savior during their lifetime. Jesus said, **"I am the way, the truth, and the life: no man cometh unto the Father, but by me"** (John 14:6). Just as Jesus Christ told Nicodemus in John 3, *"Ye must be born again."* John 10:9 – **"I am the door: by me if any man enter in, he shall be saved, and shall go in and out, and find pasture."** Church membership or attendance does not determine whether a person is saved or not saved. It has to do with a personal relationship with the Person of Jesus Christ. It is indeed a sad fact that the vast majority of humans will not be included in this calling out. The Scripture says in Matthew 7:13-14, **"Enter ye in at the strait gate: for wide *is* the gate, and broad *is* the way, that leadeth to destruction, and many there be which go in thereat: Because strait *is* the gate, and narrow *is* the way, which leadeth unto life, and few there be that find it."**

There are various beliefs regarding the Church and the Rapture relative to the Tribulation. We will define these here.

1. **Pre-Tribulation Rapture** - Christ will rapture the church before the Tribulation begins.

2. **Mid-Tribulation Rapture** - Christ will rapture the church at the Mid-point of The Tribulation.

3. **Post Tribulation** Rapture - Christ will rapture the church at the end of the Tribulation.

4. **Pre-Wrath Rapture** - Christ will rapture the church just before the Battle of Armageddon.

5. **Partial Rapture** - Christ will rapture those who are ready and leave the rest to go through the Tribulation.

6. **Multiple Rapture** - There is more than one rapture. Christ receives those who are ready.

7. **"Pan-Trib" Position** – They have no clue about future events, but think it will "all pan out in the end."

Pre-Tribulation Rapture

"For God hath not appointed us to wrath, but to obtain salvation by our Lord Jesus Christ" (1 Thes. 5:9). As we stated earlier, the Church will not go through the Tribulation. The verse above clearly states this. The Tribulation is a period of the wrath of God *upon the Nation of Israel*. Anyone else present on the earth during this time will experience the horrors as well. This verse is from Paul's Epistle to the Church at Thessalonica. Therefore, when he says, "us," he means the Body of Christ.

As we also stated above, the Tribulation is for the Jews or the Nation of Israel. According to 1 Cor. 10:32 (**"Give none offence, neither to the Jews, nor to the Gentiles, nor to the church of God"**), there are three groups of people in existence. Those groups are: Jew, Gentile, and Church of God. All of humanity can be broken down into those three groups. You are either saved, or you are a Gentile or Jew. The Tribulation is a time of judgment for the Jew, not the Gentile or the Church. There will be millions of Gentiles present in the Tribulation, but it is primarily for Israel. It is called, *"Jacob's* time of trouble."

Deterrent to Sin

The Holy Spirit is a deterrent to sin. Gen. 6:3 – **"And the LORD said, My spirit shall not always strive with man, for that he also *is* flesh: yet his days shall be an hundred and twenty years."** In 2 Thes. 2:7 we read, **"For** the mystery of iniquity doth already work: only he who now letteth *will let*, until he be taken out of the way." The Holy Spirit is "housed" in Christians. Paul said in 1 Cor. 6:19, **"What? know ye not that your body is the temple of the Holy Ghost *which is* in you, which ye have of God, and ye are not your own?"** At some time in the future the trumpet will sound and the Holy Spirit will "be taken out of the way." That is, we will hear the Trump of God and a voice saying, **"Come up hither."** The Church will be raptured out of this world. No more Holy Spirit (in the world) to strive with men. The rate of moral decay will increase exponentially.

The presence of the Holy Spirit (in Christians) all over the world is keeping the man of sin from being revealed. It is keeping a check on demon possession as well as keeping check on the level of sin in your neighborhood.

As much demon possession and sin as there is in the world today – think about what it will be like after the restraint of the Holy Spirit is gone!

Rapture Before Tribulation

Paul wrote to the Church at Thessalonica, **"For the Lord himself shall descend from heaven with a shout, with the voice of the archangel, and with the trump of God: and the dead in Christ shall rise first: Then we which are alive *and* remain shall be caught up together with them in the clouds, to meet the Lord in the air: and so shall we ever be with the Lord"** (1 Thes. 4:16-17). This "Calling Out" of the church will take place before the Tribulation. We know this for a number of reasons.

First, the passage we quoted above from 2 Thes. 2:7 indicates **"the mystery of iniquity"** (Antichrist) will not be revealed until after the Holy Spirit **("he who now letteth")** is **"taken out of the way."** That is, the Antichrist cannot be revealed until the Church is raptured out of the world.

Second, Paul wrote in 1 Thes. 5:9, **"For God hath not appointed us to wrath, but to obtain salvation by our Lord Jesus Christ."** What would be the point of subjecting the Church to the Tribulation period? The sins of Christians have already been dealt with, forgiven, and forgotten as far as the Lord is concerned. The Tribulation is for Israel, whose sin has not been dealt with and not the Church. Israel's sin has not been settled. It is *"Jacob's* time of trouble," not "the Church's time of trouble." God deals with the sins of Corporate Israel differently than He does with the Church. Proper differentiation must be made between the Church and Israel.

The Christian is not under the bondage of Mosaic Law, but indwelt with the Holy Spirit and reconciled to God through the finished work of Jesus Christ at Calvary. Eph. 2:14-17 – **"For he is our peace, who hath made both one, and hath broken down the middle wall of partition** *between us***; Having abolished in his flesh the enmity,** *even* **the law of commandments** *contained* **in ordinances; for to make in himself of twain one new man,** *so* **making peace; And that he might reconcile both unto God in one body by the cross, having slain the enmity thereby: And came and preached peace to you which were afar off, and to them that were nigh."** When there is sin in the life of the Christian, the Holy Spirit works in the heart of the believer to deal with his own sin. Paul wrote in 1 Cor. 11:31, **"For if we would judge ourselves, we should not be judged."**

The Great Tribulation is the final of seventy weeks promised to Israel in Daniel 9. This seventieth week is for the purpose of reconciliation (to God) for the Nation of Israel. Dan. 9:24 – **"Seventy weeks are determined upon thy people and upon thy holy city, to finish transgression, and to make an end of sins, and to make** reconciliation for iniquity, and to bring in everlasting righteousness, and to seal up the vision and prophecy, and to anoint the most Holy."** This Jewish judgment goes back to the conditions given for the Palestinian Covenant in Lev. 26 and Deut. 28 and has nothing to do with the Christian in the Church Age. The reader should remember that the Abrahamic Covenant was *unconditional* (Gen. 12). The Palestinian Covenant was *conditional* (Lev. 26, Deut. 28).

Old Testament Types

There are passages in the Old Testament, which are instructive for the purpose of this study. The Scriptures we will examine all speak of a group of people who escape judgment just before it begins.

Enoch

Enoch was taken out of the world and into the presence of God without dying. This happened prior to the catastrophic world judgment of Noah's flood. The Bible says in Luke 17:26, **"And as it was in the days of Noe, so shall it be also in the days of the Son of man."** Luke described the times just before the Lord returns. "The days of Noe" are found in Gen. 4-6. In Gen. 5:22-24 we read, **"And Enoch walked with God after he begat Methuselah three hundred years, and begat sons and daughters: And all the days of Enoch were three hundred sixty and five years: And Enoch walked with God: and he *was* not; for God took him."** In the New Testament, we get a better idea of what this passage means. The writer of Hebrews wrote, **"By faith Enoch was translated that he should not see death; and was not found, because God had translated him: for before his translation he had this testimony, that he pleased God"** (Heb. 11:5). We read in Jude 14,

"And Enoch also, the seventh from Adam, prophesied of these, saying, Behold, the Lord cometh with ten thousands of his saints," Again, Enoch is connected with the Second Advent of Jesus Christ and thus, is a type of the Christian taken out of the world just prior to the judgment on Israel.

Lot

Lot and his family were escorted out of Sodom before the fire and brimstone fell from heaven (Gen. 19). This is another picture of a group of people making exit just prior to the judgment of God. Gen. 19:15 – **"And when the morning arose, then the angels hastened Lot, saying, Arise, take thy wife, and thy two daughters, which are here; lest thou be consumed in the iniquity of the city."** The angels came to get Lot and his family out of the city before it was consumed in fire. Lot was inclined to linger a little longer than the angels wanted and thus we read in verse 22, **"Haste thee, escape thither; for I cannot do any thing till thou be come thither."** The judgment of God could not fall until Lot and his family were out of the city. The Church will be taken out of the world in the rapture before the Tribulation begins.

John

In Revelation two and three, Jesus Christ (Rev. 1:1, 13-18) spoke with the Apostle John and instructed him to **"Write the things which thou hast seen, and the things which are, and the things which shall be hereafter"** (Rev. 1:19). Chapters two and three follow, listing the seven churches that make up the Church Age. The last church of the age is the Laodicean Church. What comes next is the beginning of chapter four and a great event. Rev. 4:1-2 –

"After this I looked, and, behold, a door *was* opened in heaven: and the first voice which I heard *was* as it were of a trumpet talking with me; which said, Come up hither, and I will shew thee things which must be hereafter. And immediately I was in the spirit: and, behold, a throne was set in heaven, and *one* sat on the throne." Immediately after the seven churches are given, a door in heaven opens and a voice says, **"Come up hither."** There is no more mention of the church until chapter 22. This passage clearly represents the rapture of the church just prior to the Tribulation. Chapters six through eighteen are all about the Time of Jacob's Trouble. Throughout all the descriptions of the Tribulation, there is no mention of the Church. The reason for this is simple. It's gone!

During the time of the Seal, Vial, and the Trumpet judgments, the Church is in the safe harbor of Jesus Christ (2 Thes. 4:17). According to Scripture, the Antichrist cannot be revealed until the Holy Spirit is taken out of this world (Rapture). **"For the mystery of iniquity doth already work: only he who now letteth *will let*, until he be taken out of the way. And then shall that Wicked be revealed, whom the Lord shall consume with the spirit of his mouth, and shall destroy with the brightness of his coming"** (2 Thes. 2:7-8).

Looking again at Revelation, we see the Rapture in 4:1 and the rest of chapter four and five deal with the heavenly scene before John. When we get to chapter six (back on earth), the Antichrist shows up. Above, we showed how the Antichrist cannot be revealed until the Church is taken out. In Rev. 6:1-2 he shows up. Many believe this white horse rider is Jesus Christ. The white horse rider in Rev. 19 is the Lord Jesus Christ. But this is someone else. They are not the same. The white horse rider of Rev. 6 is the Antichrist.

First of all in vs. 1 we read that it is the Lamb that opens the seal resulting in this mysterious character. Since

Jesus Christ is the Lamb and the only one worthy to open the seals, it is impossible for the rider to be Jesus Christ. The rider in 6:2 has a bow and **"went forth conquering and to conquer."** Jesus Christ doesn't need a bow to conquer. In Rev. 19, He only uses a Sword that comes out of His mouth (vs. 15). Plus, at this point in the chronology the Tribulation is just beginning. Christ doesn't come until the end of the seven-year period (Rev. 19). The rider in 6:2 has a single crown because he is the god of this world (2 Cor. 4:4) and the prince of the power of the air (Eph. 2:2). Jesus Christ in Rev. 19:12 wore "many crowns."

Finally, when we look to see who follows the rider of Rev. 6, we find a red horse (vs. 4) that took peace from the earth and caused war. Next we see a black horse (vs. 5) that brings famine to the earth. Then a pale horse (vs. 8) whose name was Death, and Hell followed with him. The white horse rider of Revelation 6 cannot be Christ because His followers are not correct. In Rev. 19:14, we read that the **"armies *which were* in heaven followed him upon white horses, clothed in fine linen, white and clean."** These are the saints accompanying Jesus Christ at the Second Advent. When the Antichrist is revealed in Rev. 6:1, the Church has already been caught up to Heaven and is worshipping Jesus Christ in the beauty of holiness.

We can see the signs of the times around us today indicating that Jesus Christ will soon return. As Christians, we do not have to be concerned about entering the Tribulation. The Holy Spirit is our Comforter and will not forsake us. He has also given us Scripture to show the Church will not go through the Tribulation.

Something to Think About

Most Christians believe the Tribulation begins immediately after the Rapture. The Bible is not specifically clear about this. In fact, there is Scripture to indicate a period of time between the Rapture and the actual beginning of the seven-year period of the Tribulation. In all three Bible pictures given earlier, there is a passage of time between the escape from judgment and the actual beginning of that judgment. Let's take a closer look at each passage.

Enoch

If one takes the time to examine the genealogies and dates of the first seven chapters of Genesis and pays particular attention to Enoch, Methuselah, and Lamech, one can extrapolate the fact that the flood began six hundred and sixty-nine years after the translation of Enoch. This is a considerable passage of time between the "rapture" and the judgment of Noah's flood.

Lot

There is also a passage of time between the point when Lot leaves Sodom and when the fire and brimstone rain down on the city. Notice Gen. 19:16, **"And while he lingered, the men laid hold upon his hand, and upon the hand of his wife, and upon the hand of his two daughters; the LORD being merciful unto him: and they brought him forth, and set him without the city."** This verse shows Lot, his wife, and two daughters are escorted to (at least) the city limit of Sodom. From vs. 17 through vs. 23 there is some discussion between Lot and the angels regarding the city to which Lot would flee. In vs. 23 we read, **"The sun was risen upon the earth when Lot entered into Zoar."** Lot and his family walked out of Sodom, took time for discussion with the impatient angels, and then walked the distance and entered Zoar before the fire and brimstone judgment actually began in vs. 24. Albeit this was not a long period of time, it is sufficient to show the elapse of time between the exit of Lot and the judgment of fire.

Seven Churches

In Rev. 4:1 John (type of the Church) is caught up to Heaven and the Antichrist does not show up until Rev. 6:2. Almost two chapters pass after "the rapture" before the official beginning of the Tribulation.

In looking at these three passages, all being types of the Rapture of the Church, we see a definite period of time between the "Rapture" and the beginning of the impending judgment. So, if there is a period of time between the two events, how much time is it? There are two more Scripture passages that give additional light on this theory.

In Gen. 29:18 the Scripture says, **"And Jacob loved Rachel; and said, I will serve thee seven years for Rachel thy younger daughter."** Jacob did just that – he served Laban seven years for the "favored daughter." But in reality, it was the ill-favored daughter, Leah that was given. After being hoodwinked by Laban, Jacob served seven more years for the "favored daughter," Rachel.

In Gen. 41 Pharaoh had a nightmare. He dreamed about seven good years preceding seven bad years (famine). In fact, the point is further amplified with seven fat-fleshed kine (vs. 18), seven ill-favored kine (vs. 19), seven good ears (vs. 22), and seven withered ears (vs. 23). As you recall, Joseph interpreted the dream for Pharaoh and told him that God was about to send seven good years followed by seven bad years of famine.

These two passages of Scripture each give us some considerable food for thought and careful meditation. Could there be a period of seven years just prior to the seven-year Tribulation period? Could it be that the seven horrible years of Tribulation and famine might be preceded by seven years of great happiness, joy, prosperity, and wealth on a global scale? We don't know. There is one thing for certain though: 1 Thes. 5:9 – **"For God hath not appointed us to wrath, but to obtain salvation by our Lord Jesus Christ,"** The Church *will not* go through the Tribulation!

If there is a chance that the reader is uncertain about personal salvation in Christ, now is the time to call upon the Lord. **"For whosoever shall call upon the name of the Lord shall be saved"** (Rom. 10:13). **"But as many as received him, to them gave he power to become the sons of God,** *even* **to them that believe on his name"** (John 1:12). Be certain about this! Call upon Him now and He will save you. *You don't want to go into the Tribulation!*

CHAPTER SEVEN

GOD'S LUNAR CALENDAR

Preface

MOST CHRISTIANS PROFESS TO BELIEVE
the Bible. However when it comes to certain truths found in
Scripture, some of the saints question the Holy Spirit's words
and default to their own understanding (Jud. 17:6). For
example, the Bible says: **"These things have I written unto
you that believe on the name of the Son of God; that ye
may know that ye have eternal life..."** (1 John 5:13).
Some Christians don't think that you can know for certain
that you will go to Heaven when you die. When shown this
verse they don't think it's true and revert back to their
personal concept of understanding. Yet, there it is, written for
our benefit. Another example is found in Exodus 14. The
Bible says that Moses extended his rod out and divided the
waters and the children of Israel went through the Red Sea
on dry ground. There are many Christians that simply do not
believe that happened and would rather believe that they

actually waded across the Red Sea in some mysterious marsh where the water was only a foot deep.

In John 11 we find the shortest verse in the Bible. It simply says, **"Jesus wept."** Why did He weep? He wept because of the unbelief of His disciples. The Bible says, **"Trust in the LORD with all thine heart; and lean not unto thine own understanding"** (Prov. 3:5). The word of God trumps all our human concepts about everything. It is God's Holy word. All of the treasures found in Scripture are there in black and white. All we have to do is read it *and BELIEVE it.*

God's Lunar Calendar

When God created our solar system, He did so with twelve 30-day lunar months and a lunar calendar with a total of three hundred sixty days per year. Our modern calendar reflects three hundred sixty-five and one-quarter days per year. How do we know there were 360 days per year? How did it change to 365.25 days per year? Are there any more changes coming? This paper will address all three questions asked above.

360 Days per Year

Gen. 7:11 – **"In the six hundredth year of Noah's life, in the second month, the seventeenth day of the month, the same day were all the fountains of the great deep broken up, and the windows of heaven were opened."** After Noah, his family, and all the animals boarded the ark, they waited seven days before the rain began. The first day of the rain was recorded as the seventeenth day of the second month.

Now let us look at Gen. 8:3-4 – **"And the waters**

returned from off the earth continually: and after the end of the hundred and fifty days the waters were abated. And the ark rested in the seventh month, on the seventeenth day of the month, upon the mountains of Ararat." After one hundred fifty days the ark came to rest in the mountains of Ararat on the seventeenth of the seventh month. From the seventeenth of the second month to the seventeenth of the seventh month is a total of five months. Simple math allows us to extrapolate five thirty-day months from this time period.

In a lunar month, the "new moon" is the beginning of the cycle. The "new moon" is the phase when the earth blocks the sunlight completely and the moon is not seen. Approximately two weeks later a full moon is visible in the sky. From the Scripture, we find that the new moon not only marked the beginning of a new month, but also was a solemn feast day. **"Blow up the trumpet in the new moon, in the time appointed, on our solemn feast day. For this *was* a statute for Israel, *and* a law of the God of Jacob"** (Psm. 81:3-4). When David fled from Saul, Jonathan spoke of David's absence from the feast in 1 Sam. 20:18: **"Then Jonathan said to David, To morrow *is* the new moon: and thou shalt be missed, because thy seat will be empty."** In Isa. 66:23, we read, **"And it shall come to pass, *that* from one new moon to another, and from one sabbath to another, shall all flesh come to worship before me, saith the LORD."** The new moon is listed throughout the Old Testament as a special day and counted among feast days and Sabbaths. **"I will also cause all her mirth to cease, her feast days, her new moons, and her sabbaths, and all her solemn feasts"** (Hos. 2:11). Even the Apostle Paul mentions it in the New Testament in the same context, **"Let no man therefore judge you in meat, or in drink, or in respect of an holyday, or of the new moon, or of the sabbath *days:*"** (Col. 2:16).

A new moon (or an invisible moon) marked the beginning of a new month for the Old Testament Jew. Just as the sun, with its 24-hour cycle represented a new day, the moon was placed in the heavens as the visible monthly change. Psm. 104:19, **"He appointed the moon for seasons: the sun knoweth his going down."** The new moon is the point in the lunar cycle when the moon is between the earth and the sun. When the earth is between the sun and the moon a full moon is visible. When Moses led the children of Israel out of Egypt on the night of the first Passover (14th of the month), a full moon illuminated their way.

What Happened?

We showed from Scripture that there were at one time, three hundred sixty days in a year. There are now three hundred sixty-five and a quarter days in a year. What happened to add the five and one quarter days to the year?

Perhaps there is someone who insists that there has been no physical change in the solar system. This is simply a matter of the Jew counting thirty days and then starting a new month twelve times a year. This will not work. There must be an accounting of the additional one hundred twenty-six hours per year. Otherwise within thirty-four years we would celebrate Christmas in the middle of the summer months.

In order to change the orbit of the earth and add five and one quarter days, it would take a cataclysmic event in our solar system. The power to accomplish this feat is far beyond anything known to mortal man. A change of this enormity could only be accomplished at the hand of the solar system's Creator. Still, what happened?

Christian geologist, Donald Patten has a theory about this change. In his book, "Long Day of Joshua," he suggests that the orbits of Mars and Earth were much different than what they are now. His theory says that the two orbits came so close at one point that the gravitational pull from each planet affected the other, causing a slingshot effect, thus changing both orbits. In this interaction, both planets' solar year characteristics changed to what they are now. Is this what really happened?

There are some clues in the Scripture. Two events took place in the Old Testament, which had to do with a catastrophic change, relative to the sun, earth, and moon.

Joshua's Long Day

In Joshua 10:12-14 we read, **"Then spake Joshua to the LORD in the day when the LORD delivered up the Amorites before the children of Israel, and he said in the sight of Israel, Sun, stand thou still upon Gibeon; and thou, Moon, in the valley of Ajalon. And the sun stood still, and the moon stayed, until the people had avenged themselves upon their enemies. *Is* not this written in the book of Jasher? So the sun stood still in the midst of heaven, and hasted not to go down about a whole day. And there was no day like that before it or after it, that the LORD hearkened unto the voice of a man: for the LORD fought for Israel."**

In this passage, the sun and the moon stood still "about a whole day." According to Usher's Chronology, this event took place approximately 1451 BC. How did God accomplish this? If He had simply stopped the rotation of the earth, that would have been disastrous for every living creature on earth. He had to make the change without affecting seasons, tides, weather systems, and life. How did it happen? There must have been some change in the earth's orbit around the sun.

Ahaz's Sundial

A second astronomical miracle took place in the Scripture. This one is found listed three times in the Old Testament. Anything mentioned thrice has added significance. It is mentioned in 2 Kings 20, 2 Chron. 32, and Isa. 38. The Lord told Isaiah to go tell King Hezekiah to put his house in order because he was going to die. The King of Judah prayed and humbled himself before the Lord and asked for more time. God granted him fifteen years in addition to defeating the Assyrian king, Sennacherib, who threatened Jerusalem. We read, **"Go, and say to Hezekiah, Thus saith the LORD, the God of David thy father, I have heard thy prayer, I have seen thy tears: behold, I will add unto thy days fifteen years. And I will deliver thee and this city out of the hand of the king of Assyria: and I will defend this city. And this *shall be* a sign unto thee from the LORD, that the LORD will do this thing that he hath spoken; Behold, I will bring again the shadow of the degrees, which is gone down in the sun dial of Ahaz, ten degrees backward. So the sun returned ten degrees, by which degrees it was gone down"** (Isa. 38:5-8).

As a sign that He would fulfill His promise to the king, God moved the shadow back ten degrees on the sundial of Ahaz. Once again, some change took place in the solar system involving the orbit of earth around the sun. The sun reversed direction and moved the shadow on the sundial back ten degrees. This phenomenon was noticed by the Babylonian ambassadors who later showed up to inquire about it (2 Chron. 32:31). This was when Hezekiah showed them all the riches of Jerusalem (2 Kings 20:13). All these riches would be plundered and carried off to Babylon when Nebuchadnezzar invaded a few chapters later. This event took place roughly 713 BC.

Is it possible that these events had something to do

with the change in the number of days per year on our calendar? This writer thinks it is very possible.

Future Lunar Calendar

According to Scripture, our calendar will again be changed to reflect the former three hundred sixty-day year. We read in Rev. 11:1-3, **"And there was given me a reed like unto a rod: and the angel stood, saying, Rise, and measure the temple of God, and the altar, and them that worship therein. But the court which is without the temple leave out, and measure it not; for it is given unto the Gentiles: and the holy city shall they tread under foot forty *and* two months. And I will give *power* unto my two witnesses, and they shall prophesy a thousand two hundred *and* threescore days, clothed in sackcloth."** During the Tribulation the grand finale of the Times of the Gentiles will take place. The last three and one-half years before the Second Advent, the Gentiles will "tread under foot" the city of Jerusalem. We are given the number 1260 as the number of days in these forty-two months. Again, we have a thirty-day month. This is reinforced with Rev. 12:6 and 13:5. Somehow, by the midpoint of the Tribulation there will be change from three hundred sixty five and a quarter to three hundred sixty days per year.

Something happens during this time to change things. We read in Mat. 24:22, **"And except those days should be shortened, there should no flesh be saved: but for the elect's sake those days shall be shortened."** The Bible says in Rev .16:9, **"And men were scorched with great heat, and blasphemed the name of God, which hath power over these plagues: and they repented not to give him glory."** Joel 2:30 says, **"And I will shew wonders in the heavens and in the earth, blood, and fire, and pillars of smoke."** During the Tribulation there will be signs in the heavens and major cataclysmic changes made to the solar system. **"And I beheld when he had opened the sixth seal, and, lo, there was a great earthquake; and the sun became black as sackcloth of hair, and the moon became as blood; And the stars of heaven fell unto the earth, even as a fig tree casteth her untimely figs, when she is shaken of a mighty wind. And the heaven departed as a scroll when it is rolled together; and every mountain and island were moved out of their places. And the kings of the earth, and the great men, and the rich men, and the chief captains, and the mighty men, and every bondman, and every free man, hid themselves in the dens and in the rocks of the mountains; And said to the mountains and rocks, Fall on us, and hide us from the face of him that sitteth on the throne, and from the wrath of the Lamb:" 17 For the great day of his wrath is come; and who shall be able to stand?** (Rev. 6:12-16).

Apophis

Apophis is an asteroid orbiting the sun. It was discovered in 2004 that in 2034 its orbit would come dangerously close to earth, with the possibility of a collision. Albeit Apophis is only two kilometers in breadth, the results of it colliding with earth would be catastrophic. Scientists later down-scaled the alert and said that there would not be a collision. This scare resulted in at least two motion pictures being made about an asteroid on its way to impact our planet.

Could the scientists be wrong in their decision to lessen the danger of a collision between earth and Apophis? Could it be they want to avoid a worldwide panic? Could this asteroid be only part of the many signs in the heavens during the Tribulation? Only the Lord knows. Both of the passages sited in the Old Testament were associated with Second Advent prophecy. The fact is the Lord Jesus Christ is coming back soon and His Second Coming is not contingent upon the proximity of a stray asteroid in our solar system. Accompanying His return will be phenomena in the heavens and cataclysmic changes to our solar system. Are you ready for His return? It could happen in the next hour. If you are not certain about your personal salvation in Christ, now is the time to be saved. **"...behold, now *is* the accepted time; behold, now *is* the day of salvation"** (2 Cor. 6:2). You can be saved now by simply confessing your sin to Christ and receiving Him as your Savior. **"But as many as received him, to them gave he power to become the sons of God, *even* to them that believe on his name"** (John 1:12). Ask Him to save you now.

CHAPTER EIGHT

PREMILLENNIALISM

Preface

WHILE THE WORD MILLENNIUM IS not found in Scripture, its significance is. The word refers to a period of one thousand years. It is associated with a thousand-year period of time when Jesus Christ will sit upon the Throne of David to rule and reign with a rod of iron (Psm. 2:9, Rev. 2:27, 12:5, 19:15). The prefixes attached represent different ideas of interpretation of Scripture regarding the millennium. Amillennialism is the belief that there is no literal one thousand-year reign of Jesus Christ on earth. Postmillennialism is the belief that Christ will return at the end of the one thousand-year period, after the Christians have built the kingdom. Premillennialism is the belief that Christ will return prior to the one thousand-year period and He will rule and reign and establish His Kingdom.

This one thousand-year period, as typified in Moses'

account of the creation in Genesis, as the seventh day, or the day that God rested: **"Thus the heavens and the earth were finished, and all the host of them. And on the seventh day God ended his work which he had made; and he rested on the seventh day from all his work which he had made."** (Gen. 2:2-3). Simon Peter wrote, **"But, beloved, be not ignorant of this one thing, that one day *is* with the Lord as a thousand years, and a thousand years as one day"** (2 Pet. 3:8).

The Kingdom

When John the Baptist showed up, he heralded this millennium and termed it the "Kingdom of Heaven." **"In those days came John the Baptist, preaching in the wilderness of Judaea, And saying, Repent ye: for the kingdom of heaven is at hand"** (Mat. 3:1-2). This Kingdom was promised in the Davidic Covenant, **"And when thy days be fulfilled, and thou shalt sleep with thy fathers, I will set up thy seed after thee, which shall proceed out of thy bowels, and I will establish his kingdom. He shall build an house for my name, and I will stablish the throne of his kingdom for ever"** (2 Sam. 7:12-13). This Kingdom is mentioned in Gabriel's annunciation, **"He shall be great, and shall be called the Son of the Highest: and the Lord God shall give unto him the throne of his father David: And he shall reign over the house of Jacob for ever; and of his kingdom there shall be no end"** (Luke 1:32-33).

Peter, James, and John got a foretaste of this Kingdom at the Mount of Transfiguration. **"And after six days Jesus taketh *with him* Peter, and James, and John, and leadeth them up into an high mountain apart by themselves: and he was transfigured before them. And his raiment became shining, exceeding white as snow;**

so as no fuller on earth can white them. And there appeared unto them Elias with Moses: and they were talking with Jesus" (Mark 9:2-4). The disciples were looking for this Kingdom even after the resurrection of Christ. "When they therefore were come together, they asked of him, saying, Lord, wilt thou at this time restore again the kingdom to Israel?" (Acts 1:6).

God's plan for the Nation of Israel was that they occupy a position of dominance over all the nations of the world. "And it shall come to pass, if thou shalt hearken diligently unto the voice of the LORD thy God, to observe *and* to do all his commandments which I command thee this day, that the LORD thy God will set thee on high above all nations of the earth" (Deut. 28:1). During the reign of David and Solomon, the Nation of Israel was the most powerful force of the known world because of the God of Israel.

In today's world Israel is not a global power. The nation fell into idolatry and forsook the Lord. "And the LORD said unto Moses, Behold, thou shalt sleep with thy fathers; and this people will rise up, and go a whoring after the gods of the strangers of the land, whither they go *to be* among them, and will forsake me, and break my covenant which I have made with them. Then my anger shall be kindled against them in that day, and I will forsake them, and I will hide my face from them, and they shall be devoured, and many evils and troubles shall befall them; so that they will say in that day, Are not these evils come upon us, because our God *is* not among us?" (Deut. 31:16-17). The Lord has temporarily forsaken the Jews and allowed all the trouble and persecution to befall them. "And it shall come to pass, when many evils and troubles are befallen them, that this song shall testify against them as a witness; for it shall not be forgotten out of the mouths of their seed: for

I know their imagination which they go about, even now, before I have brought them into the land which I sware" (Deut. 31:21).

Times of the Gentiles

In Daniel 2, Nebuchadnezzar had a dream that Daniel interpreted. In this dream the king saw a great image with head of gold, breast and arms of silver, belly and thighs of brass, legs of iron, and feet and toes of iron and clay. Daniel goes on to explain that Nebuchadnezzar was the head of gold, representing Babylon. Another kingdom would then assume power, represented by the breast and arms of silver. This was Darius, king of Persia. **"In that night was Belshazzar the king of the Chaldeans slain. And Darius the Median took the kingdom, *being* about threescore and two years old"** (Dan. 5:30-31). The next world power would be the belly and thighs of brass, which was Alexander the Great and Greece. The legs of iron represented Rome. In the final days a mixture of iron and clay represent the final Gentile world power. This period of time is called the "Times of the Gentiles" in Luke 21:24.

This period began with the Babylonian captivity approximately 606 BC and will continue until the Second Advent of Jesus Christ. The final part of Nebuchadnezzar's dream was a stone smashing the feet and destroying the entire image. **"Thou sawest till that a stone was cut out without hands, which smote the image upon his feet *that were* of iron and clay, and brake them to pieces. Then was the iron, the clay, the brass, the silver, and the gold, broken to pieces together, and became like the chaff of the summer threshingfloors; and the wind carried them away, that no place was found for them: and the stone that smote the image became a great mountain, and filled the whole earth"** (Dan. 2:34-35). The stone is Jesus

Christ at the Second Advent. Note that it is likened to the threshing floors. Christ's return brings back Jewish rule and power.

Since Israel forsook their Lord, He took away their power, scattered them among the nations, and reduced them to wanderers. Hos. 9:17 – **"My God will cast them away, because they did not hearken unto him: and they shall be wanderers among the nations."** Nebuchadnezzar invaded Jerusalem, killing thousands of Jews and taking many more into captivity. He destroyed the Temple, the palaces, and the walls of Jerusalem. This event is significant enough to be recorded three times in Scripture - 2 Kings 25, 2 Chron. 36, and Jer. 52. This marks the beginning of a time when Gentile nations rule over the Jews and will remain in this position of power until Jesus Christ returns.

In Daniel's interpretation of Nebuchadnezzar's dream we read, **"And *as* the toes of the feet *were* part of iron, and part of clay, so the kingdom shall be partly strong, and partly broken. And whereas thou sawest iron mixed with miry clay, they shall mingle themselves with the seed of men: but they shall not cleave one to another, even as iron is not mixed with clay. And in the days of these kings shall the God of heaven set up a kingdom, which shall never be destroyed: and the kingdom shall not be left to other people, *but* it shall break in pieces and consume all these kingdoms, and it shall stand for ever. Forasmuch as thou sawest that the stone was cut out of the mountain without hands, and that it brake in pieces the iron, the brass, the clay, the silver, and the gold; the great God hath made known to the king what shall come to pass hereafter: and the dream *is* certain, and the interpretation thereof sure"** (Dan. 2:42-45).

The "Stone that was cut out of the mountain without hands" is Jesus Christ at the Second Advent. He comes back and smashes the image (Gentile power) into pieces. Then "**shall the God of heaven set up a kingdom.**" This is the kingdom over which Christ will rule with a rod of iron. The Bible says in Rev. 12:5 – "**And she brought forth a man child, who was to rule all nations with a rod of iron...**" In Rev. 19:15 we read, "**And out of his mouth goeth a sharp sword, that with it he should smite the nations: and he shall rule them with a rod of iron: and he treadeth the winepress of the fierceness and wrath of Almighty God.**" Jesus Christ, the King of the Jews, will rule the world when He returns. The Kingdom begins when He returns and sits on a throne in Jerusalem.

Let's look at some characteristics of Christ's iron rod reign. Under the reign of Jesus Christ, there will not be any religions, sects, or denominations allowed other than the worship of Jesus Christ, "**And the LORD shall be king over all the earth: in that day shall there be one LORD, and his name one**" (Zech. 14:9). Everyone will be required to come to Jerusalem every year to observe the Feast of Tabernacles, "**And it shall come to pass, *that* every one that is left of all the nations which came against Jerusalem shall even go up from year to year to worship the King, the LORD of hosts, and to keep the feast of tabernacles**" (Zech. 14:16). Everyone that does not come annually to Jerusalem for the Feast of Tabernacles and to worship the Lord will be excluded from receiving rain, "**And it shall be, *that* whoso will not come up of *all* the families of the earth unto Jerusalem to worship the King, the LORD of hosts, even upon them shall be no rain**" (Zech. 14:17). If they still refuse to come, they will receive a plague from the Lord, "**And if the family of Egypt go not up, and come not, that *have* no *rain*; there shall be the plague, wherewith the LORD will smite the heathen that come not up to keep the feast of tabernacles. This shall be the punishment of Egypt, and the punishment of all nations that come not up to keep the feast of tabernacles**" (Zech. 14:18-19).

Before the Kingdom can begin the Lord must return. The Kingdom described in Scripture can only be fulfilled at Christ's return. No one can accomplish the things that need to take place other than the Son of God in Person. The idea of man building the Kingdom is ludicrous in light of the word of God. The Millennial Kingdom is a visible, physical, and literal one, different from the "Spiritual Kingdom" that exists in the hearts of Christians in this age. The Spiritual Kingdom of our present age is entered by the new birth. Paul wrote about it in Romans 14:17, **"For the kingdom of God is not meat and drink; but righteousness, and peace, and joy in the Holy Ghost."** Before the Millennial Kingdom can begin, the Beast and False Prophet must be cast into the lake of fire (Rev. 19:20). Only Jesus Christ can make this happen. Satan is bound for 1000 years (Rev. 20:1-3).

Revelation Chronology

The Book of Revelation is instructive on the subject of the millennium. The book is laid out in a chronological order clearly showing Christ's return prior to the period of one thousand years referred to as the Millennium. Just as there are four accounts of the First Advent of Christ ending with the crucifixion (Matthew, Mark, Luke, and John), there are four accounts of the Tribulation ending with His Second Advent in the book of the Revelation. In our book on the Great Tribulation we go into more detail on this subject.

Chapter 1, Introduction.

Chapter 2-3, Church Age.

Chapter 4:1, Rapture.

Chapter 4:2-5:14, Heavenly scene.

Chapter 6, First account of Tribulation ending in Second Advent.

Chapter 7:1-11:19, Second account of the Tribulation ending in Second Advent.

Chapter 12:1-14:20, Third account of the Tribulation ending in Second Advent.

Chapter 15:1-19:21, Fourth account of the Tribulation ending in Second Advent.

Chapter 20:1-3, Satan bound and millennium begins.

Chapter 20:4-6, First resurrection and kingdom age.

Chapter 20:7-9, Satan loosed, Gog and Magog.

Chapter 20:10, Doom of Satan.

Chapter 20:11-15, Great White Throne.

Chapter 21:1-22:21, New Heaven and earth, New Jerusalem, eternity.

Bible Order

Bible order also instructs us regarding Premillennialism. There are numerous illustrations in Scripture of *suffering, glory, blessing*, in that order. Each example given shows tribulation followed by glory (2nd Advent), followed by blessing (Millennium).

The three books Esther, Job, Psalms show us the Bible order for Suffering (Esther), Glory (Job), and Glory (Psalms). In Esther a king dismisses a Gentile bride and takes a Jewish bride. This illustrates the end of the Times of the Gentiles. Haman is bent on exterminating all Jews and is a type of Antichrist. Then comes Job as a picture of Jew in Tribulation. At end of Job the following things take place: A giant fire-breathing dragon appears, war horses spoken of with trumpets and shouting, the Lord appears in whirlwind and turns Job's captivity. Then we get to Psalms: Psalm 1 speaks of the blessed man. Psalm 2 speaks of God the Father setting up His Son as King, **"Yet have I set my King upon my holy hill of Zion."**

Another example is found in Isa. 5:8-30 – 6:1-4. In chapter 5 we read of the woes of suffering Israel. Then this is followed by appearance of the Glory of God in chapter 6. In the book of Lamentations we find a picture of the Jew in Tribulation followed by Ezk. 1, which is another appearance of the Lord in Glory. In Ezk. 7, again the suffering of Israel is followed by the appearance of the Glory of God in Ezk. 8:1-2. In Ezk. 9 we have another picture of the Jews in Tribulation followed by appearance of the Glory of God in chapter 10. In Isaiah 10 we read of the tribulation followed by the Kingdom of God in chapter 11. Again, in Isa. 13 we see the tribulation followed by the Kingdom of God in chapter 14.

If you look for them, there are more examples like the ones given. The principle is given again and again in the Scripture. This principle is suffering, glory, blessing. Christ came as the Suffering Servant at His first coming. He was resurrected in Glory and is presently seated at the right hand of God. When He returns, He will end the suffering and begin the Millennium. This will be a time of rest and blessing not only for the Nation of Israel, but also for the entire creation (Rom. 8:22). In addition, there is blessing now for the one who enters the other Kingdom.

Kingdom of God

There is a kingdom that we can enter now without waiting for the literal, physical, visible Kingdom, which is coming soon. This is called the Kingdom of God and it is a spiritual kingdom where Jesus Christ rules and reigns right now. Paul said, **"For the kingdom of God is not meat and drink; but righteousness, and peace, and joy in the Holy Ghost"** (Rom. 14:17). The only way to enter this kingdom is through the new birth. Jesus Christ told Nicodemus, **"Jesus answered and said unto him, Verily, verily, I say unto thee, Except a man be born again, he cannot see the kingdom of God. Nicodemus saith unto him, How can a man be born when he is old? can he enter the second time into his mother's womb, and be born? Jesus answered, Verily, verily, I say unto thee, Except a man be born of water and** *of* **the Spirit, he cannot enter into the kingdom of God."** (John 3:3-5)

If there is a chance that the reader is uncertain about personal salvation in Christ, now is the time to call upon the Lord. **"For whosoever shall call upon the name of the Lord shall be saved"** (Rom. 10:13). **"But as many as received him, to them gave he power to become the sons of God,** *even* **to them that believe on his name"** (John 1:12). Call upon Him now and He will save you.

CHAPTER NINE

THE OTHER VICTORY OF CALVARY

Preface

THE APOSTLE PAUL SAID IN 1 COR. 1:23, **"But we preach Christ crucified, unto the Jews a stumblingblock, and unto the Greeks foolishness."** Therefore, we should preach about Jesus Christ on the cross of Calvary. I can remember the first few years of my salvation, sitting under the ministry of Dr. J.B. Buffington at Calvary Baptist Church in Lakeland, Florida. He preached on the seven sayings of Christ on the cross for seven consecutive Sundays. Each one was a tremendous message. We've all heard numerous sermons on the cross. However, there is one aspect of the cross that I have never heard expounded. That aspect will be the focus of this booklet.

The world in which we live contains invisible things. They are all around us. An example would be the wind. John wrote, **"The wind bloweth where it listeth, and thou**

hearest the sound thereof, but canst not tell whence it cometh, and whither it goeth:" (John 3:8). There are dust particles all around us that we cannot see. We breath them in and out and can only see them if they are illuminated by rays of sunlight. All around us are radio waves carrying voices, pictures, data, and other information. We cannot see them, but they are there.

There is also a world of spirit beings that is invisible to us. God Himself is invisible. The Scripture says in 1 Tim. 1:17, **"Now unto the King eternal, immortal, invisible, the only wise God, be honour and glory for ever and ever. Amen."** In addition, there are angels and devils (demons) that are invisible. The Bible says in Col. 1:16, **"For by him were all things created, that are in heaven, and that are in earth, visible and invisible, whether they be thrones, or dominions, or principalities, or powers: all things were created by him, and for him:"** The phrase, "principalities and (or) powers" is found four times in Scripture and three of those four speak of spirit beings (Eph. 3:10, Col. 2:15, 16, Titus 3:1). The phrase also speaks of position of power and authority.

If He wants to, God can open our eyes to these invisible things. There are a few places in Scripture where He does just that.

In Gen. 21 it was time to cast out the bondwoman, Hagar. Abraham gave her bread and a bottle of water and sent her and Ishmael into the wilderness of Beersheba. When the provisions were spent, she cast the child under a shrub and went a good way off and wept. The Angel of the Lord came and opened her eyes to a well of water. She filled the bottle and gave the child drink.

In Gen. 22 Abraham was instructed to take Isaac into the land of Moriah and offer him there for a burnt offering. As Abraham stretched forth his hand to slay his son, the Angel of the Lord called him and opened his eyes to a ram caught in a thicket by his horns.

In Num. 22 Balaam's ass saw the Angel of the Lord and Balaam didn't. Then the Lord opened Balaam's eyes.

In 2 Kings 6 Elisha prayed and asked God to open the eyes of his servant, who then was able to see a multitude of horses and chariots of fire surrounding their position.

In Luke 24 Cleopas and another disciple were walking to Ammaus and were joined by the Lord Jesus. They did not recognize Him. They spent hours together talking about the Scripture. When the Lord broke bread with them He opened their eyes and they recognized Him. He then disappeared before their eyes!

In John 20 Mary Magdalene showed up at the tomb early Sunday morning. She spoke with a man she thought to be the gardener. Then the Lord opened her eyes and she saw that the man was actually the Lord.

These are just a few instances where the Lord opened the eyes of mortal men to the existing unseen world. There is another way that we can see into the unseen world. The Scripture says in Heb. 11:1-3, **"Now faith is the substance of things hoped for, the *evidence of things not seen*. For by it the elders obtained a good report. Through faith we understand that the worlds were framed by the word of God, so that things which are seen were not made of things which do appear."** In addition, Paul tells us in Rom. 1:20, **"For the invisible things of him from the creation of the world are clearly seen, being understood by the things that are made, even his eternal power and Godhead; so that they are without excuse:"** Through faith and by "things that are made" we can see into the unseen world surrounding the cross of Calvary.

Before we get into our text, there is one more element of groundwork, which first needs to be established. The Old Testament gives us illustrations that help us understand Bible truths. Nothing in Scripture is without significance. The Bible says in Prov. 30:5, **"Every word of God is pure."** When reading through the Bible, we find certain reoccurring events, such as:

1. Someone departs and someone pursues them.

2. Someone is being pursued and someone helps them escape out an upper window.

3. Someone is being sought after and someone hides them from the pursuers.

4. Someone vanishes and people search for them for a period of time.

When we come across this Bible phenomenon we should understand that there is some significance to these reoccurrences. We may not understand them, but the Holy Spirit does not put anything in Scripture that does not have a purpose.

There is a similar reoccurring situation that we will focus on. In the Bible, we find someone who wants to take over a position of power and they fail in their attempt. This results in an embarrassing situation and in some cases lethal. Let's look at them:

1. In Num. 16 an Israelite named Korah led a group of 250 leaders in the tribe of Levi to challenge the authority of Moses and Aaron. They said to Moses, **"Ye take too much upon you, seeing all the congregation are holy, every one of them, and the LORD is among them: wherefore then lift ye up yourselves above the congregation of the LORD?"** (vs. 3) In subsequent verses the Bible says, **"And it came to pass, as he had made an end of speaking all these words, that the ground clave asunder that was under them: And the earth opened her mouth, and swallowed them up, and their houses, and all the men that appertained unto Korah, and all their**

goods. They, and all that appertained to them, went down alive into the pit, and the earth closed upon them: and they perished from among the congregation" (vs. 31-33).

2. In 1 Kings 1, David's son, Adonijah decides that he should be king since the aged David is on his death bed and the opportunity is right for him. With the help of General Joab and Abiathar, the priest, he sets himself up as the next king with a great banquet. Meanwhile Nathan the prophet hears about this and warns Bathsheba, who tells King David. David gives them instructions to anoint Solomon as king in his stead and makes it official. Then word gets back to Adonijah at the banquet and he realizes his attempted takeover is an embarrassing failure.

3. The book of Esther provides the best illustration of the truth with the character named Haman. Mordecai saves the life of the king and it is recorded in the chronicles. The king, unable to sleep one night, finds himself reading the chronicles and learns about the attempt on his life. He sees that nothing is done to reward Mordecai for his loyalty. When the self-exalting Haman enters, the king asks him what should be done to the one whom the king wishes to honor? His answer blows up in his face and he faces the embarrassing results. Then later after he passes a law to exterminate all the Jews in the land, including the queen, his plan to elevate himself comes crashing down on his head and he is hanged on the gallows he made for Mordecai.

Each one of these passages shares a similar thread. Someone attempts to exalt himself and take over a position of power and authority. We have seen the coup d'état element in three different passages of Scripture. There is yet another similar passage which needs to be examined in the light of the first three. In Isaiah 14, we find the following verses:

12 How art thou fallen from heaven, O Lucifer,

son of the morning! how art thou cut down to the ground, which didst weaken the nations!

13 For thou hast said in thine heart, I will ascend into heaven, I will exalt my throne above the stars of God: I will sit also upon the mount of the congregation, in the sides of the north:

14 I will ascend above the heights of the clouds; I will be like the most High.

15 Yet thou shalt be brought down to hell, to the sides of the pit.

16 They that see thee shall narrowly look upon thee, and consider thee, saying, Is this the man that made the earth to tremble, that did shake kingdoms;

In these verses, we read about the ultimate grab for power and authority. The Devil actually made an attempt to elevate himself above God. This attempt resulted in his fall from the exalted position of "anointed cherub that covereth." We learn this from the study of Ezekiel 28. Verse 14 of that chapter says, **"Thou art the anointed cherub that covereth; and I have set thee so: thou wast upon the holy mountain of God; thou hast walked up and down in the midst of the stones of fire."** Satan was not satisfied with his position and wanted more power and authority.

While Satan was removed from his former position of power, he is still the prince of the power of the air (Eph. 2:2) and still has tremendous power. The Devil is no one to "toy around" with. **"Yet Michael the archangel, when contending with the devil he disputed about the body of Moses, durst not bring against him a railing accusation, but said, The Lord rebuke thee"** (Jude 9). Even Michael has to observe certain heavenly protocols.

Note verse 12 above is written in the past tense, but Satan's ejection from heaven has not yet taken place. It happens in Rev. 12:9. It is not uncommon to find future events in the Bible written about in the past tense. For example, the White Throne Judgment found in Rev. 20:11. There are plenty more examples throughout the book of Revelation. The devil is still in heaven, standing before God, accusing the brethren (Job 1, 2, 1 Kings 22:22, 2 Chron. 18:18, Zech. 3:1-2, Rev. 12:10). The most important aspect of the Isaiah passage is found in verses 15 and 16. That is, the devil's attempt fails and he is brought down, ultimately to the pit. Note the similarity in the three previously mentioned examples above. Someone attempts to take over, the attempt is foiled, and the perpetrator is shamefully rebuked or executed.

With this in mind, let us now approach the subject of

The Other Victory of Calvary

During the Last Supper Christ told the disciples that one of them would betray Him. Naturally, all the disciples wondered whom. John wrote, **"Jesus answered, He it is, to whom I shall give a sop, when I have dipped *it*. And when he had dipped the sop, he gave *it* to Judas Iscariot, *the son* of Simon. And after the sop Satan entered into him. Then said Jesus unto him, That thou doest, do quickly"** (John 13:26-27). We have just seen that Satan entered into Judas during the last supper. Judas Iscariot actually became Satan incarnate.

Now let's look at Luke's gospel. Luke 22:47-53 says, **"And while he yet spake, behold a multitude, and he that was called Judas, one of the twelve, went before them, and drew near unto Jesus to kiss him. But Jesus said unto him, Judas, betrayest thou the Son of man with a kiss? When they which were about him saw what would follow, they said unto him, Lord, shall we smite with the sword? And one of them smote the servant of** the high priest, and cut off his right ear. And Jesus answered and said, Suffer ye thus far. And he touched his ear, and healed him. Then Jesus said unto the chief priests, and captains of the temple, and the elders, which were come to him, Be ye come out, as against a thief, with swords and staves? When I was daily with you in the temple, ye stretched forth no hands against me: but this is your hour, and the power of darkness." In this passage, we read of a lynch mob, led by Judas, to arrest Jesus Christ. Judas led this group and through previous arrangements (Mat. 26:14-16), had agreed to identify Jesus Christ with a kiss.

This mob showed up right after Christ prayed in the garden of Gethsemane. The Bible says in the passage above they came with "swords and staves." There were probably several carrying torches since this took place late in the evening before the last Passover. Visualize Judas standing in front of the Lord Jesus, with the torch-bearing mob behind him. Somewhere nearby were Peter, James, and John. When Simon Peter sensed that this was not a friendly encounter, he drew his sword and sliced off the right ear of Malchus (John 18:10). The Lord immediately and miraculously replaced the severed ear and rebuked Simon. The scene continues with Christ addressing the crowd and pointing out that they never made any attempt to abduct Him when He **"was daily with them in the Temple."** Then Jesus Christ looked into the eyes of Judas Iscariot, or Satan incarnate, and said, **"but this is your hour and the power of darkness."**

One might say that this was Satan's finest hour. That is, from that point until the following afternoon around six o'clock, Satan would have his way with Jesus Christ through the human agency of Annas, Caiaphas, the Jewish High Priest, the chief priests, scribes, elders, false witnesses, Pontius Pilate, Herod, then back to Pilate and his Praetorian guard, and finally into the hands of the Roman soldiers who nailed him to the cross.

Let us now look beyond the physical sufferings of Christ on the cross as depicted in the four Gospels and scrutinize what went on in the "unseen world" during "Satan's hour." We have already seen how God can open the eyes of certain people (and even animals) and allow them to visualize what is normally invisible. We also pointed out the Holy Spirit's ability to illuminate Scripture, thus enabling one to "see" into this spiritual realm. As we examine some passages in the Old Testament, pray and ask God to open your eyes.

Psm. 22:1, **"My God, my God, why hast thou forsaken me?** *why art thou so* **far from helping me,** *and from* **the words of my roaring?"** The first verse of this Psalm immediately identifies it with the Cross of Calvary. This same phrase is recorded in Mat. 27:46 and Mark 15:34 by the Lord Jesus while on the cross.

Verse 2-3, **"O my God, I cry in the daytime, but thou hearest not; and in the night season, and am not silent. But thou** *art* **holy, O** *thou* **that inhabitest the praises of Israel."** God the Father could not look upon sin. Jesus Christ became sin on the cross and thus, His Father "hearest not."

Verse 6, **"But I** *am* **a worm, and no man; a reproach of men, and despised of the people."** Jesus Christ likened Himself to a worm, the vilest form of a serpent. He said in John 3:14, **"And as Moses lifted up the serpent in the wilderness, even so must the Son of man be lifted up:"** Again Christ compared Himself to the epitome of all sin, the serpent of Scripture.

Verse 7, **"All they that see me laugh me to scorn: they shoot out the lip, they shake the head,** *saying,***"** Three times in the New Testament the phrase, *"And they laughed him to scorn,"* is found (Mat. 9:24, Mark 5:40, Luke 8:53). Each time the subject is the Lord Jesus.

Verse 8, **"He trusted on the LORD** *that* **he would deliver him: let him deliver him, seeing he delighted in him."** The Bible says in Mat. 27:43, **"He trusted in God; let him deliver him now, if he will have him: for he said, I am the Son of God."** The context of Psm. 22 is, without a doubt, Christ on the cross. Now let's move forward to verse 11. At this point there is a subtle change in the text with the beginning of a new paragraph.

Verse 11, **"Be not far from me; for trouble** *is* **near; for** *there is* **none to help."** Under the inspiration of the Holy Ghost, David writes, "trouble is near." This is the harbinger of the world unseen by the writers of the four Gospels.

Verse 12, **"Many bulls have compassed me: strong** *bulls* **of Bashan have beset me round."** If we allow the word of God to be our dictionary, we will find the word "compassed" means to "encircle with harmful intent." The word is found forty-four times in Scripture and thirty-seven of them match this definition. Let's look at some of them:

2 Sam. 22:5, **"When the waves of death compassed me, the floods of ungodly men made me afraid;"** Here, the immediate context is David's deliverance from the hands of King Saul. As we shall see, this passage is Messianic in nature and speaks of the unseen world closing in on Jesus Christ on the cross.

2 Sam. 22:6, **"The sorrows of hell compassed me about; the snares of death prevented me;"** Again, we see the same scene in the subsequent verse from David.

Psm. 18:4, **"The sorrows of death compassed me, and the floods of ungodly men made me afraid."**

Psm. 18:5, **"The sorrows of hell compassed me about: the snares of death prevented me."** Notice this verse is identical to 2 Sam. 22:6.

Psm. 40:12, **"For innumerable evils have**

compassed me about:"

Psm. 109:3, "They compassed me about also with words of hatred; and fought against me without a cause."

Psm. 116:3, "The sorrows of death compassed me, and the pains of hell gat hold upon me: I found trouble and sorrow."

Psm. 118:12, "They compassed me about like bees; they are quenched as the fire of thorns: for in the name of the LORD I will destroy them."

Jonah 2:3, "For thou hadst cast me into the deep, in the midst of the seas; and the floods compassed me about: all thy billows and thy waves passed over me."

Jonah 2:5, "The waters compassed me about, *even* to the soul: the depth closed me round about, the weeds were wrapped about my head."

In each of the above verses, the subject is compassed (or surrounded) with:

1. Waves of death

2. Sorrows of hell

3. Sorrows of death

4. Innumerable evils

5. Words of hatred

6. Something likened to bees

7. Water

Each of these has to do with the "cup" from which Jesus Christ "drank" and the "baptism," which He experienced at Calvary. This is mentioned in Mark 10:38, **"But Jesus said unto them, Ye know not what ye ask:**

can ye drink of the cup that I drink of? and be baptized with the baptism that I am baptized with?" This cup also is mentioned by Christ when He prayed in Gethsemane, **"And he went a little further, and fell on his face, and prayed, saying, O my Father, if it be possible, let this cup pass from me: nevertheless not as I will, but as thou *wilt*"** (Mat. 26:39). (Jesus Christ's prayer was not to be delivered from the horrible death of the cross. It had to do with Christ "becoming" sin, and as such, God the Father would turn His back upon Him. It was the broken fellowship with the Father that Christ did not want to face. Hence, His cry, **"My God, My God, why hast thou forsaken me?"**)

It should be noted here that the "baptism" mentioned above is associated with a passage mentioned in Mat. 12:39-40, **"But he answered and said unto them, An evil and adulterous generation seeketh after a sign; and there shall no sign be given to it, but the sign of the prophet Jonas: For as Jonas was three days and three nights in the whale's belly; so shall the Son of man be three days and three nights in the heart of the earth."** There were certain scribes and Pharisees who asked for a sign. Jesus Christ told them the only sign would be the prophet Jonah. When we look at chapter two of Jonah, we find some instructive things about the unseen world.

In the context of this first chapter Jonah has been thrown overboard into the stormy waters and swallowed by a great fish (1:15-17). The whale, swimming to the bottom of the sea, begins the digestive process of his most recent meal and heads in the general direction of Nineveh.

Jonah 2:1-2, **"Then Jonah prayed unto the LORD his God out of the fish's belly, And said, I cried by reason of mine affliction unto the LORD, and he heard me; out of the belly of hell cried I, *and* thou heardest my voice."** Jonah prayed unto the Lord just as did Jesus Christ on the cross. Jonah found himself in the "belly of hell," just as did Jesus Christ in payment for the sin of mankind.

Verse 3, **"For thou hadst cast me into the deep, in the midst of the seas; and the floods compassed me about: all thy billows and thy waves passed over me."** Compare this verse to Psm. 69:2 and 15. **"I sink in deep mire, where *there is* no standing: I am come into deep waters, where the floods overflow me."**

Psm. 69:15, **"Let not the waterflood overflow me, neither let the deep swallow me up, and let not the pit shut her mouth upon me."** Psm. 69 is another Messianic Psalm and gives light on Christ's suffering on the cross. In these two verses Christ is "baptized" in "deep waters." He is beneath the "floods" and is "swallowed" by the deep. The context clearly indicates that it is not something that He enjoyed.

Jonah 2:4, **"Then I said, I am cast out of thy sight; yet I will look again toward thy holy temple."** Again, we see that Christ was "cast out of thy sight" as God the Father turned His back on His Son during Calvary.

Verse 5, **"The waters compassed me about, *even* to the soul: the depth closed me round about, the weeds were wrapped about my head."** The seaweed was a type of crown of thorns.

Verse 6, **"I went down to the bottoms of the mountains; the earth with her bars *was* about me for ever: yet hast thou brought up my life from corruption, O LORD my God."** Christ went into the heart of the earth during Calvary (Mat. 12:40). We also see in this verse the death of Jonah. **"Yet hast thou brought up my life from corruption"** speaks of death brought back to life. The age-old cry of the liberals regarding the impossibility of a man surviving three days and three nights in the belly of a whale is a moot point. Jonah did not live through it. He died – just as did the Lord Jesus Christ on Calvary.

Verse 7-9, **"When my soul fainted within me I remembered the LORD: and my prayer came in unto thee, into thine holy temple. They that observe lying vanities forsake their own mercy. But I will sacrifice unto thee with the voice of thanksgiving; I will pay *that* that I have vowed. Salvation *is* of the LORD."** Christ paid the sin debt of mankind and made salvation and freedom from sin available once and for all.

Verse 10, **"And the LORD spake unto the fish, and it vomited out Jonah upon the dry *land*."** By this time, the whale had swum the distance to Nineveh and Jonah is resurrected from his "death." He is back on "dry land." Psm. 18:16 says, **"He sent from above, he took me, he drew me out of many waters."**

The Apostle Paul, a steadfast student of the Old Testament understood this when he wrote, **"Who shall descend into the deep? (that is, to bring up Christ again from the dead)"** (Rom. 10:7).

Let us now return Psm. 22:12 and finish with this verse before proceeding to verse thirteen. **"Many bulls have compassed me: strong bulls of Bashan have beset me round."** The second half of his verse is also interesting. It indicates that "strong bulls" surrounded Christ on the cross. When David wrote this Psalm he was being hunted by King Saul, who wanted him dead. David found himself surrounded by Saul's army (1 Sam. 23:26) and cried out for God's help. At no time during David's flight from Saul was he surrounded by literal bulls. In the prophetic aspect of the verse (Christ on the cross), there was no livestock present at Golgotha. However, the subject says, "Many bulls have compassed me: strong bulls of Bashan have beset me round."

The king of Bashan was Og, who was a remnant of the giants (Deut.3:11). Bashan was known as the "land of the giants," (Deut. 3:13). Bashan was given to Reuben, Gad, and the half-tribe of Manasseh, who remained on the east side of

Jordan. Bashan was known for its cattle and oak trees. The area is now called Syria. However, none of this background information sheds any light on the passage. In our context, the subject reports being surrounded with bulls, which are beasts of the field.

We find another interesting passage in Gen. 3:1, **"Now the serpent was more subtil than any beast of the field which the LORD God had made."** Further investigation reveals that "beasts of the field" include not only cattle, but carnivorous animals as well (Ezek. 34:8). However, Gen. 3:14 shows us that in this particular case, the serpent was considered "cattle." **"And the LORD God said unto the serpent, Because thou hast done this, thou *art* cursed above all cattle, and above every beast of the field; upon thy belly shalt thou go, and dust shalt thou eat all the days of thy life:"** Therefore, before it was cursed, the serpent was some sort of hoofed and horned beast. In Isaiah 34:14 we find a creature called a Satyr. Any dictionary or encyclopedia will identify this creature as made up of the bottom half of a goat and the top half of a man with pointed ears, tail, and horns (Gen. 6:4, Lev. 18:23). Could this have been the form of the serpent before it was cursed? We don't know. We can only speculate. We do know however, that the serpent (like "bulls") was considered to be "cattle." Christ, while on the cross referred to being surrounded by beasts called "bulls."

Verses 13, **"They gaped upon me *with* their mouths, *as* a ravening and a roaring lion."** The subjects of this verse are the bulls mentioned in verse twelve. To "gape" is to gawk or stare. The phrase is used one other time in Scripture. Job 16:9-11, **"He teareth *me* in his wrath, who hateth me: he gnasheth upon me with his teeth; mine enemy sharpeneth his eyes upon me. They have gaped upon me with their mouth; they have smitten me upon the cheek reproachfully; they have gathered themselves**

together against me. God hath delivered me to the ungodly, and turned me over into the hands of the wicked." Job is suffering the grief of his dead children. He is in pain from sore boils that cover his body (Job 2:7) as he sits in the ash heap. He lost everything he owned. Here again, we are allowed a glimpse at the unseen world of suffering experienced by the Lord Jesus. **"He teareth me in his wrath, who hateth me."** Gen. 22:13 (above) says, **"They gaped upon me *with* their mouths, *as* a ravening and a roaring lion."** A lion "tears in his wrath." The devil is compared to a roaring lion in 1 Pet. 5:8. **"He gnasheth upon me with his teeth:"** This phrase takes us to Psm. 35:16 where the context is also Christ on the cross. There was no one who physically gnashed on Christ with their teeth while He was on the cross in the four Gospels. There was no one who "tore" Him while on the cross. The Praetorian guard whipped him before the crucifixion, but that was spoken of as "stripes" (Isa. 53:5). Yet according to two places in Scripture someone or something was gnawing on Christ with their teeth while He was on the cross. **"And turned me over into the hands of the wicked."** Christ was surrounded by "the wicked," or to be more specific, "spiritual wickedness in high places" (Eph. 6:12).

Verse 14-15, **"I am poured out like water, and all my bones are out of joint: my heart is like wax; it is melted in the midst of my bowels. My strength is dried up like a potsherd; and my tongue cleaveth to my jaws; and thou hast brought me into the dust of death."** We are back to the Lord's physical suffering in these verses.

Verse 16, **"For dogs have compassed me: the assembly of the wicked have inclosed me: they pierced my hands and my feet."** You never read about any dogs surrounding the Lord while He was on the cross. In Scripture, dogs are unclean beasts and nothing good is said about them. In Rev. 22:15 dogs are associated with sorcerers, whoremongers, murderers, idolaters, liars, and they are not allowed into New Jerusalem.

Verse 17-19, **"I may tell all my bones: they look** *and* **stare upon me. They part my garments among them, and cast lots upon my vesture. But be not thou far from me, O LORD: O my strength, haste thee to help me."** In these three verses we are back to the physical realm of Calvary.

Verse 20, **"Deliver my soul from the sword; my darling from the power of the dog."** This verse is remarkably similar to Psm. 35:17, which says, **"Lord, how long wilt thou look on? rescue my soul from their destructions, my darling from the lions."** These two verses are the only occurrences of the word, "darling" in Scripture. Both verses cry for deliverance and from beasts.

Verse 21, **"Save me from the lion's mouth: for thou hast heard me from the horns of the unicorns."** The beast of Revelation 13:2 is said to have a mouth like that of a lion, **"and his mouth as the mouth of a lion."**

Now, let us summarize what we have gleaned from these Messianic passages in the Old Testament and apply them to our thesis.

1. While on the cross, Jesus Christ was compassed about with beasts (dogs, bulls, etc.).

2. These beasts gaped upon him with their mouths.

3. The mouths of these beasts were likened to the mouth of a ravenous lion.

4. He was compassed with the sorrows of death, sorrows of hell, innumerable evils, snares of death, words of hatred, and wickedness.

5. He experienced the pains of hell, trouble, and sorrow.

6. Those that surrounded Him were compared to

bees and the fire of thorns.

In the process of paying the sin debt of the world, Jesus Christ suffered untold and unimaginable agonies and sorrows, both physical *and spiritual.* We showed how Satan entered Judas and Christ told him, **"this is your hour"** (Luke 22:53). It was at Calvary that the devil intended to elevate his position even higher. Perhaps he even figured on achieving his goal of Isaiah 14. At any rate he thought he had the Lord Jesus pinned to the mat in the subsequent crucifixion and death.

If indeed these were Satan's thoughts, it stands to reason that he would have all his "lieutenants" around to witness his victory, just as Adonijah was surrounded by all his friends and associates at the banquet in 1 Kings 1. He was taking over the throne and had all his high-ranking officials with him. His two highest ranking officials were Joab (in charge of the military) and Abiathar, the priest (1 Kings 1:7). In the case of Haman in Esther, it was his family and certain friends (Est. 5:10, 14) who stood behind him and made ready to enjoy a new position in the court. In Numbers 16 when Korah intended to take over Moses' authority, he was flanked by a number of high-ranking Israelites. The Scripture says, **"And they rose up before Moses, with certain of the children of Israel, two hundred and fifty princes of the assembly, famous in the congregation, men of renown"** (Num. 16:2). In each of the above-listed attempts to take over someone else's power, there is a leader and a hierarchy of followers. In Paul's epistle to the Ephesians we find another of these chains of command. **"For we wrestle not against flesh and blood, but against principalities, against powers, against the rulers of the darkness of this world, against spiritual wickedness in high *places*"** (Eph 6:12). Here is the devil's high command – his highest-ranking officials, if you will.

It stands to reason, by the passages we pointed out in

the Old Testament, that when Satan made his move to "take over," he would have all his helpers with him. It is our belief that this is the very assembly that encompassed the Lord Jesus at Calvary. He was surrounded by all the principalities, powers, and spiritual wickedness of the universe. And the leader of the group was the prince of the power of the air, the god of this world, Satan himself. This was the "unseen gallery" that was on hand to view the ugly scene. Matthew, Mark, Luke, and John didn't see them. The Roman soldiers didn't see them. The two malefactors didn't see them. The only one who saw them was their victim. Christ described them as "beasts."

At the high point of this wicked group's activity something took place that caused an abrupt change in the proceedings. Everything was going their way and then the Lord Jesus "spoiled the fun." It was similar to when Adonijah and his guests were enjoying the banquet and a messenger arrived with news that Solomon had just been officially anointed and crowned King (1 King 1:41-50). It was also like the moment in Esther 7:6 when Esther pointed her finger at Haman and said, **"The adversary and enemy is this wicked Haman."** We are also reminded of the Lord saying, **"Separate yourselves from among this congregation, that I may consume them in a moment"** (Num. 16:20-21). It was after that that the ground opened up and swallowed Korah and his entire rebellious group.

There is yet another illustration in the Scripture of this sudden turn of events that is worthy of our attention. In Judges 3:15-21 we read about Ehud, who was used of God to deliver Israel out of trouble. Ehud, a left-handed Benjamite, fabricated a short, double-bladed dagger and kept it strapped to his right thigh. The Bible says, **"And he brought the present unto Eglon king of Moab: and Eglon *was* a very fat man. And when he had made an end to offer the present, he sent away the people that bare the present.**

But he himself turned again from the quarries that were by Gilgal, and said, I have a secret errand unto thee, O king: who said, Keep silence. And all that stood by him went out from him. And Ehud came unto him; and he was sitting in a summer parlour, which he had for himself alone. And Ehud said, I have a message from God unto thee. And he arose out of *his* seat. And Ehud put forth his left hand, and took the dagger from his right thigh, and thrust it into his belly: And the haft also went in after the blade; and the fat closed upon the blade, so that he could not draw the dagger out of his belly; and the dirt came out." (Jud. 3:17-22).

Albeit Ehud was not trying to take over any governmental authority and elevate himself, this passage of Scripture is extremely significant in our study of Christ's unseen "other victory" on Golgotha's hill. Ehud approached Eglon, the wicked king of Moab as a secret messenger following the presentation of a gift. We are not told what Eglon was expecting or why he had everyone leave the room before he received the message, but that's what took place. Ehud told the king he had a secret message from God. When he got close enough to whisper into his ear, he drew his dagger and planted it into the king's belly.

Why is this passage instructive for us? In Scripture, a two-edged dagger or sword is a type of the word of God. Heb. 4:12 states, **"For the word of God is quick, and powerful, and sharper than any twoedged sword, piercing even to the dividing asunder of soul and spirit, and of the joints and marrow, and is a discerner of the thoughts and intents of the heart."** Additionally, Paul wrote, **"And take the helmet of salvation, and the sword of the Spirit, which is the word of God"** (Eph. 6:17). It is our belief that at the zenith of the Lord Jesus Christ's suffering on the cross He got up close to the devil and whispered something to him. Whatever it was He said was like a knife in his belly and it brought the devil's celebration to a close. It also amounted to a colossal embarrassment to Satan before all the host of heaven. The Scripture says in Col. 2:15, **"And having spoiled principalities and powers, he made a shew of them openly, triumphing over them in it."** The Lord Jesus made a perfect fool of the devil in front of his own cohorts.

The devil was humiliated and defeated. This is also given to us in Scripture. **"But thou hast cast off and abhorred, thou hast been wroth with thine anointed. Thou hast made void the covenant of thy servant: thou hast profaned his crown *casting by it* to the ground. Thou hast broken down all his hedges; thou hast brought his strong holds to ruin. All that pass by the way spoil him: he is a reproach to his neighbours. Thou hast set up the right hand of his adversaries; thou hast made all his enemies to rejoice. Thou hast also turned the edge of his sword, and hast not made him to stand in the battle. Thou hast made his glory to cease, and cast his throne down to the ground. The days of his youth hast thou shortened: thou hast covered him with shame. Selah"**(Psm. 89:38-45).

The verses following Satan's vow to ascend above the stars of God in Isa. 14 are as follows: **"Yet thou shalt be brought down to hell, to the sides of the pit. They that see thee shall narrowly look upon thee, *and* consider thee, *saying, Is* this the man that made the earth to tremble, that did shake kingdoms;"** (Isa. 14:15-16).

What was it that the Lord said to Satan? The Scripture doesn't say. However, there is a passage in Isa. 50 that is very interesting. **"I gave my back to the smiters, and my cheeks to them that plucked off the hair: I hid not my face from shame and spitting. For the Lord GOD will help me; therefore shall I not be confounded: therefore have I set my face like a flint, and I know that I shall not be ashamed"** (Isa. 50:6-7).Verses six and seven identify the speaker as the Lord Jesus and the scene as Calvary. The passage continues with verse 8 – **"He is near that justifieth me; who will contend with me? let us stand together: who is mine adversary? let him come near to me."** Christ asks, "Who will contend with me?" The obvious answer is Satan. Could this verse have been part of what was said to Satan? The Lord may have looked into the devil's dead eyes and asked, "Who is mine adversary? Let him come near to me. Step in a little closer Satan. I've got something to tell you…" Perhaps the Lord Jesus looked at him and asked, "Is this all you've got? Are you my adversary? Are you kidding me? You call this an attempt to take over? You think you are going to defeat me with this?

Another passage is found in Isaiah 44:8, which reads, **"Fear ye not, neither be afraid: have not I told thee from that time, and have declared it? ye are even my witnesses. Is there a God beside me? yea, there is no God; I know not any."** Perhaps the Lord Jesus said to the devil, **"Is there a God beside me? Yea, there is no God; I know not any."** Perhaps He followed that by saying, "You call yourself a god? I'd walk right past you looking for a god." **"And having spoiled principalities and powers, he made a shew of them openly, triumphing over them in it."**

We don't know what it was Christ uttered to Satan. We can rest assured that it was the word of God and it cut him like a double-bladed sword. It defeated him and made him look like a fool before all the host of heaven. There is a verse in Proverbs that says, **"There is that speaketh like the piercings of a sword:"** (Prov. 12:18).

We quoted Isa. 50:6-8 above. The verse that follows says: **"Who is among you that feareth the LORD, that obeyeth the voice of his servant, that walketh in darkness, and hath no light? let him trust in the name of the LORD, and stay upon his God"** (Isa. 50:10).

We serve a mighty and all-powerful God. It is our prayer that this treatise will serve to challenge the reader to **"Study to shew thyself approved unto God, a workman that needeth not to be ashamed, rightly dividing the word of truth"** (2 Tim. 2:15). **"For all those *things* hath mine hand made, and all those *things* have been, saith the LORD: but to this *man* will I look, *even* to *him that* is poor and of a contrite spirit, and trembleth at my word"** (Isa. 66:2).

CHAPTER TEN

CHRIST'S SUBTERRANIAN REDEMPTIVE WORK

OF THE MANY JUDGMENTS FOUND in Scripture, there are seven that stand out in significance above the others. Those seven main judgments are as follows (the order listed is not necessarily chronological):

1. Judgment Seat of Christ

2. White Throne Judgment

3. Judgment of the Nations

4. Judgment on Satan and his angels

5. Judgment on Israel (Tribulation)

6. Believer's self judgment

7. Judgment on sin (Calvary)

It is the Judgment on sin at Calvary that we will discuss in this paper. There are those who may take issue with the seven judgments listed above. Some believe, for example that the White Throne Judgment and the Judgment of the Nations are the same. Our division will not be discussed in this paper. The reader is directed to our paper on the Judgment of the Nations for the Scripture supporting this division.

The Judgment on sin is by far the most significant of the seven mentioned as far as the sinner is concerned. Since the Bible states, **"All have sinned and come short of the glory of God"** (Rom. 3:23), indicating that virtually all men are sinners, the details of the judgment upon sin should be welcome news indeed to all of us. In this paper we will look at the three days and three nights following Christ's redemptive work on the cross. When those present on Golgotha heard Jesus Christ lift up His voice and say, *"It is finished"* (John 19:30), none of them but the penitent thief would know anything about what would transpire during the next three days. It would be early Sunday morning before any of those witnesses would see Him again. The writer of Hebrews wrote, **"Now faith is the substance of things hoped for, the evidence of things not seen"** (Heb. 11:1). Through the eyes of faith, we are going to follow the Lord Jesus in His death and tag along on His journey to the heart of the earth. We are going to see what went on during those three days and three nights. The things we will write about were those "things not seen."

We should also note that it was on a Wednesday that Christ was crucified and not the traditional belief of Friday as His day of Passion. This statement is documented with numerous passages of Scriptural evidence in our booklet on "Good Friday or Good Wednesday." The only way to get three nights and three days, beginning at sundown and ending on the first day of the week (Mat. 28:1, Mark 16:2, Luke 24:1, John 20:1), is to start on Wednesday afternoon. Note also that when the Scripture says in Mark 16:9, **"Now when *Jesus* was risen early the first *day* of the week, he appeared**

first to Mary Magdalene...” the writer is not talking about early Sunday morning. Remember, the Jewish day begins at sundown the previous day. When the passage says that **“Jesus was risen early the first day of the week,”** that would mean right after sundown on Saturday evening. Therefore when Mary came to the empty tomb in John 20:1 (in the morning), His resurrection would have been approximately twelve hours previous. With all this in mind, let us examine the Scriptures to learn what went on during the three days prior to His appearing to Mary and the disciples after His resurrection.

The Bible says, **“For the wages of sin *is* death, but the gift of God *is* eternal life through Jesus Christ our Lord”** (Rom. 6:23). Let me remind you that no one is without sin. Death came as result of Adam’s sin of disobeying God and eating of the forbidden fruit. **“But of the tree of the knowledge of good and evil, thou shalt not eat of it: for in the day that thou eatest thereof thou shalt surely die”** (Gen. 2:17). From the time Adam ate the fruit his body began the process of dying. Eventually, his body would physically die. This is the first death and since Adam is the father of all of humanity and we are all made in his image (Gen. 5:3), we will all eventually die.

The second part of this judgment is far worse than the first. **“And death and hell were cast into the lake of fire. This is the second death”** (Rev. 20:14). Here we get to the real payment for the sin debt. **“The wages of sin is death.”** The only way to pay for sin is first to die a physical death and then burn in hell for all eternity.

In Gen. 5 we are given **“the book of the generations of Adam.”** The end of verse 5 says, **“and he died.”** The end of verse 8 says **“and he died.”** The end of verse 11 says **“and he died.”** The end of verse 14 says **“and he died.”** The end of verse 17 says **“and he died.”** The end of verse 20 says **“and he died.”** The end of verse 27 says

"and he died." The end of verse 31 says **"and he died."** The only other time the phrase, **"the book of the generations"** is found in Scripture, is in Matthew 1 and it is the book of the generations of Jesus Christ. The phrase, **"and he died"** is not found in the chapter. Of course the reason for this is found in Paul's writings. **"For as in Adam all die, even so in Christ shall all be made alive"** (1 Cor. 15:22).

Let me repeat the fact that since we are all sinners, and the wages of sin is death, all must die the first and second death and spend eternity in the lake of fire…unless there is another option. Thank God there *is* another option available for sinners. The option is someone else takes your place and goes to hell on your behalf and pays your sin debt.

Rom. 4:5 says, **"But to him that worketh not, but believeth on him that justifieth the ungodly, his faith is counted for righteousness."** According to this verse, works don't count toward our "option" but **"believing on him that justifieth the ungodly"** does. Man is saved from the death penalty by believing, not working. **"For by grace are ye saved through faith; and that not of yourselves: it is the gift of God: Not of works, lest any man should boast"** (Eph. 2:8-9). Our good works are compared to filthy rags in Isa. 64:6 - **"But we are all as an unclean *thing*, and all our righteousnesses *are* as filthy rags; and we all do fade as a leaf; and our iniquities, like the wind, have taken us away."**

In Rom. 4:8 the Scripture says, **"Blessed *is* the man to whom the Lord will not impute sin."** The verse just prior to that one states, **"…Blessed *are* they whose iniquities are forgiven, and whose sins are covered."** In theological terms, this is called imputation. That is, our sinfulness and unrighteousness is not imputed to us, but Christ. In turn, His righteousness is imputed to us. Or in plainer words, we "get credit" for His righteousness and He "gets credit" for our sinfulness. Toward the end of Rom. 4

Paul speaks of Abraham's belief in the word of God and says, **"And therefore it was imputed to him for righteousness. Now it was not written for his sake alone, that it was imputed to him; But for us also, to whom it shall be imputed, if we believe on him that raised up Jesus our Lord from the dead"** (4:22-24). Because he simply believed the word of God, the righteousness of God was imputed to him. He got credit for being righteous by believing. We can have the same thing. Christ's righteousness is imputed to us by believing in Him and His finished work on Calvary. By having imputed righteousness, we don't have to pay the price of sin (eternal death in the lake of fire). Remember, you can't earn this by works. It only comes from believing and receiving.

Now let's look at a picture of this in the Old Testament. In Gen. 27 we read the account of how Jacob stole his brother, Esau's blessing. As the elder brother, Esau was to get the family blessing. However, Jacob valued this commodity much higher than did his older sibling. Jacob's mother, Rebekah masterminded the plot when she heard her husband instruct Esau, **"Bring me venison, and make me savoury meat, that I may eat, and bless thee before the LORD before my death"** (vs. 7). While Esau is out hunting a deer, Rebekah quickly prepares some goat stew and puts goat skins on the backs of Jacob's hands and on the back of his neck. By doing this, he was able to make his father, Isaac think that it was Esau and not Jacob. This resulted in Jacob getting the blessing that was to go to the elder brother.

Just as the person of Esau was "imputed" to Jacob by wearing the skins of the goats, the righteousness of Jesus Christ is imputed to us by receiving Him as our Savior by *believing* Him. God the Father smells the scent of His Son and His righteousness on our raiment because we are "clothed" in Christ's righteousness. Again, this comes by receiving Him as Savior. **"But as many as received him, to them gave he power to become the sons of God, *even* to them that**

believe on his name" (John 1:12).

All this came as a result in the work that Christ did on the cross of Calvary. They nailed Him to the cross and after six hours of agony, He died. They placed His body in a tomb and three days later He arose from the dead. What did He do during that time? Where did He go? What was accomplished? Did He meet with anyone? These questions and others will be answered in the remaining pages of this paper.

In Mat. 12 certain of the scribes and Pharisees approached Jesus Christ and wanted a sign from Him. His reply was, **"An evil and adulterous generation seeketh after a sign; and there shall no sign be given to it, but the sign of the prophet Jonas: For as Jonas was three days and three nights in the whale's belly; so shall the Son of man be three days and three nights in the heart of the earth,"** (12:39-40).

In this passage, the Lord gives us the first of several revelations regarding His activities during the three-day and three-night period. He likens this time to what happened to Jonah. Therefore, if we study Jonah, we can understand better what happened to the Lord Jesus during this time. What *did* happen to Jonah? In Jonah 1 and 2 we find out. Jonah was cast into the sea. There are twenty places in the Scripture where something is cast into the sea (our search included the words, "cast" and "sea"). Eighteen of those twenty have to do with demise or death.

Jonah told the men aboard the ship, **"Take me up, and cast me forth into the sea; so shall the sea be calm unto you: for I know that for my sake this great tempest *is* upon you"** (1:12). In 1 Cor. 15 Paul contrasts the earthly with the heavenly and likens this to the "first Adam" and the "last Adam." The first Adam brought death and the last brought life. The first Adam could very well have made the statement above in Jonah 1:12. It was because of his sin that the rest of mankind (or those aboard the wind-tossed ship) owes the debt of sin. But once Jonah is cast into the sea, **"the sea ceased from her raging"** (1:15). Therefore, sinful men cast the last Adam into the "sea" and the sin debt was paid for all of mankind who are willing to receive this payment of debt.

Immediately after Jonah was cast into the sea a great fish swallowed him up (vs. 17). The Bible says, **"And Jonah was in the belly of the fish three days and three nights."** Christ likened Himself to Jonah, who was not only in the belly of the whale, but also under the surface of a huge body of water, referred to in Scripture as "the great deep," "the floods," "the sea," "the depths of the sea," "the channels of waters," "many waters," and "great waters." In Psm. 18 these waters are compared to the "sorrows of hell," "the snares of death," and "the floods of ungodly men." Jonah 2 likens these waters to "the belly of hell."

In the second chapter of Jonah we find a picture of Christ on the cross and the three days following.

Verse 3 – **"For thou hadst cast me into the deep, in the midst of the seas; and the floods compassed me about: all thy billows and thy waves passed over me."** The torments, agony, and suffering Christ went through on the cross were compared to a man taken down under the sea and being surrounded with great depths of water – drowning.

Verse 4 – **"Then I said, I am cast out of thy sight; yet I will look again toward thy holy temple."** When Christ was on the cross, the sins of mankind were imputed to Him. He "became sin" and as such, God the Father could no longer have fellowship with Him.

Verse 5 – **"The waters compassed me about, *even* to the soul: the depth closed me round about, the weeds were wrapped about my head."**

Jonah was completely surrounded by water, as were Pharaoh and his men in Ex. 15:5 – **"The depths have** covered them: they sank into the bottom as a stone." The Song Moses and the Children of Israel sung looks beyond the Red Sea to the Second Advent of Christ and the demise of the Great Dragon. The Leviathan (the great fire-breathing dragon) of Job 41 is located in this large body of water as indicated by verses 7, 31, and 32. The surface of this water is mentioned in the creation account in Genesis 1 as, **"the face of the deep"** (vs. 2). In Genesis 2 this water is divided by a great firmament (the universe). The location of this great body of water is mentioned in Psm. 148:4 – **"Praise him, ye heavens of heavens, and ye waters that be above the heavens."** This body of water was the source for the huge amount of water needed to submerge the earth in Noah's flood, as indicated in Gen. 7:11 – **"In the six hundredth year of Noah's life, in the second month, the seventeenth day of the month, the same day were all the fountains of the great deep broken up, and the windows of heaven were opened."** This large body of water separates the universe from the Third Heaven (the location of God's Throne) and is typified in Scripture by the miraculous crossing of the Red Sea, Jordan River, and Christ walking on the sea. It is also mentioned in Christian song lyrics such as the reference to "crossing Jordan" when a saint dies and goes home to Glory. **"The weeds were wrapped about my head"** – The latter part of verse 5 references the seaweed, also in the belly of the whale, and takes us again to Calvary with the crown of thorns wrapped about Christ's head.

Vs. 6 – **"I went down to the bottoms of the mountains; the earth with her bars *was* about me for ever: yet hast thou brought up my life from corruption, O LORD my God."** The whale took Jonah to the bottom of the sea, typifying Christ's trip to the heart of the earth (Mat. 12:40). The mention of "bars" has to do with the location of the Old Testament saints, which will be mentioned later. The mention of "corruption" indicates the death of Jonah. Corruption only comes after the spirit and soul leave the body. Jonah's cry, **"Yet hast thou brought up my life from corruption"** indicates God resurrected him from death. This, of course, voids all the liberal critics of the Scripture, who contend that the book of Jonah is a myth. The idea that no one could remain alive three days in the belly of a whale is the proof of this. The fact is, Jonah died and was brought back to life – just as Christ died and was brought back to life.

Vs. 7-9 – **"When my soul fainted within me I remembered the LORD: and my prayer came in unto thee, into thine holy temple. They that observe lying vanities forsake their own mercy. But I will sacrifice unto thee with the voice of thanksgiving; I will pay** *that* **that I have vowed. Salvation** *is* **of the LORD."** Jonah gets right with God and agrees to go to Nineveh to warn them of the impending judgment of God.

Vs. 10 – **"And the LORD spake unto the fish, and it vomited out Jonah upon the dry** *land*.**"** The three-day and three-night ordeal is complete and Jonah is brought up out of the water and back to dry land.

Jonah is not the only comparison to Christ's sufferings to being tormented under the surface of water. When we look the Messianic Psalms we find more evidence of this truth. Psm. 18:4-5 says, **"The sorrows of death compassed me, and the floods of ungodly men made me afraid. The sorrows of hell compassed me about: the snares of death prevented me."** These are the very torments Christ suffered. In verses 15-17 we read, **"Then the channels of waters were seen, and the foundations of the world were discovered at thy rebuke, O LORD, at the blast of the breath of thy nostrils. He sent from above, he took me, he drew me out of many waters. He delivered me from my strong enemy, and from them which hated me: for they were too strong for me."** It is interesting to note in this passage when the Savior is relieved of His suffering, it is compared to being drawn out of water.

Psm. 40:2 - **"He brought me up also out of an horrible pit, out of the miry clay, and set my feet upon a rock, *and* established my goings."**

Psm. 69, another Messianic Psalm, should be mentioned also in this study. Verses 1 and 2 state, **"Save me, O God; for the waters are come in unto *my* soul. I sink in deep mire, where *there is* no standing: I am come into deep waters, where the floods overflow me."** The context of this Psalm is the cross. Verse 15 says, **"Let not the waterflood overflow me, neither let the deep swallow me up, and let not the pit shut her mouth upon me."**

In Mat. 20 and Mark 10 James and John made a special request of the Savior: **"Grant unto us that we may sit, one on thy right hand, and the other on thy left hand, in thy glory"** (Mark 10:37). Christ's reply was, **"Ye know not what ye ask: can yet drink of the cup that I drink of" and be baptized with the baptism that I am baptized with?"** The cup and baptism Christ spoke of in this passage was His suffering. The "cup" was God's wrath upon sin and the "baptism," as we have shown with the Scripture, picture of Christ's suffering compared to being immersed in water. So not only does water baptism show the death, burial, and resurrection of Jesus Christ, but it also shows the horrible suffering He underwent on the cross.

There are three places in Scripture where we read of horrible suffering. Descriptions of suffering are certainly not limited to these three places, however, these locations in Scripture more indicative than others of a particular *kind* of suffering. These passages describe the suffering of: 1) the Jew in the Tribulation, 2) a man in hell, and 3) the suffering of Christ on the cross. Of the three places mentioned, certain the Psalms are the first. The other two are the books of Job and Lamentations. I will list a few of these passages from these books in order to illustrate the suffering of Christ on the cross.

"Though I speak, my grief is not asswaged: and *though* I forbear, what am I eased? But now he hath made me weary: thou hast made desolate all my company. And thou hast filled me with wrinkles, *which* is a witness *against me*: and my leanness rising up in me beareth witness to my face. He teareth *me* in his wrath, who hateth me: he gnasheth upon me with his teeth; mine enemy sharpeneth his eyes upon me. They have gaped upon me with their mouth; they have smitten me upon the cheek reproachfully; they have gathered themselves together against me. God hath delivered me to the ungodly, and turned me over into the hands of the wicked. I was at ease, but he hath broken me asunder: he hath also taken *me* by my neck, and shaken me to pieces, and set me up for his mark. His archers compass me round about, he cleaveth my reins asunder, and doth not spare; he poureth out my gall upon the ground. He breaketh me with breach upon breach, he runneth upon me like a giant. I have sewed sackcloth upon my skin, and defiled my horn in the dust. My face is foul with weeping, and on my eyelids is the shadow of death;" (Job 16:6-16).

"*Is it* nothing to you, all ye that pass by? behold, and see if there be any sorrow like unto my sorrow, which is done unto me, wherewith the LORD hath afflicted *me* in the day of his fierce anger. From above hath he sent fire into my bones, and it prevaileth against them: he hath spread a net for my feet, he hath turned me back: he hath made me desolate *and* faint all the day. The yoke of my transgressions is bound by his hand: they are wreathed, and come up upon my neck: he hath made my strength to fall, the Lord hath delivered me into *their* hands, *from whom* I am not able to rise up.The Lord hath trodden under foot all my mighty men in the midst of me: he hath called an assembly against me to crush my young men: the Lord hath trodden the virgin, the daughter of Judah, as in a winepress. For these *things* I weep; mine eye, mine eye runneth down with water, because the comforter that should relieve my soul is far from me: my children are desolate, because the enemy prevailed. Zion spreadeth forth her hands, *and there is* none to comfort her: the LORD hath commanded concerning Jacob, *that* his adversaries *should be* round about him: Jerusalem is as a menstruous woman among them (Lam. 1:12-17).

"I am the man *that* hath seen affliction by the rod of his wrath. He hath led me, and brought *me into* darkness, but not *into* light. Surely against me is he turned; he turneth his hand *against* me all the day. My flesh and my skin hath he made old; he hath broken my bones. He hath builded against me, and compassed *me* with gall and travail. He hath set me in dark places, as *they that be* dead of old. He hath hedged me about, that I cannot get out: he hath made my chain heavy. Also when I cry and shout, he shutteth out my prayer. He hath inclosed my ways with hewn stone, he hath made my paths crooked. He *was* unto me *as* a bear lying in wait, *and as* a lion in secret places. He hath turned aside my ways, and pulled me in pieces: he hath made me desolate. He hath bent his bow, and set me as a mark for the arrow. He hath caused the arrows of his quiver to enter into my reins. I was a derision to all my people; *and* their song all the day. He hath filled me with bitterness, he hath made me drunken with wormwood. He hath also broken my teeth with gravel stones, he hath covered me with ashes. And thou hast removed my soul far off from peace: I forgat prosperity. And I said, My strength and my hope is perished from the LORD: Remembering mine affliction and my misery, the wormwood and the gall" (Lam. 3:1-19).

These are just few of the passages from these three books that show the despair, gloom, darkness, dreariness, and suffering of the three different contexts given.

The Heart of the Earth

When people died in the Old Testament, they went to the heart of the earth. There was a place for the saints as well as a place for the damned. This place is spoken of as prison. Psm. 142:7 – **"Bring my soul out of prison, that I may praise thy name: the righteous shall compass me about; for thou shalt deal bountifully with me."** The book of Job speaks of this place in Job 3:17-18 – **"There the wicked cease *from* troubling; and there the weary be at rest. There the prisoners rest together; they hear not the voice of the oppressor."** Notice the division between the "wicked" and the "weary." Two different compartments are revealed in Luke 16:22, 23 – **"And it came to pass, that the beggar died, and was carried by the angels into Abraham's bosom: the rich man also died, and was buried; and in hell he lift up his eyes, being in torments, and seeth Abraham afar off, and Lazarus in his bosom."** We learn from this passage that there is a stark difference between the two compartments. Lazarus is in a place called "Abraham's Bosom," also called "Paradise" by Christ and the penitent thief just before their deaths. There is a great gulf fixed between the two and no one can cross from one to the other (Luke 16:26).

Have you ever noticed how many prisons there are mentioned in Scripture? Joseph was sold by his brethren for 20 pieces of silver and ended up in an Egyptian prison on false charges. It is interesting to note that during Joseph's prison sentence there were two fellow inmates, one of whom was released from prison and the other was not. Also Joseph's brother Simeon had to spend some time in prison awaiting the return of his brothers for more corn. Samson was put in the prison house after his eyes were put out. Micaiah had to go to prison after prophesying bad news to King Ahab. Jeremiah spent time in prison. John the Baptist was sent to prison by Herod. Jesus Christ Himself was a prisoner the night before his crucifixion. When Pilate unsuccessfully tried to get the crowd to release Jesus and crucify Barabbas, Christ was referred to as a "prisoner" in this passage (Mat. 27). Note also that, just as in the case of Joseph, one was released from prison and one was not. Simon Peter spent some time in prison. Saul of Tarsus sent many innocent disciples of Christ to prison. After his conversion to Christ, Paul spent time there also. Many others in Scripture spent time in prison.

Obviously the "hell" compartment of the heart of the earth is a prison where the inmates never get out. The "Paradise" or "Abraham's Bosom" section was also a prison. These inmates eventually were released. Again, some released some not released.

The Scripture says in Isa. 14:16-17 – "...*Is* this the man that made the earth to tremble, that did shake kingdoms; *That* made the world as a wilderness, and destroyed the cities thereof; *that* opened not the house of his prisoners?" The context of Isa. 14 is Lucifer. Thus, the Devil is the keeper of this prison in the heart of the earth. The Lord Jesus Christ is the one who sets the prisoners free. Isa. 42:5-7 – "Thus saith God the LORD, he that created the heavens, and stretched them out; he that spread forth the earth, and that which cometh out of it; he that giveth breath unto the people upon it, and spirit to them that walk therein: I the LORD have called thee in righteousness, and will hold thine hand, and will keep thee, and give thee for a covenant of the people, for a light of the Gentiles; To open the blind eyes, to bring out the prisoners from the prison, and them that sit in darkness out of the prison house."

Isa. 61:1 – "**The Spirit of the Lord GOD *is* upon me; because the LORD hath anointed me to preach good tidings unto the meek; he hath sent me to bind up the brokenhearted, to proclaim liberty to the captives, and the opening of the prison to *them that* are bound;**" Here again, we see that there are captives and prisoners who are eventually set free by the Lord. This was the passage that Christ quoted in the synagogue in Luke 4. He spoke of Himself.

We learn in Luke 23:43-44 that the penitent thief was the final sinner that entered into Paradise. "**And he said unto Jesus, Lord, remember me when thou comest into thy kingdom. And Jesus said unto him, Verily I say unto thee, To day shalt thou be with me in paradise.**" The Gospel according to Luke continues, "**And the sun was darkened, and the veil of the temple was rent in the midst. And when Jesus had cried with a loud voice, he said, Father, into thy hands I commend my spirit: and having said thus, he gave up the ghost**" (Luke 23:45-46).

This is the point that Christ's perfect and sinless body died of the wounds received at the hands of the Roman soldiers. (The Lord laid His life down of His own will according to John. 10:17, 18.) The Lord commended His spirit into the hands of His Father and went to the heart of the earth. With Him, He took the sins and wickedness of the men of all the ages. The sin of mankind was "imputed" to Him. Christ said in John 3:14, "**And as Moses lifted up the serpent in the wilderness, even so must the Son of man be lifted up:**" This was a direct reference to Num. 21:8-9 when Moses fashioned a brazen serpent and put it on a pole. "**And the LORD said unto Moses, Make thee a fiery serpent, and set it upon a pole: and it shall come to pass, that every one that is bitten, when he looketh upon it, shall live. And Moses made a serpent of brass, and put it** upon a pole, and it came to pass, that if a serpent had bitten any man, when he beheld the serpent of brass, he lived." The serpent is a symbol for the Devil (Gen. 3:1, Rev. 20:2). Christ likened Himself to the epitome of all sin and evil. He did not *become* the serpent, He *likened* Himself to it. No one could fail to see the reference to Calvary in the Messianic Psm. 22 where we read, **"But I *am* a worm, and no man; a reproach of men, and despised of the people."**

Jesus Christ took the sins of all the world and went to hell to complete His once-and-for-all payment of sin. Remember, the wages of sin is death and the death comes in two parts. The first part is physical death – Christ died on the cross. The second part is suffering the eternal torments of hell. Both the first and second of these horrible aspects of penalty were accomplished on the cross. We showed how the Lord suffered unspeakable torments while on the cross. Now it was time for the Lord to take those sins and deposit them in the fires of hell.

Wearing Someone Else's Clothes

Throughout the Scriptures we find certain scenarios that repeat themselves in various places. They never fail to have significance. Sometimes the significance is difficult to understand and must be assumed by faith. 2 Timothy 3:16 says, **"All scripture *is* given by inspiration of God, and *is* profitable for doctrine, for reproof, for correction, for instruction in righteousness:"**

One of those reoccurring scenarios is the idea of someone wearing someone else's clothing for a certain purpose. Let me give a few examples to illustrate:

1. Earlier we noted Jacob's endeavor to steal his older brother's blessing by clothing himself in the skins of an animal. The purpose here was to deceive his elderly father

(Isaac) into thinking that it was actually his brother Esau that was serving up the savory stew.

2. In 1 Kings 14 Jereboam's wife disguised herself in the clothing of a common woman (rather than a King's wife) in order to ask counsel of Ahijah, the prophet in Shiloh regarding her sick son.

3. In 1 Kings 22:29-40 and 2 Chron. 18:29 Micaiah the prophet told Ahab he would fall in battle the following day. In effort to prevent this from happening, Ahab wore Jehoshephat's robes into battle, thinking he would escape the fate of doom.

4. In 1 Sam. 17 David refused to wear King Saul's armor into battle. Saul evidently had the notion that the armor would aid David in his effort against the giant. David refused the offer of someone else's attire.

5. In Rev. 19 at the Second Advent of Jesus Christ, the saints will be dressed in fine linen, clean and white, which represents imputed righteousness.

There are some additional items of interest with regard to garments that need to be mentioned before we make our point.

1. In Gen. 37 Joseph wore the coat of many colors that Jacob had made for him. This coat was stripped off and left in the presence of his wicked brethren.

2. In Gen. 39 Joseph's coat was stripped off of him by Potiphar's wife as he ran from the presence of wickedness.

3. At Calvary Christ's garments were stripped off of Him and were parted among those who crucified Him.

4. In Lev. 13 we find the Levitical protocol for Leprosy. If the garment contained in its warp and woof the red or green color of leprosy it was to be burned (vs. 52). Leprosy is a picture of sin.

5. In Psm. 73:6 pride and violence are spoken of as a garment that is worn. **"Therefore pride compasseth them about as a chain; violence covereth them *as* a garment."**

6. In Dan. 3:20-27 Shadrach, Meshach, and Abednego were bound and cast into the burning fiery furnace. One might say they were "clothed" with rope bindings. When they came out of the fire the ropes were burned off, but the flame had not touched the skin or the hair on their bodies.

When Jesus Christ went to the cross, our sins were imputed to Him. He died in our place. His garments were removed and He "put on" the coat or garment of our sin. He wore the garments of someone else (as in the illustrations given above) for a specific purpose. He "wore" those garments into the fires of hell. Those garments were burned off of Him just as the ropes were burned off Shadrach, Meshach, and Abednego. Those garments of sin were to be burned just like the disease-filled garments of the leper in Lev. 13. Those filthy garments were stripped off of Christ and left in the presence of the wicked, burning in hell for eternity. Those "garments of sin" are spoken of in Jude 23 – **"And others save with fear, pulling *them* out of the fire; hating even the garment spotted by the flesh."**

The Keys of Hell and Death

Christ gained entrance into the different compartments in the heart of the earth with keys. Rev. 1:18 – **"I *am* he that liveth, and was dead; and, behold, I am alive for evermore, Amen; and have the keys of hell and of death."** These compartments, mentioned earlier, are both spoken of as a prison, also mentioned earlier. These compartments have gates. Mat. 16:18 – **"And I say also unto thee, That thou art Peter, and upon this rock I will build my church; and the gates of hell shall not prevail against it."** (notice plural "gates") Using His keys, Christ opened the first gate and dumped off his raiment of sin in the fires of hell. Then He went to Abraham's Bosom (Paradise) and unlocked this gate. 1 Pet. 3:18,19 – **"For Christ also hath once suffered for sins, the just for the unjust, that he might bring us to God, being put to death in the flesh, but quickened by the Spirit: By which also he went and preached unto the spirits in prison;"**

At this point let us briefly discuss exactly who these "spirits in prison" are. There are three schools of thought here:

1. These spirits in prison are the angels that kept not their first estate. We find them noted in Jude 6 – **"And the angels which kept not their first estate, but left their own habitation, he hath reserved in everlasting chains under darkness unto the judgment of the great day."** These angels were those (sons of God) who cohabited with the daughters of men in Gen. 6 and produced a race of giants. This is a rather controversial issue among many and has to do with the definition of the "sons of God." This is a phrase used only for angels in the Old Testament. In Psm. 82:6-7 we find a passage that supports this view. **"I have said, Ye are gods; and all of you are children of the most High. But ye shall die like men, and fall like one of the princes."** The subjects of this passage are spoken of as "gods" and "children of the most High," but are said to "die like men." If they "die like men" then they must not *be* men, but angels. Additionally, verse 20, the verse following those given above (1 Pet. 3:18, 19), supports this view.

2. The second school of thought is that these spirits are "familiar" or "unclean" spirits. The vast majority of uses of the word "spirits" in Scripture is found with this context.

3. The third school of thought is the "spirits in prison" are those held captive in Paradise, or the Old Testament saints. In spite of the majority of uses of "spirits" in Scripture, there are passages using the word for men. For

example:

Heb. 12:23 – "To the general assembly and church of the firstborn, which are written in heaven, and to God the Judge of all, and to the spirits of just men made perfect,"

If we were to take position three, what message would Christ have to preach for those in the other two categories? If these spirits are the Old Testament saints, then we have a definite message that Christ could have preached. When Christ walked toward Emmaus with Cleopas and the other disciple, the Bible says, **"And beginning at Moses and all the prophets, he expounded unto them in all the scriptures the things concerning himself"** (Luke 24:27). If there ever was a message Jesus Christ could preach to the Old Testament saints held in Abraham's Bosom, this would be the one! In this case Christ would have gone back much farther than Moses. Let's look at some of the possibilities of Christ preaching this message to those present in Paradise immediately after Calvary.

1. Since Adam and Eve would have been present, perhaps Christ explained to them about the lamb that was slain to provide skins for them in the garden.

2. Abel would have been there. Christ may have explained to him why his sacrifice was accepted and his brother's not.

3. Abraham and Isaac were there. The Lord Jesus probably told them all about the significance of the Father offering his only begotten son for a sacrifice.

4. Jacob and Joseph would have been there to hear Christ preach. Perhaps He explained to them how Joseph was used of God as a type of Christ in feeding the children of Israel during a time of famine.

5. Moses and Aaron were there. Maybe Christ

explained to them the significance of the High Priest and the veil that screened the ark.

6. Joshua was present and maybe the Lord told him about how one day He would come back and see to it that Israel received all of the land promised to them in a great national restoration and revival.

7. David was there. He probably told him how he was used as a type of Christ in killing Goliath. Surely the Lord explained that David was a type of Israel fleeing into the wilderness and living in caves with the Antichrist in pursuit.

8. Jonah would have been there. Surely Christ would have explained to him his suffering was only a type of the suffering Christ would endure.

9. There are countless others who would have been present that day when the Prophet that Moses said would come finally arrived. They all no doubt recognized Him as the long-awaited Messiah. Their Savior had finally come!

Then what happened?

Eph. 4:8-10 – **"Wherefore he saith, When he ascended up on high, he led captivity captive, and gave gifts unto men. (Now that he ascended, what is it but that he also descended first into the lower parts of the earth? He that descended is the same also that ascended up far above all heavens, that he might fill all things.)"**

Psm. 68:18 – **"Thou hast ascended on high, thou hast led captivity captive: thou hast received gifts for men; yea,** *for* **the rebellious also, that the LORD God might dwell** *among them.***"**

The phrase used in these passages, "led captivity captive," is the act of freeing those who are held prisoner with the idea that they are now "voluntary captives" of the one who set them free. Again, here is a scenario that is repeated in Scripture. In Gen. 14 Lot and his group are taken captive. Abraham and his men come to rescue them. In Numbers 21 Israelites are taken captive by King Arad. Their brethren come after them and set them free. In 1 Sam. 30 David's camp is spoiled and taken captive by Amalekites. David and his men go after them and release them and bring them home with all the spoil. These are all pictures of what is to take place in the future (Eccl. 1). The final episode of this scenario will be the release of the Nation of Israel from the bonds of Satan. This will take place at the end of the Tribulation and the result will be Jewish National Revival and recognition of Jesus Christ as their Messiah. Moses leading the children of Israel out of Egypt depicts this very event.

Isa. 14:17 – **"*That* made the world as a wilderness, and destroyed the cities thereof; *that* opened not the house of his prisoners?"** The subject of this passage is Lucifer. He did not want his prisoners to be released. Mark 3:27 – **"No man can enter into a strong man's house, and spoil his goods, except he will first bind the strong man; and then he will spoil his house."** Jesus Christ bound the strong man (Satan) and spoiled his "house." He took the Devil's captives and they became Christ's "captives."

Christ's payment of sin with His own blood (God's blood) made it possible for the sins of the Old Testament saints to be erased. Heb. 10:4 – **"For *it is* not possible that the blood of bulls and of goats should take away sins."** Their sins were temporarily put away, but not once and for all. The Old Testament sacrifices were only temporary measures until the promised Messiah showed up and made the required payment. Now that this payment was made, these inhabitants of Abraham's Bosom could put on a clean, white, linen coat, representing the righteousness of Jesus Christ. That also meant they could accompany Him to Glory. John 17:24 – **"Father, I will that they also, whom thou hast given me, be with me where I am; that they may behold my glory, which thou hast given me: for thou**

lovedst me before the foundation of the world." With their new coats of imputed righteousness, the Old Testament saints were led out of the prison in the heart of the earth and taken up to the sides of the north in the third heaven. Later, Paul would write, **"How that he was caught up into paradise, and heard unspeakable words, which it is not lawful for a man to utter"** (2 Cor. 12:4). This passage shows how Paradise was moved from the heart of the earth to a direction that is "up" or Glory.

With the consummation of the New Testament (Heb. 9:16), the death of a saint means his or her soul and spirit will go immediately to wherever the Lord is. Paul wrote, **"We are confident, *I say*, and willing rather to be absent from the body, and to be present with the Lord"** (2 Cor. 5:8). Abraham's Bosom is an empty compartment in the heart of the earth. The body goes to the grave and corrupts awaiting the resurrection. Some day in the future there will be a shout, the sound of a trumpet, and we'll go up.

"For the Lord himself shall descend from heaven with a shout, with the voice of the archangel, and with the trump of God: and the dead in Christ shall rise first: Then we which are alive *and* remain shall be caught up together with them in the clouds, to meet the Lord in the air: and so shall we ever be with the Lord. Wherefore comfort one another with these words" (1 Thes. 4:16-18).

CHAPTER ELEVEN

THE WAY OF CAIN

APPROXIMATELY FOUR THOUSAND years before the crucifixion of Jesus Christ, God instructed Adam and his family in the proper manner in which to deal with the sin problem. The evidence of this is found in Gen. 4:4. Abel was obedient to the Lord's command to offer the blood of a lamb while Cain sought his own means of atonement. In the subsequent verses, we learn that God only accepted one of the two offerings. When we read the Scripture, we learn that all the thousands of innocent animals sacrificed to the Lord in the Tabernacle and the Temple were types of Jesus Christ. One day He would come to make the one final sacrifice on Golgotha.

Ever since Cain, man has sought ways to circumvent God's clear instructions regarding atonement. Since Jesus Christ paid the sin debt for all mankind on Calvary, man has tried everything imaginable to do it for himself. The men of Babel thought that by building a tower, they could get to heaven (Gen. 11). Some thought that worshipping a gold calf would bring salvation (Ex. 32), while others burned incense to Moses' brass serpent (2 Kings 18:4). This list goes on, but there is a common denominator of all these "religions." That is, they all reject God's clear instructions regarding the SIN OFFERING. They either ignore it or make an attempt to deal with it in their own way *just like Cain.*

In our modern times man has not changed. The Way of Cain (Jude 11) is still the most popular form of religion. It comes in many sizes, shapes, colors, and varieties. To avoid receiving Christ as Savior and accepting His blood atonement, some will adopt the religion of Humanism – that is, they lead a politically correct life, give to charities, and do good deeds, etc. Some will say the rosary and take the "Holy Eucharist" on a weekly basis. Some will observe a Sabbath, which was given only to Israel as a sign (Ex. 31:16-17). Some will join a church; some will get baptized; some will ride bicycles, wearing white shirts with neckties, and pass out literature. Some will live "a good life" and try to make the world a better place in which to live. Some will pray to Buddha. Some will pray to Allah. Some will eat only fruit and vegetables and abstain from meats. And some will bow down and worship a statue of the Queen of Heaven (Jer. 44).

Again, the Way of Cain is, any form of religion **OTHER** than trusting the finished work of Jesus Christ as atonement for sin. Satan's desire is to take as many souls to hell with him as possible. The only way anyone can go to hell is by **NOT RECEIVING CHRIST AS SAVIOR**. Any form of religion that does not promote a personal relationship with Jesus Christ as Savior has its origin in Satan (1 John 3:12).

A few years ago my pastor (at that time) approached me with some pamphlets that had been given to a church member. The member was not certain as to the doctrinal content and gave the material to the pastor. Since he had never heard of this religious sect, he asked me to read the material and summarize the content in a brief paper. This paper is the net result of that encounter. I have chosen to remove the name of this particular group from this writing since this is not an attack on that particular sect, but rather a Biblical explanation of the Way of Cain.

This particular group's core beliefs align with those of Cain's. That is, "We will preach and teach some doctrine **OTHER** than salvation by grace through the shed blood of Jesus Christ." In their literature, they make a number of false claims. They claim the only name for God is "Yahovah" [sic]. The truth is this word is not found in the Bible. Contrary to their claim, there are many names for the Lord in the Bible. The name, JEHOVAH (all capital letters) is found four times in Scripture. The phrase, "the LORD" (all capital letters) refers to the name "JEHOVAH" in Scripture. In the English language, the "J" is pronounced as a "Jay." In other languages (including Hebrew, Spanish, German, et al), it is pronounced with a "ya" sound. Additionally, there IS one name that stands out among all the rest. Acts 4:10-12 **"Be it known unto you all, and to all the people of Israel, that by the name of Jesus Christ of Nazareth, whom ye crucified, whom God raised from the dead... which is become the head of the corner. Neither is there salvation in any other: for there is none other name under heaven given among men, whereby we must be saved."** Therefore, when it comes to the salvation of your soul, the only name you need to be concerned with is JESUS.

This group claims salvation comes only by keeping the Law of Moses. The truth is no one has ever kept the Law of Moses except Jesus Christ (and even He made a habit of breaking the Sabbath). Even if someone *could* keep the Old Testament Law, it could not keep you from going to hell. Paul said in Titus 3:5, **"Not by works of righteousness which we have done, but according to his mercy he saved us, by the washing of regeneration, and renewing of the Holy Ghost;"** According to the Apostle Paul, we can't be saved by keeping the Old Testament Law. Gal. 2:16 - **"Knowing that a man is not justified by the works of the law, but by the faith of Jesus Christ, even we have believed in Jesus Christ, that we might be justified by the faith of Christ, and not by the works of the law: for by the works of the law shall no flesh be justified."**

The sinner must realize that he is a sinner. **"For all have sinned, and come short of the glory of God"** (Rom. 3:23). **"The wages of sin is death"** (eternal lake of fire – Rev. 20:14). God loved you in spite of your sin and gave His only Son to die and go to hell (Mat. 12:40) in your place. **"For God so loved the world, that he gave his only begotten Son, that whosoever believeth in him should not perish, but have everlasting life."** (John 3:16). By receiving Christ, you can be saved and have life eternal. **"But as many as received him, to them gave he power to become the sons of God,** *even* **to them that believe on his name:"** (John 1:12). Salvation in Christ is the only way anyone can escape the torments of eternal damnation. 1 Tim 2:5, **"For** *there is* **one God, and one mediator between God and men, the man Christ Jesus;"** John 14:6, **"Jesus saith unto him, I am the way, the truth, and the life: no man cometh unto the Father, but by me."**

The group claimed (in a tract entitled "The Christian Conspiracy") Christianity removed the name "Yahovah" from the Scriptures. As we mentioned above, the name, JEHOVAH is mentioned four times in Scripture and the phrase, "the LORD" (JEHOVAH) is mentioned over 6900 times. They claim (in the same tract) that Christianity has attempted to change the weekly Sabbath from Saturday to Sunday.

The Sabbath was a sign given only to the Nation of Israel. **"Wherefore the children of Israel shall keep the sabbath, to observe the sabbath throughout their generations,** *for* **a perpetual covenant. It** *is* **a sign between me and the** children of Israel for ever: for *in* six days the LORD made heaven and earth, and on the seventh day he rested, and was refreshed." (Ex. 31:16-17). Christians observe Sunday, the first day of the week, as a time to meet to worship. The basis for this is found in Acts 20:7, **"And upon the first *day* of the week, when the disciples came together to break bread, Paul preached unto them, ready to depart on the morrow;"** Also, the first day of the week was the time set apart for the giving of tithes and offerings, **"Upon the first *day* of the week let every one of you lay by him in store, as *God* hath prospered him, that there be no gatherings when I come"** (1 Cor. 16:2). The Sabbath is not for a New Testament Christian. Paul said, **"Let no man therefore judge you in meat, or in drink, or in respect of an holyday, or of the new moon, or of the sabbath *days*"** (Col. 2:16).

Additional false claims were made by this group, which we chose to ignore. The real issues here are not the false claims of any particular religious sect but a clear rejection of Scripture. Let's take a close look at Genesis 4 where Cain made his error. In verse 3 we read, **"And the LORD had respect unto Abel and to his offering"** (a lamb). In verse 5 we read, **"But unto Cain and to his offering he had not respect..."** From the context of this passage, both brothers were fully aware of God's instructions for the proper sin offering. This is evident in verse 7, where God said, **"If thou doest well, shalt thou not be accepted?"** In plainer words, The LORD was pleading with Cain (Jer. 2:9) to obey the clear instructions He had given earlier (Gen. 3:21). But, as in the case of all the varieties of the "Way of Cain," the common thread is a simple rejection of the word of God. *Rejecting God's word is the ultimate rationale for Cain and his followers.*

Cain obeyed the Scripture *in part* – that is, he *did* bring an offering to the LORD (vs. 3). Some individual sects of the

"Way of Cain" are indeed making some effort to obey the Scripture. They have taken certain parts of the word of God and embraced them. However, they rejected (as did Cain) the part about the blood sacrifice made by Jesus Christ at Calvary.

There are three essential warnings in Scripture regarding this very sin. They are clear warnings about adding to and taking away from Scripture: First: Deut. 4:2 – **"Ye shall not add unto the word which I command you, neither shall ye diminish *ought* from it, that ye may keep the commandments of the LORD your God which I command you."** Second: Prov. 30:6 – **"Add thou not unto his words, lest he reprove thee, and thou be found a liar."** Third: Rev. 22:19 – **"And if any man shall take away from the words of the book of this prophecy, God shall take away his part out of the book of life, and out of the holy city, and *from* the things which are written in this book."**

From these three passages, it is clear that we are to take all of the word of God and not reject the parts that we don't like. Obviously, this group does not care much for the New Testament. They have eliminated it from their Bible. Jehudi had the same problem in Jeremiah 36.

Conclusion

There is available to all, including the individual religious sects of the world, the same plea from the LORD that Cain received. Take advantage of the free gift that God has made available to every sinner. **"...Come. And let him that is athirst come. And whosoever will, let him take the water of life freely"** (Rev. 22:17). Jesus Christ said in Mat. 11:28, **"Come unto me, all ye that labour and are heavy laden, and I will give you rest."** The plan for salvation was given earlier in this paper. Read it again, pray and ask Christ to save you from your sin and grant you eternal life. He is waiting for you

CHAPTER TWELVE

THE COURSE OF ABIA

Introduction

AT THE END OF THE GOSPEL ACCORDING
to John, the Apostle says something of great significance. The
final verse of the book states, **"And there are also many
other things which Jesus did, the which, if they should
be written every one, I suppose that even the world itself
could not contain the books that should be written.
Amen"** (John 21:25). The idea here is that although John's
Gospel was relatively small compared to all that Jesus Christ
said and did; what *was* said was sufficient to accomplish what
the Holy Spirit had in mind not only for the Gospel of John,
but for the entire sixty-six books of the canon of Scripture.
Moreover, *this passage indicates that there is absolutely nothing
contained in the word of God that is without significance.* Christ said
in Mat. 5:18, **"For verily I say unto you, Till heaven and**

earth pass, one jot or one tittle shall in no wise pass from the law, till all be fulfilled." This verse supports this idea. Not even a Hebrew punctuation mark will fail to come to pass. Even the punctuation marks in the word of God have significance.

It is with this in mind that we approach the subject of the Course of Abia. For many this is an unknown subject. It is this writer's intent to show why this is worthy of our study. There is nothing mentioned in Scripture (see paragraph above) that is not worthy of time spent in study. Otherwise it would not be in Scripture. Luke mentions our subject in the first chapter of his Gospel. It came as a clue, given by the Holy Spirit as to the time of the birth of Jesus Christ.

The Anointed One

All four Gospels of the New Testament tell the story of first coming of the long-awaited Jewish Messiah. This personage is found throughout the Old Testament both typologically and prophetically. There are passages that hint of a miraculous birth of a very special person sent from God.

Gen. 3:15 – "...her seed..."

Gen. 49:10 – "Until Shiloh come;"

Deut. 18:18 – "I will raise them up a Prophet from among their brethren, like unto thee, and will put my words in his mouth; and he shall speak unto them all that I shall command him."

Psm. 2:2 – "His anointed"

Psm. 16:10 – "For thou wilt not leave my soul in hell; neither wilt thou suffer thine Holy One to see corruption."

Psm. 22:1-18 – "My God My God, why hast thou forsaken me..."

Psm. 45:11 – "So shall the king greatly desire thy beauty: for he *is* thy Lord; and worship thou him."

Mic. 5:2 – "But thou, Bethlehem Ephratah, *though* thou be little among the thousands of Judah, *yet* out of thee shall he come forth unto me *that is* to be ruler in Israel; whose goings forth have *been from* of old, from everlasting."

Isa. 7:14 – "Therefore the Lord himself shall give you a sign; Behold, a virgin shall conceive, and bear a son, and shall call his name Immanuel."

Luke 7:20 – "When the men were come unto him, they said, John Baptist hath sent us unto thee, saying, Art thou he that should come? or look we for another?"

There are many additional like-passages we could quote regarding the coming Messiah. The wise men of Mat. 2 knew very well of the coming Messiah and were familiar with all of the Old Testament passages that spoke of Him.

"There was in the days of Herod, the king of Judaea, a certain priest named Zacharias, of the course of Abia: and his wife *was* of the daughters of Aaron, and her name *was* Elisabeth" (Luke 1:5). The context of the first two chapters of Luke is the birth of Jesus Christ and a glimpse of His early life. The phrase, "of the course of Abia" is a clue inserted into the text by the Holy Spirit for the benefit of the reader who desires additional information about "when" the Savior's birth took place. Upon further investigation, we learn that many years prior to our text King David organized his work force into "courses" to maximize efficiency. David was a man after God's own heart (1 Sam. 13:14) and the LORD is a God of order.

In 1 Chron. 24 David organized several groups of workers into courses. In other words, he organized them in rotations where they worked for a period of time and then were off for a period of time. When it came to the Levites, the period of time worked was seven days. Among those who were organized were: Aaron's sons the priests (1 Chron. 24:1-29), the other sons of Levi, including the Kohathites (1 Chron. 24:20-25) and the Merarites (1 Chron. 24:26-31), the singers and musicians (1 Chron. 25:1-7), the Gate Keepers (1 Chron. 26:13-19), the Levite Treasurers (1 Chron. 26:20-28), the Officers and Judges (1 Chron. 26:29-32), the Military Officers (1 Chron. 27:1-15), and the Princes of the twelve tribes (1 Chron. 27:16-22).

David taught his son Solomon this same order. When King Solomon later organized his men to procure materials for the Temple, 30,000 men worked in three courses. Ten thousand men worked for a month and then they went home for two months (1 Kings 5:13-14).

In 1 Chron. 24:1-29 we find the order of the priests. In the text we read about the order of the twenty-four priests was determined by lot (vs. 5, 7). The first lot "came forth to Jehoiarib…" and so forth. The eighth lot (vs. 10) was Abijah. This is the English translation from Hebrew and Abia (Luke) is the English translation from Greek. This continues to verse 19, giving all twenty-four names of the priests and their order. This order is referred to as the priest's "course."

In Lev. 8:35 we learn that the priest was to serve in the Tabernacle for a period of seven days. **"Therefore shall ye abide *at* the door of the tabernacle of the congregation day and night seven days, and keep the charge of the LORD, that ye die not: for so I am commanded."** They were not allowed to leave the court of the Tabernacle for seven days. Later, when Solomon built the Temple on Mt. Moriah, he incorporated chambers within the Temple as quarters for the priests. In the early days of the Tabernacle they were required to stay in tents in the court.

There are fifty-two weeks in the year and twenty-four courses of priests. Obviously the priests rotated twice per year in their courses for a total of forty-eight weeks. What about the other four weeks in the year?

The Israelites were instructed in Ex. 23:14, **"Three times thou shalt keep a feast unto me in the year."** Verse 17 says, **"Three times in the year all thy males shall appear before the Lord GOD"** (Deut. 16:16, 1 Kings 9:25, and 2 Chron. 16:16-17). When all these males came to the Tabernacle (later the Temple) they were not to come empty-handed.

"Three times in a year shall all thy males appear before the LORD thy God in the place which he shall choose; in the feast of unleavened bread, and in the feast of weeks, and in the feast of tabernacles: and they shall not appear before the LORD empty: Every man shall give as he is able, according to the blessing of the LORD thy God which he hath given thee" (Deut. 16:16-17). The three times they were to show up were the Feasts of the Lord. They were to bring offerings when they came.

The first of the three times was the Feast of the Passover, followed by Unleavened Bread, and First Fruits. This first group of feasts took place within a two-week period. Fifty days (from First Fruits) later the third occasion for the trip to appear before the LORD was Pentecost. The third trip came in the seventh month and included the Feasts of Trumpets, Day of Atonement, and Tabernacles. Again these last three feasts all took place within a period of a few weeks.

In our study of the five offerings of Lev. 1-5 we found that there were five different offerings. First was the Burnt Offering (Lev. 1), then the Meat Offering (Lev. 2), then the Peace Offering (Lev. 3), then the Sin Offering (Lev. 4), and finally the Trespass Offering (Lev. 5). The first three were voluntary and the last two were mandatory. In these five offerings, the Israelite was required to bring something to the Priest to offer before the Lord on his behalf. This included bullocks, goats, rams, lambs, pigeons, doves, calves, wheat, corn barley, grapes, and other crops (all sustenance for the priests). There were thousands of Hebrews that came three times per year to bring their offerings to the Lord. In addition, at the time of Passover the Israelite was not to kill his lamb at his home. This was only done the first time in Ex. 12. From then on they were to bring the lamb to the priest as indicated in Deut. 16:5-6.

In light of this information we can see how a single priest working his one-week course at the time of one of these seven feasts would be overworked. It would be impossible for him to kill and offer all of those animal sacrifices by himself. Therefore, all the priests would need to be on duty during these days of non-stop priestly duties. During the first set of three feasts (Passover, Unleavened Bread, and First Fruits) all the priests would be on duty in the Tabernacle or Temple for two weeks (The Feast of Unleavened Bread is a week-long). Then on the Feast of Pentecost they would all have to work. Again in the seventh month all would work on the first day of the month – the Feast of Trumpets. Then on the tenth day of the month they would all show up to work. The Feast of Tabernacles on the fifteenth day would last a full week (Lev. 23). These feasts would overlap the duty roster for the courses and all would need to work for another period of two weeks during this month.

The priests would all work (at the same time) two weeks during the first month and two weeks during the seventh month. Pentecost, Trumpets, and Day of Atonement would again require all the priests to work on those feast days. These four "feast weeks" plus the forty-eight weeks of courses made up the entire 52-week year for the priests. The first priest of the courses would naturally begin at the beginning of the Jewish year (our April) and there would normally be some overlap since the first day of the month rotates each year (sometimes on Monday, Tuesday, etc.).

Take a standard Gregorian calendar and chart the twenty-four courses or weeks of the priests beginning at April – The first week of April would be Jehoiarib, the second would be Jedaiah, and so forth through Maaziah, the twenty-fourth (1 Chron. 24:7-18). Then start again with Jehoiarib (first) and continue through to the 24th course. April, or Nissan or Abib is the first month of the Jewish year (Ex. 12). Then place the four weeks of "all priests on duty" into their proper places according the dates of the feasts given in Lev. 23. The days of the week constantly shift from one year to the next. For example, some years there might be two weeks of courses before the first "all priests" week in the first month. The next year there may be three weeks between the two. Additionally, the Jewish month begins about a week to ten days before ours. This can be confusing if you allow it. The conclusion of this paper will be the same if you choose to sync up with the Jewish calendar or stay with the Gregorian (modern) calendar.

In Luke 1 we read, **"There was in the days of Herod, the king of Judaea, a certain priest named Zacharias, of the course of Abia:"** Zacharias was on his regular course of duty in the Temple in Jerusalem. According to our chart this would have been about the tenth week of the year, or around the first week of June. During his time inside the Temple that day Gabriel, the angel of the Lord appeared, standing next to the Golden Altar (Luke 1:11). Gabriel instructs Zacharias that his wife Elisabeth will bear him a son and he is to name the child John (vs. 13). The priest and his wife are both senior citizens as indicated by Zacharias himself with the phrase, "well stricken" in years. The idea here is that he and his wife are well past the age of parenthood and their reproductive organs have long-since "dried up" (Hos. 9:16). It is interesting to note that the only other place the phrase is used in Scripture is with Abraham and Sarah. Gen. 18:11 – **"Now Abraham and Sarah *were* old *and* well stricken in age; *and* it ceased to be with**

Sarah after the manner of women." The same situation took place in both occasions. Both couples were well beyond the age of bearing children and were visited by a supernatural being that announced to them that they would indeed produce a child in their old age. Both couples reacted with a measure of skepticism to the news and were promptly rebuked for their lack of faith. Both couples enjoyed a miraculous birth from the Lord.

In our text, Zacharias finished his course of Temple duty and couldn't wait to get home to Elisabeth with the exciting news (vs. 23-24). The result was the conception of John the Baptist "after those days." This means that the 40-week human gestation period began approximately the 11th or 12th week of the Jewish year, or around the middle of June.

Six Months Later

In our text, Gabriel visits a certain virgin named Mary who is espoused to a man named Joseph, both of whom are of the house of David. Mary is told that she is highly favored and will conceive and bring forth a Son of the Holy Ghost, whose name will be Jesus (vs. 26-35). As she absorbs this information she is told further, that her cousin Elisabeth is also with child (vs. 36) and **"this is the sixth month with her..."** The text says in verse 35, **"The Holy Ghost shall come upon thee..."** indicating the conception would be in the near future from that time. After that encounter, **"Mary arose in those days, and went into the hill country with haste..."** to visit her cousin Elisabeth. As soon as Mary entered her cousin's house and spoke to Elisabeth something took place. **"And it came to pass, that, when Elisabeth heard the salutation of Mary, the babe leaped in her womb; and Elisabeth was filled with the Holy Ghost"** (Luke 1:41). By this time Mary was obviously carrying the Lord Jesus within her because of the reaction that follows.

Elisabeth pronounces a blessing on Mary and the fruit of her womb (vs. 42). She then refers to her as "the mother of my Lord" (vs. 43). Then verse 49 – **"For he that is mighty hath done to me great things; and holy *is* his name."** The promise from Gabriel of the miraculous conception of verse 35 is now spoken of in the past tense.

Thus Mary's 40-week gestation period begins approximately six months into Elisabeth's time. On our chart that would place Christ's conception at about the 39th or 40th week of the year, or around the fourth week of the ninth month (December). That means the birth of Christ would take place some 40 weeks later, or around the second week of the seventh month (October). This conclusion initiates a closer look at the three feasts of the Lord which take place during this approximate period.

According to Lev. 23 the 1st day of the seventh month is the Feast of Trumpets (vs. 23-25). The prophetic significance of this feast is the regathering of Israel in the last days before the Second Advent of Jesus Christ. Since the Balfour Declaration in 1917, Palestine has seen a gradual increase in the Jewish population. As result of the world learning of Hitler's Holocaust and the murder of over six million Jews in Europe, the League of Nations voted to grant a portion of Palestine back to the Jews in 1948 as their homeland. In 1914 there were 60,000 Jews in Palestine. Now there are over 5.2 million Jewish residents in Palestine. The Jewish people are returning to their land in fulfillment of the Feast of Trumpets – when the trumpet was sounded and the people gathered.

On the tenth day of the same month, the Day of Atonement took place. This was the day the priest went behind the veil and sprinkled the blood on the Mercy Seat. This was a day that the Jews were to "afflict themselves" or observe a time of "mourning." This happened once each year and was the time when Israel's sins were forgiven for another year. Prophetically, this is the future time of Israel's National Revival. This is the future time when they recognize their Messiah for whom He really is and they mourn for their sins. Zech. 12:10-12 – **"And I will pour upon the house of David, and upon the inhabitants of Jerusalem, the spirit of grace and of supplications: and they shall look upon me whom they have pierced, and they shall mourn for him, as one mourneth for his only son, and shall be in bitterness for him, as one that is in bitterness for *his* firstborn. In that day shall there be a great mourning in Jerusalem, as the mourning of Hadadrimmon in the valley of Megiddon. And the land shall mourn..."** Israel will see Jesus Christ and, **"And one shall say unto him, What are these wounds in thine hands? Then he shall answer, Those with which I was wounded in the house of my friends"** (Zech. 13:6).

On the 15th day of the seventh month was the Feast of Tabernacles. This feast lasted seven days (Lev. 23:34). The Hebrews would gather after the harvest and celebrate the bountiful harvest given by Jehovah. They brought offerings from their crops and presented them to the priests. Prophetically, this represents the Millennial rest for Israel after their regathering and national conversion to the Messiah. The regathering has been taking place over the last 90 years. Israel's National Revival and restoration of the land (all of it) will take place at the end of the Great Tribulation. Following the Tribulation will be the Thousand-year reign of Jesus Christ the King (Feast of Tabernacles).

Based upon this study of Scripture, it appears that Christ's true day of birth could very well have been on The Day of Atonement or the 10th day of the Jewish 7th month. This assumption is based on the information given in the previous pages. It should be noted that these are estimates only and precise dates cannot be extrapolated from Scripture due to the evolution of our modern calendar as well as approximations in the human gestation period (some babies are early – some late). Nonetheless, what more appropriate day could our Savior have been born than on the Jewish Feast, the Day of Atonement? Jesus Christ is "Atonement" personified.

December 25th

December 25th, our traditional date of the celebration of our Savior's birth is not supported in Scripture, but has a rather dubious origin. One of the oldest and most idolatrous practices in Scripture is the worship of the Sun. Warnings against this are found in a number of places:

Deut. 4:19 **"And lest thou lift up thine eyes unto heaven, and when thou seest the sun, and the moon, and the stars, even all the host of heaven, shouldest be driven to worship them, and serve them, which the LORD thy God hath divided unto all nations under the whole heaven."**

Deut. 17:3 **"And hath gone and served other gods, and worshipped them, either the sun, or moon, or any of the host of heaven, which I have not commanded;"**

Jer. 8:2 **"And they shall spread them before the sun, and the moon, and all the host of heaven, whom they have loved, and whom they have served, and after whom they have walked, and whom they have sought, and whom they have worshipped: they shall not be gathered, nor be buried; they shall be for dung upon the face of the earth."**

Ezk. 8:16 **"And he brought me into the inner court of the LORD'S house, and, behold, at the door of the temple of the LORD, between the porch and the altar, _were_ about five and twenty men, with their backs toward the temple of the LORD, and their faces toward the east; and they worshipped the sun toward the east."**

This practice went on long before Joshua led the Children of Israel into the Promised Land. The Canaanites practiced this religion at the time the Israelites came to occupy Palestine. This was a major reason the Lord instructed the Israelites to get rid of the Canaanites when they arrived in the land.

The day that these people celebrated the birth of their sun god (Sol) was on the winter solstice (Babylon Mystery Religion by Ralph Woodrow, 1966). This is also the day of the festival in honor of the birth of Tammuz (Ezk. 8:14), the son of the Queen of Heaven (Jer. 7:18, 44:17-19, 25, The Two Babylons by Alexander Hislop, 1916). The Queen of Heaven is the mother and child image and is also known as Ashtaroth (Jud. 10:6), Ishtar, Astarte, Ashtoreth (I Kings 11:5), Ashtart, Baalat, Isis, and Semiramis. In China the mother goddess is called Shingmoo (Holy Mother) and she is pictured with child in her arms and a nimbus (round shining sun) surrounding the head of the child. Ancient Germans worshipped "Hertha" with the child in her arms. The Scandinavians called her "Disa," also pictured with child. To the Druids she was "Viro-Paritura" and to the Etruscans she was "Nutria." In India she was called "Indrani" and in Asia she was known as "Cybele." She was the wife of Baal and the Queen of Heaven in every country she was found. She is found in the New Testament as Diana of the Ephesians (Acts 19:24, 27, 28, 34, 35). In modern times she can be seen in Roman Catholic Church literature, paintings, and statuary. The main festival for the Queen of Heaven (and her many aliases) is the winter solstice, on or near the 25th of December. The winter solstice represents the farthest distance from the sun in the earth's orbit. This is the time of the longest night and shortest day. The summer solstice is just the opposite and occurs six months later.

We Are Not Bashing Christmas

The purpose of this paper is not to censure December 25th as our Christmas holiday. It is the traditional date of our holiday to celebrate the birth of Jesus Christ, irrespective of its true origin. Our country should celebrate our Savior's birth and this is the date that it is done. We understand Jeremiah 10:1-5 speaks of a Christmas tree and is referred to the "way of the heathen." Again, we are not campaigning against this traditional holiday. We acknowledge that this is a time for celebrating the birth of Christ and a time for families to be together.

The Scripture commands us to **"Study to shew thyself approved unto God, a workman that needeth not to be ashamed, rightly dividing the word of truth"** (2 Tim. 2:15). One of the most important dates in Scripture is the birth of the Lord Jesus Christ. He came to redeem a hellbound populous of their burden of sin. Should it not be the desire of the student of the word of God to learn all he can about our Savior? **"It is written, Man shall not live by bread alone, but by every word that proceedeth out of the mouth of God"** (Mat. 4:4).

We have shown from Scripture how Jesus Christ was not born in December, but in the Jewish month of Ethanim (1 King 8:2). We proved this in a rather complex manner. There is an easier method to reach the same conclusion. We learn in Luke 3:23 that Christ began His ministry at the time of His baptism at (or near) the age of 30 (Num. 4:23). In the Gospel of John there are four Passovers mentioned: Passover #1, John 2:13, Age: 30 ½; Passover #2, John 5:1, Age: 31 ½; Passover #3, John 6:4, Age: 32 ½; Passover #4, John 13:1, Age: 33 ½.

The first one took place six months after He began His ministry. The last one was the day He was killed (14th day of first month of Jewish calendar). He was 33 ½ years old at the time of His death. When you subtract six months from that date, you are right at the date we have shown to be His birthday – right around the time of the Day of Atonement.

It is our desire that these studies have served to open the eyes of some to the riches of the Scripture. While we celebrate the birth of our Savior on the 25th of December every year, we can be cognizant of our study in the Scriptures of His true date of birth. The real importance of the matter is the fact that Christ *was* born and lived and died on a cross and paid the huge sin debt that we owed. He is no longer on the cross, but making intercession for us daily before God the Father. He is there for us, hearing and answering our prayer. He wants to save the souls of our lost brethren, both Jew and Gentile. He's coming back soon to call His bride home to be with Him. Our prayer is that this paper will pique the interest of many who will give themselves wholly to the study the most fascinating book ever written to **"shew themselves approved unto God."** May we desire to learn more about Jesus Christ and enjoy the riches He has for us in His blessed word. May the Lord bless you as you read and study the word of God.

Send a request to drcharlieedwards@gmail.com for a free copy of an Excel spreadsheet illustration of what we said in this paper. This graphic display will make it easier to visualize the Course of Abia.

CHAPTER THIRTEEN

THE BAREFOOT PRIEST

Preface

THE APOSTLE PAUL ONCE SAID **"O the depth of the riches both of the wisdom and knowledge of God! how unsearchable *are* his judgments, and his ways past finding out!"** (Rom. 11:33). He spoke of the word of God. His choice of nouns, "wisdom, knowledge, and judgments" all refer to Scripture. In addition, "his ways" speak of the same. As far as we are concerned everything we know and understand about God comes from the written word of God. Thus, "his ways" can only speak of the Scriptures. The passage speaks of God's word as that which has "depth." Anyone who has spent time searching the Scripture understands this concept. It matters not how many times one has read the Bible from cover to cover, there is always (and always will be) something else, something new, something fresh, or something missed or unrevealed on previous reads. This verse in Romans indicates that there is a wealth of wisdom and understanding yet to be discovered. May the Holy Spirit open our eyes and hearts to the wonders of His blessed word.

Preparatory to our study of the Barefoot Priest, there is some ground to cover relative to understanding our thesis. We must take a hard look at a very peculiar substance known to all of us. The subject of blood abounds in Scripture. There is no book that is bloodier than the word of God. Let us look at some Bible information about blood:

Innocent Blood

Innocent blood is a phrase used in Scripture for the shedding of blood and thus the death of an innocent person, whose blood should not have been shed. Long before the Lord instructed Moses to write the Ten Commandments, capital punishment was in effect. **"Whoso sheddeth man's blood, by man shall his blood be shed: for in the image of God made he man"** (Gen. 9:6). In plainer words, once murder has taken place and "innocent blood" has been shed, there is an unsettled account. This account is not closed until the murderer's blood has been shed (his death). Cain took the life of his brother and by God's standard Cain's blood should have been shed. However, the law was not given until after the deed was done (Rom. 5:13). Thus we have an unsettled account, typifying our world today.

Further study of innocent blood brings to light other truths. God provided safe harbor for those who accidentally shed innocent blood. These were known as Cities of Refuge, where someone in this situation could flee from an avenging blood relative of the deceased. If a man killed someone unintentionally, he did not deserve to die. The scripture gives an example of this scenario in Deut. 19:5 – **"As when a man goeth into the wood with his neighbour to hew wood, and his hand fetcheth a stroke with the axe to cut down** the tree, and the head slippeth from the helve, and lighteth upon his neighbour, that he die; he shall flee unto one of those cities, and live:" If an Israelite killed someone intentionally and flees to a city of refuge, the people of the city are to give him up to the avenger of blood (Num. 35). The "cities" mentioned were the cities of refuge given for this purpose. **"If thou shalt keep all these commandments to do them, which I command thee this day, to love the LORD thy God, and to walk ever in his ways; then shalt thou add three cities more for thee, beside these three: That innocent blood be not shed in thy land, which the LORD thy God giveth thee *for* an inheritance, and *so* blood be upon thee"** (Deut. 19:9-10). When innocent blood is shed the land is defiled and under a curse until the murderer's blood is shed. **"So ye shall not pollute the land wherein ye *are*: for blood it defileth the land: and the land cannot be cleansed of the blood that is shed therein, but by the blood of him that shed it. Defile not therefore the land which ye shall inhabit, wherein I dwell: for I the LORD dwell among the children of Israel"** (Num. 35:33-34).

Jeremiah informed the Israelites that if they killed him, they would bring innocent blood upon themselves and the city – **"But know ye for certain, that if ye put me to death, ye shall surely bring innocent blood upon yourselves, and upon this city, and upon the inhabitants thereof: for of a truth the LORD hath sent me unto you to speak all these words in your ears"** (Jer. 26:15). King Manasseh brought innocent blood upon his kingdom with the death of countless babies murdered in Baal worship. **"Moreover Manasseh shed innocent blood very much, till he had filled Jerusalem from one end to another; beside his sin wherewith he made Judah to sin, in doing *that which was* evil in the sight of the LORD"** (2 Kings 21:16). In doing this the king caused the people of the land to be guilty of blood. In 2 Kings 24:4 we find that God would not pardon innocent blood. **"And also for the innocent blood that he shed: for he filled Jerusalem with innocent blood; which the LORD would not pardon."** In Psm. 106:37-38 Palestine became polluted with blood. **"Yea, they sacrificed their sons and their daughters unto devils, And shed innocent blood,** *even* **the blood of their sons and of their daughters, whom they sacrificed unto the idols of Canaan: and the land was polluted with blood."** In Joel's writings we learn that innocent blood can be the cause of the land becoming a desolate wilderness. **"Egypt shall be a desolation, and Edom shall be a desolate wilderness, for the violence** *against* **the children of Judah, because they have shed innocent blood in their land"** (Joel 3:19). In 1 Kings 2:31 King Solomon ordered the execution of Joab (who had shed the innocent blood of Abner and Amasa - 1 Kings 2:5) for the purpose of removing blood guiltiness. **"And the king said unto him, Do as he hath said, and fall upon him, and bury him; that thou mayest take away the innocent blood, which Joab shed, from me, and from the house of my father"** (1 Kings2:31).

Let us take another look at Gen. 9:6 - **"Whoso sheddeth man's blood, by man shall his blood be shed: for in the image of God made he man."** According to Scripture, when innocent blood contacts the ground it radiates a signal, heard by God, making request for judgment. **"What hast thou done? the voice of thy brother's blood crieth unto me from the ground"** (Gen. 4:10). Cain was thereafter under a curse from God for shedding his brother's blood (Gen 4:11). In the Tabernacle, the priest was to sprinkle innocent blood on the horns of the Golden Altar every year. Ex. 30:10 – **"And Aaron shall make an atonement upon the horns of it once in a year with the blood of the sin offering of atonements: once in the year shall he make atonement upon it throughout your generations: it** *is* **most holy unto the LORD."** During the Tribulation the blood on the horns of that same altar will cry out for judgment. Rev. 9:13 – **"And the sixth angel sounded, and I heard a voice from the four horns of the golden altar which is before God,"** This cry will result in the deaths of one-third of the world population (14-21). Unavenged blood again cries out to God and makes request for judgment in Rev 6:9-10 - **"And when he had opened the fifth seal, I saw under the altar the souls of them that were slain for the word of God, and for the testimony which they held: And they cried with a loud voice, saying, How long, O Lord, holy and true, dost thou not judge and avenge our blood on them that dwell on the earth?"**

In Proverbs 6:16-18 there are seven things that the Lord hates. The third one is **"hands that shed innocent blood."** **"These six things doth the LORD hate: yea, seven are an abomination unto him: A proud look, a lying tongue, and hands that shed innocent blood..."**

In Deut. 21 we find a provision given to Israel to guard against the land becoming cursed (Deut. 11:28) by innocent blood. In the first nine verses of the chapter the Hebrews are given instructions for cleansing the land of innocent blood which was mysteriously shed (vs. 1). The elders and judges are to determine the closest city to the discovered corpse (vs. 2). The elders of that city are to take a heifer and sever its head next to the body of the dead man (vs. 3-4). The priests were to be present while the elders wash their hands over the beheaded heifer. While doing so, they are to say, **"...Our hands have not shed this blood, neither have our eyes seen *it*. Be merciful, O LORD, unto thy people Israel, whom thou hast redeemed, and lay not innocent blood unto thy people of Israel's charge..."** (vs. 7-8). The Scripture adds, **"...And the blood shall be forgiven them. So shalt thou put away the *guilt of* innocent blood from among you, when thou shalt do *that which is* right in the sight of the LORD"** (vs. 8-9).

In this case someone shed the blood of an innocent man. His blood soaked into the ground, thus creating an imbalance or open account (see above). Until the murderer's blood is shed and "neutralizes" the ground, there is a curse on the land and the people of the land are guilty of innocent blood. No one knows where or who the murderer is and thus God's people are in a difficult situation. The Lord gives His people a special clause in the Law to remedy the dilemma. They are instructed to shed the blood of an innocent animal next to where the dead man's blood soaked into the ground. The heifer's blood erupts when the head is severed and spills on the cursed ground. The elders of the "guilty" city are to recite the prayer beseeching God to remove the blood guiltiness. The key to this passage is verse 5 where it mentions **"the priests the sons of Levi."** The verse states, they **"shall come near; for them the LORD thy God hath chosen to minister unto him, and to bless in the name of the LORD: and by their word shall every controversy and every stroke be *tried*;"** If the priests were not present the whole affair was in vain for the above mentioned reasons. Here we find the sin of the shedding of innocent blood resolved with innocent blood, only under the supervision of the Levite priest.

More Innocent Blood

Hundreds of thousands of animals were killed at the Brazen Altar in the Tabernacle and the Temple. The blood of these animals served as a temporary atonement for the sins of the Old Testament saints. The Scripture says in Heb. 10:4, **"For *it is* not possible that the blood of bulls and of goats should take away sins."** The sacrifices made at the Brazen Altar sufficed until Jesus Christ made the ultimate blood sacrifice on Calvary (Heb. 9:10). The Lord gave Moses detailed instructions regarding the sacrificial blood-letting. The priests were to shed the blood of the sacrifice on the north side of the altar. **"And he shall kill it on the side of the altar northward before the LORD: and the priests, Aaron's sons, shall sprinkle his blood round about upon the altar"** (Lev. 1:11).

Explicit instructions were given to the priest regarding the blood from the animals. The blood (innocent blood) was to be poured out on the ground at the bottom of the altar. **"And he shall put *some* of the blood upon the horns of the altar which is before the LORD, that *is* in the tabernacle of the congregation, and shall pour out all the blood at the bottom of the altar of the burnt offering, which *is* at the door of the tabernacle of the congregation"** (Lev. 4:18; see also 4:25, 30, 34, 8:15, 9:9). The priest was to make certain the blood came in contact with the ground. **"Only thou shalt not eat the blood thereof; thou shalt pour it upon the ground as water"** (Deut. 15:23). Bloodshed was required for remitting sin, **"And almost all things are by the law purged with blood; and without shedding of blood is no remission"** (Heb. 9:22).

The Ultimate Innocent Blood

After Judas Iscariot sold out Christ for thirty pieces of silver he "repented himself" and stated to the priests, **"Saying, I have sinned in that I have betrayed the innocent blood"** (Mat. 27:4). And when Pilate tried to talk the Jews out of crucifying the Lord Jesus they demanded that Christ be crucified and cried, **"...His blood *be* on us, and on our children"** (Mat. 27:25). For over two thousand years Israel has had blood-guilty hands. The shedding of Christ's blood was a one-time event that will never be repeated. Christ's atoning work on Calvary did away with the Levitical sacrifices during the present dispensation. These sacrifices will return again in the future (Ezk. 43-46).

The Priest in the Tabernacle

During the days of the operation of the Tabernacle the Israelites brought their animal sacrifices to the door of the Tabernacle and turned them over to the priest to carry out the offering (Lev. 1-5). On days of Holy Convocation (Lev. 23) there would have been thousands of Israelites bringing their animals for a team of Levite priests to sacrifice at the Brazen Altar. All of these animals had to be killed on the north side of the altar (Lev. 1:11) and the majority of the blood was to be poured out at the bottom of the altar (Lev. 4:18). The priest would be working and walking around in this bloody area. He was to drain the blood from the carcass and cut it in pieces. Therefore, his hands and feet would be completely covered with blood – innocent blood.

Depending upon the offering and the protocol for the Holy Convocations (see our notes on The Five Offerings and The Feasts of the Lord), the priest was to slay the animal, take of its blood, and enter the Tabernacle. Before entering the Tabernacle (proper) he had to go to the Brazen Laver to wash his hands *and his feet* before entering into the Holy Place (Ex. 30:18-21). If he entered into the Tabernacle with innocent blood on his hands or feet, he would be put to death – **"…they shall wash with water, that they die not;"** (Ex. 30:20).

When the Laver is described in Exodus 30:18-21 the reader will notice that no dimensions are given for its construction. When we consider its use and magnitude in the ministry of the priests in the Tabernacle it would have made sense for it to have a practical shape. In light of prophetic significance which will be discussed later, we envision something in the order of a shallow round pool perhaps ten feet in diameter. In the center it may have had a pedestal supporting a shallow tub of approximate diameter of three feet. Or another way to explain its appearance might be something similar to a child's pool with about eight inches of water and a birdbath-affair in the middle. With this shape the priest could stand in the shallow water while washing both hands and feet. Again, this is speculation as no dimensions or clues to its shape other than its purpose for the priest to wash his hands and feet. It must also be somewhat portable for transportation.

The dimensions are given for the laver in the Temple, but the reader will notice that no "foot" is mentioned for the Temple Laver. Why? Solomon's kingdom (including the Temple) depicts the Millennial reign of Christ. With respect to the Tabernacle, Christ's Second Advent is *in the future*. However the Second Advent will be *in the past* during the Millennium and thus no "foot" on the Temple Laver. This will make more sense later in this treatise.

The Priest Wore No Shoes

When we study the garments of the Priest in Exodus 28 we notice a subtle absence of footwear. Details are given for his mitre, linen breeches (undergarment), breastplate, ephod, robe, girdle, and broidered coat, but there are no shoes mentioned. Further, when examining the detail given to other parts of the Tabernacle, we recognize that this omission was not by accident. Why?

During the time Moses was up on Mt. Sinai (Horeb) for a 40-day meeting with God (when He gave Moses all the instructions and plans for construction of the Tabernacle) the Children of Israel were camped at the foot of the same mountain. It was on this same mountain just a few months earlier that Moses kept Jethro's sheep (Ex. 3:1). During that same time the Angel of the LORD appeared to him in the burning bush. When Moses approached to get a closer look, God called out to him from the midst of the bush, **"Moses,**

Moses… put off thy shoes from thy feet, for the place whereon thou standest *is* holy ground" (Ex. 3:2-5). The ground was holy or set apart and therefore God wanted Moses' feet to be bare and in contact with the ground.

Approximately forty years later Moses was dead and Joshua had just led the Israelites across the Jordan River. They were encamped near the river and Jericho just before its conquest. Joshua saw a man with a drawn sword (Josh. 5:13). He approached him and asked, **"Art thou for us, or for our adversaries? And he said, Nay; but *as* captain of the host of the LORD am I now come. And Joshua fell on his face to the earth, and did worship, and said unto him, What saith my lord unto his servant? And the captain of the LORD'S host said unto Joshua, Loose thy shoe from off thy foot; for the place whereon thou standest *is* holy. And Joshua did so"** (13-15). The Holy Spirit gives us a second geographic position referred to as "holy" and instructs His servant to remove his shoes so that his bare feet are in contact with the ground.

The Tabernacle was disassembled and moved many times during the forty years of wilderness wanderings. Wherever the Ark rested was Holy Ground. The priest's feet had to be in contact with that ground while in the Tabernacle. When the priests carried the Ark they were barefoot. When the Children of Israel crossed the Jordan River, they did so after the barefoot priests went first. **"And it shall come to pass, as soon as the soles of the feet of the priests that bear the ark of the LORD, the Lord of all the earth, shall rest in the waters of Jordan, *that* the waters of Jordan shall be cut off *from* the waters that come down from above; and they shall stand upon an heap"** (Josh. 3:13).

When a priest was consecrated in the Tabernacle, blood was applied to the great toe of his right foot (Ex. 29, Lev. 8, 14). The priest's feet were bare the entire time he was in the Tabernacle. The priest was a type of our Great High

Priest, the Lord Jesus Christ (Heb. 4:14). With every mention of Christ's feet, there is no indication He wore shoes or sandals. His feet are always in view, unimpeded by footwear.

In His pre-incarnate visage: **"And they saw the God of Israel: and *there was* under his feet as it were a paved work of a sapphire stone, and as it were the body of heaven in *his* clearness"** (Ex. 24:10). **"And, behold, there cometh one of the rulers of the synagogue, Jairus by name; and when he saw him, he fell at his feet,"** (Mark 5:22). **"For a *certain* woman, whose young daughter had an unclean spirit, heard of him, and came and fell at his feet:"** (Mark 7:25). **"And stood at his feet behind *him* weeping, and began to wash his feet with tears, and did wipe *them* with the hairs of her head, and kissed his feet, and anointed *them* with the ointment"** (Luke 7:38). There are many other similar passages about people falling to Christ's feet with no mention of His shoes.

There is only one mention of Christ's shoes in Scripture and it was used in metaphor – **"He it is, who coming after me is preferred before me, whose shoe's latchet I am not worthy to unloose."** (John 1:27). This occurrence is mentioned in all four Gospels: Mat. 3:11, Mark 1:7, and Luke 3:16. It is noteworthy that when Mark, Luke, and John write of John the Baptist's statement about Christ's footwear, they all speak of the *removal* of His shoes. Matthew speaks of "bearing" His shoes. At the time John said these words, he had never seen Christ. It was after this that he said, **"Behold the Lamb of God, which taketh away the sin of the world."**

When Christ was crucified and His garments parted – there were no shoes.

Christ sent His disciples out barefooted in Mat. 10:5-15. **"Provide neither gold, nor silver, nor brass in your purses, Nor scrip for *your* journey, neither two coats,** neither shoes, nor yet staves: for the workman is worthy of his meat" (vs. 9-10). Paul wrote, "And how shall they preach, except they be sent? as it is written, How beautiful are the feet of them that preach the gospel of peace, and bring glad tidings of good things!" (Rom. 10:15).

Everywhere Christ went was Holy Ground. His feet were in contact with the ground.

After His resurrection He was without shoes: Mat. 28:9 – "And as they went to tell his disciples, behold, Jesus met them, saying, All hail. And they came and held him by the feet, and worshipped him." Luke 24:39 – "Behold my hands and my feet, that it is I myself: handle me, and see; for a spirit hath not flesh and bones, as ye see me have." Luke 24:40 – "And when he had thus spoken, he shewed them *his* hands and *his* feet."

John saw Him in the book of Revelation without shoes: "And his feet like unto fine brass, as if they burned in a furnace; and his voice as the sound of many waters" (Rev. 1:15).

He will be without shoes when He treads the winepress of His wrath: "Wherefore *art thou* red in thine apparel, and thy garments like him that treadeth in the winefat? I have trodden the winepress alone; and of the people *there was* none with me: for I will tread them in mine anger, and trample them in my fury; and their blood shall be sprinkled upon my garments, and I will stain all my raiment" (Isa. 63:2-3). "The righteous shall rejoice when he seeth the vengeance: he shall wash his feet in the blood of the wicked" (Psm. 58:10).

We have shown how the priest ministered in the Tabernacle without shoes. He trod through the blood of countless innocent beasts. His feet were covered with blood when he went to the laver. He stepped into the shallow "foot" of the laver and walked the few steps to the hand-washing basin, thus rinsing the blood off his feet. Then he entered the Tabernacle to minister before God. He did not enter the Tabernacle with blood on his feet or hands, **"that he die not"** (Ex. 30:20).

Christ's Second Advent and His Path to Jerusalem

There will be a time in the future when a variation of this same scenario will be repeated. As the Tabernacle Priest, Christ will tromp through blood and get it on His feet and His raiment (Isa. 63:1-4, Rev. 19:13). He will walk through the foot of the laver to wash it off (Mat. 14:25-26, Mark 6:49, John 6:19).

When Jesus Christ returns in His Glory there is a route given in Scripture for His return to Jerusalem. (See Dr. Ruckman's booklet, "The Route of the Second Advent.")

He goes first to Mt. Sinai. When Moses blessed the Children of Israel just before his death, **"And he said, The LORD came from Sinai, and rose up from Seir unto them; he shined forth from mount Paran, and he came with ten thousands of saints: from his right hand** *went* **a fiery law for them."** (Deut. 33:2). We know that this passage is a reference to the Second Advent because of the mention of the Lord being accompanied "with ten thousands of saints." This same site was where He came before – **"And mount Sinai was altogether on a smoke, because the LORD descended upon it in fire: and the smoke thereof ascended as the smoke of a furnace, and the whole mount quaked greatly"** (Ex. 19:18). Mt. Sinai was the first place someone was instructed to remove their shoes because of holy ground. It was also the location of the end of the wilderness wanderings and the beginning of the official trek to the Promised Land. **"The LORD our God spake unto** us in Horeb, saying, Ye have dwelt long enough in this mount" (Deut. 1:6).

"Who *is* this that cometh out of the wilderness like pillars of smoke, perfumed with myrrh and frankincense, with all powders of the merchant?" (Song 3:6). This passage is another Second Advent passage that speaks of someone "that cometh out of the wilderness," which is where Mt. Sinai is located. We know it is Sinai because of the "pillars of smoke," spoken of in Ex. 19:18 (quoted above). "Perfumed with myrrh and frankincense" speaks of Christ. We know this because of the gifts brought to him by the wise men in Mat. 2:11. Also the Messianic Psm. 45 tells us, "All thy garments *smell* of myrrh, and aloes, *and* cassia, out of the ivory palaces, whereby they have made thee glad" (Psm. 45:8).

From Sinai He goes through Seir and Edom as shown in Judges 5 in the Song of Deborah. "LORD, when thou wentest out of Seir, when thou marchedst out of the field of Edom, the earth trembled, and the heavens dropped, the clouds also dropped water. The mountains melted from before the LORD, *even* that Sinai from before the LORD God of Israel" (Jud. 5:4-5). The reader should notice that the Lord is moving from Sinai northward in essentially the same path that Moses led the Children of Israel in Numbers 10-14, mentioned again in Deuteronomy 2. Moses' attempt to take the Israelites into the Promised Land failed at Kadesh Barnea in Numbers 14. Subsequently they ended up wandering in the wilderness until a new generation became adults. This is also the same path Joshua led the Children of Israel with the Ark of God out front being carried by the barefoot priests. He mentions Seir and Edom in the passage from Judges 5 above. It was Edom who would not allow Moses and the Israelites to pass through their land in Numbers 20. This was never forgotten by Moses and the Lord and is mentioned again in Deut. 2:29. When Christ returns in His glory the Edomites won't be a problem for Him.

"**Who *is* this that cometh from Edom, with dyed garments from Bozrah? this *that is* glorious in his apparel, travelling in the greatness of his strength? I that speak in righteousness, mighty to save. 2 Wherefore *art thou* red in thine apparel, and thy garments like him that treadeth in the winefat? 3 I have trodden the winepress alone; and of the people *there was* none with me: for I will tread them in mine anger, and trample them in my fury; and their blood shall be sprinkled upon my garments, and I will stain all my raiment. 4 For the day of vengeance *is* in mine heart, and the year of my redeemed is come. 5 And I looked, and *there was* none to help; and I wondered that *there was* none to uphold: therefore mine own arm brought salvation unto me; and my fury, it upheld me. 6 And I will tread down the people in mine anger, and make them drunk in my fury, and I will bring down their strength to the earth.**" (Isa. 63:1-6). If the reader will look at a Bible map he will see the cities and geographic areas mentioned as King Jesus continues His bloody northward advance. On this march Christ's bare feet are treading the winepress (above). The blood of millions of the murderous (Gen 9:6) enemies of Israel and God is being shed and soaking into the ground. The Lord's garments are splattered and "dyed" red in His northward progression. This is the vengeance requested by all the innocent blood shed for all ages of this world. All the open and unbalanced accounts are settled during this bloody affair.

"**God came from Teman, and the Holy One from mount Paran. Selah. His glory covered the heavens, and the earth was full of his praise. 4 And *his* brightness was as the light; he had horns *coming* out of his hand: and there *was* the hiding of his power. 5 Before him went the** pestilence, and burning coals went forth at his feet. 6 He stood, and measured the earth: he beheld, and drove asunder the nations; and the everlasting mountains were scattered, the perpetual hills did bow: his ways *are* everlasting. 7 I saw the tents of Cushan in affliction: *and* the curtains of the land of Midian did tremble. 8 Was the LORD displeased against the rivers? *was* thine anger against the rivers? *was* thy wrath against the sea, that thou didst ride upon thine horses *and* thy chariots of salvation? 9 Thy bow was made quite naked, *according* to the oaths of the tribes, *even thy* word. Selah. Thou didst cleave the earth with rivers. 10 The mountains saw thee, *and* they trembled: the overflowing of the water passed by: the deep uttered his voice, *and* lifted up his hands on high. 11 The sun *and* moon stood still in their habitation: at the light of thine arrows they went, *and* at the shining of thy glittering spear. 12 Thou didst march through the land in indignation, thou didst thresh the heathen in anger. 13 Thou wentest forth for the salvation of thy people, *even* for salvation with thine anointed; thou woundedst the head out of the house of the wicked, by discovering the foundation unto the neck. Selah. 14 Thou didst strike through with his staves the head of his villages: they came out as a whirlwind to scatter me: their rejoicing *was* as to devour the poor secretly. 15 Thou didst walk through the sea with thine horses, *through* the heap of great waters." (Hab. 3:3-15) Teman is a descendent of Esau and is from Edom. Mount Paran (mentioned in vs. 1). All this area is between Sinai and the Kings Highway, up the east side of the Dead Sea. When Christ the King and His accompanying army get to the Jordan River above the Dead Sea He walks across the surface of the water as He walked on the Sea of Galilee in Matthew 14, Mark 6, and John 6. In doing so, His feet are cleansed of blood. See verse 15 above. This is also analogous to the priest who has blood all over his bare feet and washes his feet in the laver before entering the Tabernacle. Reference also the priest's bare feet carrying the Ark through the Jordan River in Joshua 3. The reader should also notice the reference to Genesis 3:15, "...her seed; it shall bruise thy head..." in verses 13 and 14 above. This represents Christ's victory over Satan at His Second Advent. This crossing point on the Jordan River would also be the same as where Elijah and Elisha crossed and where John the Baptist baptized the Lord Jesus. This Second Advent crossing is mentioned also in Hab. 3:15, **"Thou didst walk through the sea with thine horses, *through* the heap of great waters."**

Christ's bare feet touch the ground on the Mount of Olives. **"And his feet shall stand in that day upon the mount of Olives, which *is* before Jerusalem on the east, and the mount of Olives shall cleave in the midst thereof toward the east and toward the west, *and there shall be* a very great valley; and half of the mountain shall remove toward the north, and half of it toward the south"** (Zech. 14:4). The topography of the Jerusalem area will change at this time.

Christ will then enter Jerusalem through the Eastern Gate (Ezk. 44:1-2).

King Jesus will enter the Temple and into the Holy of Holies and sit down on His Throne of Glory (Rev. 8:3 shows us the position of Christ's throne relative to the Golden Altar).

"And the LORD shall be king over all the earth: in that day shall there be one LORD, and his name one" (Zech. 14:9).

Removal of the Shoe

In the Old Testament when a man refused to perform

the duty of the husband's brother (to marry the widow and raise up the seed of the deceased brother), the widow would spit in his face and remove his shoe before the elders (Deut. 25:5-10). This is illustrated in the Book of Ruth when Boaz redeemed Naomi's land and took Ruth as his wife to raise up seed to her deceased husband. The man who was next of kin refused to redeem the land and marry Ruth because he did not want to mar his own inheritance (Ruth 4:6). Since he knew Boaz was next in line and was willing to perform the duty, he removed his shoe in confirmation of the denial. The removal of the shoe not only confirmed his refusal to marry the woman, but also validated the change of ownership of the specific property involved. **"Now this was *the manner* in former time in Israel concerning redeeming and concerning changing, for to confirm all things; a man plucked off his shoe, and gave *it* to his neighbour: and this *was* a testimony in Israel. Therefore the kinsman said unto Boaz, Buy *it* for thee. So he drew off his shoe"** (Ruth 4:7-8).

When Jesus Christ returns He will be without shoes, thus confirming a change of ownership of the entire Palestinian area in addition to the rest of the world – Rom. 4:13, **"For the promise, that he should be the heir of the world, *was* not to Abraham, or to his seed, through the law, but through the righteousness of faith."** He will redeem all the land for Israel, but He won't marry the woman (Rev. 12:1). The woman (Israel) will be reunited with God the Father (Hos. 2:14-23, Isa. 54:5, Jer. 3:1, 14, 20, 31:32), who is currently divorced from her (Isa. 50:1).

It is interesting to note that Boaz, by taking a Gentile bride and redeeming the property for Naomi was a type of Christ the Redeemer. By contrast, the near kinsman who refused was the one who removed his shoe. In the context he was a type of God the Father whose inheritance (Israel) he did not want to mar (Deut. 4:21, 9:26, Psm. 28:9, 33:12, Isa.

19:25, et al). So, when Jesus Christ returns He will cast His shoe over Edom (Psm. 108:9) and will tread the winepress (this is always done barefooted) of His wrath (Isa. 63:2-3, Rev. 14:19, 19:15). After that He may dismount His white horse and walk across the Jordan River (similar to the priest walking in the foot of the laver) and thus wash the blood from His feet before entering the Temple in Jerusalem.

Moses, Joshua, Boaz, and the Tabernacle Priests were all types of Christ who had something to do with the removal of shoes. David was also a type of Christ. There is an interesting passage found in 2 Samuel: **"And David went up by the ascent of *mount* Olivet, and wept as he went up, and had his head covered, and he went barefoot: and all the people that *was* with him covered every man his head, and they went up, weeping as they went up"** (2 Sam.15:30).

We might wonder at what point during His ministry did Christ become shoeless? Perhaps He was always that way from a child. We simply do not know. It is possible that He wore shoes or sandals up until a certain point in time. The passages sited in this paper imply He wore no shoes. But if He did wear them up until a certain point prior to that, what was that point? I would like to submit a possible answer to this question: Three times we are told of the Sadducees that approached Christ and inquired about the hypothetical seven brothers who married the same woman to raise up seed. This situation is mentioned in Matthew 22, Mark 12, and Luke 20. Their main question was about whose wife the woman would be in the resurrection. But the Sadducees did not believe in the resurrection. It appears their intentions were like that of the Pharisees, to make Christ look bad and try to "entangle Him in His talk" (Mat. 22:15). But just suppose they knew of some event that had recently taken place regarding Jesus' family and were subtly raising that point to the subject Himself. What if they were being more direct with their question than what appears to be the surface truth here?

There is another passage that might be related to this very situation. Something took place in Matthew 12, Mark 3, and Luke 8 regarding Jesus' mother and His brethren. In all three passages we read where Mary and Christ's brothers came to where He was and desired to speak with Him. They were unable to do so because of the crowd of people. They sent a messenger to Jesus to let Him know, to which He responded, **"Who is my mother? And who are my brethren? ...behold my mother and my brethren!"** In other words He distanced Himself from His immediate family and associated Himself with His disciples and the people who came to hear what He had to say. We were never told what it was they wanted to discuss with the Elder Brother of the family.

Here is our theory: Could it possibly be that one of Jesus' four step-brothers got married and before he and his wife were able to have children he died? Perhaps this brother was the groom in the marriage feast in John 2 where Mary appeared to be in charge. This would also explain why Christ and His disciples were invited. And could it be that the reason Mary and the remaining brothers came to see Jesus that day was to inquire about Him performing the duty of the husband's brother? (Deut. 25:5-10). Obviously the Lord had no intention of fulfilling this Levitical requirement. He had more important things to accomplish in His short ministry. In Luke 2:49 He said to His mother, **"How is it that ye sought me? wist ye not that I must be about my Father's business?"** This was said in mild rebuke of His mother's concern for His safety relative to His calling from God the Father. Then it was at the marriage feast in John 2 that she told Him, **"They have no wine."** His reply was, **"Woman, what have I to do with thee? mine hour is not yet come."** So, when Mary and His brethren came to speak with Him in Matthew 12, Mark 3, and Luke 8 the third rebuke is given by His rebuff and thus His refusal to perform the duty of the husband's brother. According to Deut. 25:9 this refusal was followed by being spit upon in the face and the removal of the shoes.

The passages sited above regarding the Sadducees asking Jesus about the seven brothers may have been related to this event. Perhaps they knew of His refusal and were badgering Him with this knowledge. Since they did not believe in a resurrection, their motives were clearly something other than achieving a true understanding of prophecy. Perhaps that motive was to make the Savior look bad by dealing with the Mosaic Law He seemed to be ignoring. Additionally, all three of the Sadducees passages occur before the passage where Christ's mother and brethren come to see Him. So, chronologically, it is a plausible conjecture. Again, this is only a theory and there is no way to prove it. But as it stands, it could have happened.

Conclusion

Based upon the many passages of Scripture examined in this paper, we submit to you that: Moses and Joshua were instructed to "...put off thy shoes from off thy feet..." (Ex. 3:5 and Josh. 5:15). Both of these men were types of Christ. The priests (also types of Christ) were barefoot in the Tabernacle. They walked through pools of blood and washed the blood off in water before entering the Tabernacle as a type of what will take place at the Second Advent of Jesus Christ. Jesus Christ was barefoot during his three and one-half year ministry in Palestine as the anti-type for the Tabernacle Priest. Christ will return with no shoes. He will accomplish His "strange work" (avenging innocent blood) without shoes (Isa. 28:21). At the Second Advent of Christ all the blood that is shed will soak into the ground and satisfy the cries of the unavenged and innocent blood of all ages (Gen. 4:10, Rev. 14:20) as prophesied by Christ in Matthew

23:35 and Luke 11:50-51 – **"That the blood of all the prophets, which was shed from the foundation of the world, may be required of this generation; From the blood of Abel unto the blood of Zacharias, which perished between the altar and the temple: verily I say unto you, It shall be required of this generation."**

It is worthy of note that in the passage from Luke 11 quoted above, Zacharias "perished between the altar and the temple." This is the position of the Laver, where the innocent blood was washed from the feet of the priests.

In this paper we have spoken about Christ returning to avenge the innocent blood of all ages. The First Advent of Jesus Christ was for the shedding of His own innocent blood for the purpose of redeeming the souls of all mankind. This paper would be incomplete and pointless without pointing to Christ as our one and only Atonement for sin. If you have never accepted Christ as Savior, do so now.

As with all our papers in this Doctrinal Series, our prayer is that these studies will pique the interest of the reader to study the Scriptures to show himself approved unto God (2 Tim. 2:15).

CHAPTER FOURTEEN

GOD'S TRANSPORT TO HELL

Introduction

THE IDEA OF GOD ALMIGHTY, THE Creator of the universe, having a "transport" to a place called Hell is repugnant to the natural man. The suggestion of transportation to this destination is one thing, but the notion that God would assign a person to permanent damnation in the fires of hell is completely unfathomable (by the world's standards). The reason for this is found in the writings of the Apostle Paul. He wrote in 1 Cor. 2:14, **"But the natural man receiveth not the things of the Spirit of God: for they are foolishness unto him: neither can he know *them*, because they are spiritually discerned."** In other words, the unregenerate man is completely unable to comprehend this concept. On the other hand, when a man who is regenerated by the Holy Spirit in the New Birth approaches the Scripture with a genuine attitude of, **"Open thou mine eyes, that I may behold wondrous things out**

of thy law" (Psm. 119:18), his prayer is answered.

God created man and put him on the earth. He gave him the opportunity to make his own choice of light or darkness. In John's Gospel we read, **"And this is the condemnation, that light is come into the world, and men loved darkness rather than light, because their deeds were evil"** (John 3:19). Historically, the majority of men have chosen darkness rather than light. Scripture again confirms the ugly fact that most people who live and die on earth will experience this "Transport to Hell." We read in Matthew 7:13-14 where Christ said these ominous words, **"Enter ye in at the strait gate: for wide *is* the gate, and broad *is* the way, that leadeth to destruction, and many there be which go in thereat: Because strait is the gate, and narrow is the way, which leadeth unto life, and few there be that find it."**

God told the Israelites before they entered the Promised Land, **"Behold, I set before you this day a blessing and a curse; A blessing, if ye obey the commandments of the LORD your God, which I command you this day: And a curse, if ye will not obey the commandments of the LORD your God, but turn aside out of the way which I command you this day, to go after other gods, which ye have not known"** (Deut. 11:26-28). God put them in the land and gave them two options: 1) obey His commandments and enjoy all the blessings He promised them, 2) turn aside from His commandments and bring on the curse of God. This is a vivid picture of how the Lord operates. He gives us two options – heaven and hell. It is up to the individual to make a choice between the two. According to the passage sited above, most choose hell. When they die God holds them to their choice of darkness and they experience God's Transport to Hell.

The question has been asked, "Where do we go when

we die?" Before this question can be answered properly more information is required. Was this question asked before or after Jesus Christ died on the cross? Does the question refer to an Old Testament saint or New? If it refers to an unsaved person, is it before or after the cross? We can go a step further and inquire by what means of transportation does one go to wherever they go? It is the objective of this paper to offer a Biblical answer to these questions. There is only one true source of information for our research available. Any attempt to answer these questions apart from the Holy Bible is an exercise in futility. For obvious reasons, the word of God is the only book on the subject which will offer us authoritative answers.

When Old Testament saints died, they went to a place called Abraham's Bosom. Christ spoke to the repentant thief while on the cross about this same place and referred to it as "Paradise." This place was located in the heart of the earth. In Luke 16 we find the death of two people – one saved (Lazarus) and one lost (the rich man). The Holy Spirit put this passage in Scripture to explain further about our subject. There are some who claim this passage is a parable. Religious sects that do not believe in a literal hell consign this passage to allegory. Unfortunately (for them) we are not given the privilege to "cherry pick" the Scripture and decide which passages we like or don't like. We have to take all of it or none of it. This same response was experienced by Ezekiel when he prophesied of Christ's Second Advent and spoke of a burning unquenchable fire which Christ will ignite during this great event (Ezk. 20:45-49, Isa. 30:30-33, Jer. 21:12-14, Mat. 3:12, Mark 9:43-49). The response from those who did not care for the concept said, **"...Doth he not speak parables?"** (Ezk. 20:49). The idea of a literal burning hell has never been a popular concept. This writer does not relish the notion of an unquenchable fire where people go who reject Jesus Christ's atonement. However, this truth is found throughout Scripture. To deny this it is to deny the word of

God. When the word of God speaks in parables, it is announced as such. When it is not announced it should be taken as a literal truth (Mat. 13:3, 10, 13, 18, 24, 31, 33, 34, 35, 36, 53, 15:15, 53, 21:33, 45, 22:1, 24:32, Mark 2:23, et al). Luke 16:22 – **"And it came to pass, that the beggar died, and was carried by the angels into Abraham's bosom…"** While the book of Luke is found in the New Testament, the New Testament did not officially begin until Christ gave up the Ghost on Golgotha. According to Hebrews 9:16-17, **"For where a testament *is*, there must also of necessity be the death of the testator. For a testament *is* of force after men are dead: otherwise it is of no strength at all while the testator liveth."** So, technically the Old Testament was still in effect until Christ died. In these two verses we learn the answer to two of the questions above. The Old Testament saints went to Abraham's Bosom and the method of conveyance was two or more angels. Abraham's Bosom and hell were located in the heart of the earth. They were two different places and were separated by a great gulf.

What about the rich man in the passage sited? That latter part of verse 22 and all of 23 (of Luke 16) give us the answer: **"…the rich man also died, and was buried; And in hell he lift up his eyes, being in torments…"** How did the rich man get to hell? Before we address this question, let us answer the remaining question from earlier. Where does the New Testament saint go when he dies?

When the born-again Christian dies, his body is buried and begins corruption. His soul and spirit are released from the body and are immediately in the presence of Jesus Christ. We know this because Paul wrote, **"We are confident, *I say*, and willing rather to be absent from the body, and to be present with the Lord"** (2 Cor. 5:8). On the same subject, Paul also wrote, **"I knew a man in Christ above fourteen years ago, (whether in the body, I cannot tell; or whether out of the body, I cannot tell: God**

knoweth;) such an one caught up to the third heaven. And I knew such a man, (whether in the body, or out of the body, I cannot tell: God knoweth;) How that he was caught up into paradise, and heard unspeakable words, which it is not lawful for a man to utter" (2 Cor. 12:2-4). In this passage the Apostle refers to his own experience of dying (Acts 14:19) and departing this world to ascend to the third heaven. He also refers to this place as "Paradise." Paradise (Abraham's Bosom) was at one time in the heart of the earth. In the passage quoted above, it is found in the third heaven. (For more details on this subject, see our paper entitled, "Christ's Subterranean Redemptive Work.")

When Christ died on the cross and paid our sin debt, He went to the heart of the earth and "led captivity captive," according to Ephesians 4:8, **"Wherefore he saith, When he ascended up on high, he led captivity captive, and gave gifts unto men."** The gifts Christ gave to the inhabitants of Abraham's Bosom were the linen garments John wrote about in Rev. 19:8 – **"And to her was granted that she should be arrayed in fine linen, clean and white: for the fine linen is the righteousness of saints."** These garments were not available before the consummation (Christ's death) of the New Testament (Heb. 9:16). When Jesus Christ gave up the Ghost the Old Covenant was broken (Psm. 89:39) and the veil in the Temple was rent in twain (Eph. 2:14). The Scripture says in Heb. 9:12, **"Neither by the blood of goats and calves, but by his own blood he entered in once into the holy place, having obtained eternal redemption *for us*."** The Old Testament saints being held prisoner in Abraham's Bosom (Paradise) were required to stay there because the blood of bulls and goats could not take away sin. They could not exist in the presence of God (Third Heaven) without the sins permanently removed. After Christ shed His own blood (which DOES take away sin) these saints could be ushered into the Third Heaven and into the presence of the Lord. Christ's shed blood was the provision for that garment of fine linen John wrote about. That garment depicts Christ's righteousness.

While Christ was in the heart of the earth three days and three nights (Mat. 12:40), He visited the occupants of Abraham's Bosom, presented them with a coat of righteousness, and escorted them to the Third Heaven. Therefore, when someone dies who knows Christ as Savior, they are immediately in the presence of the Lord. 2 Cor. 5:8 – **"We are confident, *I say*, and willing rather to be absent from the body, and to be present with the Lord."**

Unsaved Dead

Today in New Testament times when an unsaved person dies, he goes to the same place the Old Testament unsaved went – Hell. This place of unspeakable torment is found in the heart of the earth. Both Abraham's Bosom and Hell were in the heart of the earth, but one was kept separate from the other. We learn from Luke 16 that Lazarus (the beggar) was "comforted." Luke 16:25, **"But Abraham said, Son, remember that thou in thy lifetime receivedst thy good things, and likewise Lazarus evil things: but now he is comforted, and thou art tormented."** Like the saved person, when the unsaved person dies, his body is buried and decays. The soul and spirit are released from the body but instead of going up to the Third Heaven, they go down to hell.

How is it that for one person death releases the soul and spirit to go up to heaven and for another the soul and spirit go down to hell? Let us take a look at Scripture and see what the Holy Spirit says about this phenomenon.

Earthly – Heavenly

In John 3 Jesus Christ explains to Nicodemus that he must be born again. Nicodemus doesn't understand and Christ instructs him about the difference in the physical birth and the new birth. He illustrates by contrasting unlike things. He compares the water birth to the spirit birth. Then He compares the spirit birth to the wind. Then He compares some additional unlike elements. John 3:12 – **"If I have told you earthly things, and ye believe not, how shall ye believe, if I tell you *of* heavenly things?"** Christ compares the physical birth to "earthly things" and the new birth to "heavenly things." Later in the same chapter He is discussing John the Baptist with His disciples and again gives the contrast of earthly and heavenly. John 3:31 – **"He that cometh from above is above all: he that is of the earth is earthly, and speaketh of the earth: he that cometh from heaven is above all."** As if to punctuate His twice-used contrast of earthly and heavenly, He gives us verse 36, **"He that believeth on the Son hath everlasting life: and he that believeth not the Son shall not see life; but the wrath of God abideth on him."** His comparison is boiled down to two different locations – heaven and hell.

Later, Paul uses the same contrast in 1 Cor. 15:45-49: **"And so it is written, The first man Adam was made a living soul; the last Adam *was made* a quickening spirit. Howbeit that was not first which is spiritual, but that which is natural; and afterward that which is spiritual. The first man *is* of the earth, earthy: the second man *is* the Lord from heaven. As *is* the earthy, such *are* they also that are earthy: and *as is* the heavenly, such *are* they also that are heavenly. And as we have borne the image of the earthy, we shall also bear the image of the heavenly. Now this I say, brethren, that flesh and blood cannot inherit the kingdom of God; neither doth**

corruption inherit incorruption." Here, the Apostle uses the earthly-heavenly contrast to illustrate the same thing John did, but with a slight twist. Paul speaks of the first Adam as being of the flesh, or earthly. The last Adam (Christ) was heavenly and a quickening Spirit. Again, the flesh is contrasted with the spirit or, the natural man (Adam) contrasted with the born-again man (Christ-filled), or earthly contrasted with heavenly.

In Philippians 3:18-19 Paul points out that those who walk after the flesh are the enemies of Christ's Atonement. Note the preoccupation of this group with earthly things. **"For many walk, of whom I have told you often, and now tell you even weeping, *that they are* the enemies of the cross of Christ: Whose end *is* destruction, whose God *is their* belly, and whose glory *is* in their shame, who mind earthly things."**

James picks up this line of thought and goes a little deeper with the earthly side. James 3:14-16 – **"But if ye have bitter envying and strife in your hearts, glory not, and lie not against the truth. This wisdom descendeth not from above, but *is* earthly, sensual, devilish. For where envying and strife *is*, there is confusion and every evil work."**

Earthly Bound to Earth

The unsaved or earthly people are bound to this world (earth) by the cords of sin. Prov. 5:22, **"His own iniquities shall take the wicked himself, and he shall be holden with the cords of his sins."** Psm. 102:20, **"To hear the groaning of the prisoner; to loose those that are appointed to death."** The Lord has the power to break these cords of sin that connect the sinner to this earth. Psm. 107:14 – **"He brought them out of darkness and the** shadow of death, and brake their bands in sunder." Isa. 58:6 – *"Is* not this the fast that I have chosen? to loose the bands of wickedness, to undo the heavy burdens, and to let the oppressed go free, and that ye break every yoke?"

In Luke 4 Jesus went into the Synagogue and read from Isaiah 61:1, "The Spirit of the Lord *is* upon me, because he hath anointed me to preach the gospel to the poor; he hath sent me to heal the brokenhearted, to preach deliverance to the captives, and recovering of sight to the blind, to set at liberty *them that are* bruised..." Isaiah used the word, "bound" instead of bruised, but both illustrate the same point. Isaiah spoke of those who were "bound" with the shackles of sin being set at liberty. Christ used the word "bruised." Psm. 105:17-18 shows that the bruises come from iron shackles (of sin). Paul said in Gal 5:1 – "Stand fast therefore in the liberty wherewith Christ hath made us free, and be not entangled again with the yoke of bondage." This bondage comes from the shackles of sin connecting the earthly man to this world.

In Col. 2 Paul wrote about a spiritual operation where something gets cut in the process of salvation. "In whom also ye are circumcised with the circumcision made without hands, in putting off the body of the sins of the flesh by the circumcision of Christ: Buried with him in baptism, wherein also ye are risen with *him* through the faith of the operation of God, who hath raised him from the dead" (Col. 2:11-12). What is it that gets cut? Whatever it is that connects the believer to the sins of the flesh. That is, cords, bands, and shackles of sin. They are severed in a spiritual operation and compared to the token of the Abrahamic Covenant. In the Old Testament, circumcision of the Hebrew male symbolized the cutting away of the flesh where it has to do with the seed. Ultimately the seed was the coming Messiah that would bruise the head of the serpent (Gen. 3:15). The Bible says in Heb. 4:12, **"For the word of God *is* quick, and powerful, and sharper than any twoedged sword, piercing even to the dividing asunder of soul and spirit, and of the joints and marrow, and *is* a discerner of the thoughts and intents of the heart."** The word of God is a razor-sharp spiritual sword capable of severing those bands of sin connecting the "joints and marrow" (flesh, earthly) to the soul and spirit. So, when a sinner receives Jesus Christ as Savior, he undergoes a spiritual circumcision which cuts the cords that bind the sinner to this world and the flesh (earthly).

Conclusion

With all this in mind, let us go back and answer the question about the mode of transportation. When the saved person's body dies, the soul and spirit separate from the body. Since that person has been through the spiritual operation mentioned in Col. 2:11, this person is not affected by the pull of the earthly cords of this world. Since this person is "in Christ" and "born-again" he has not only the water birth (flesh), but also the spiritual birth (heavenly). John 12:26 says **"If any man serve me, let him follow me; and where I am, there shall also my servant be:"** Paul wrote in 2 Cor. 5:6, 8, **"Therefore *we are* always confident, knowing that, whilst we are at home in the body, we are absent from the Lord...We are confident, *I say*, and willing rather to be absent from the body, and to be present with the Lord."** As soon as the saved person dies there is absolutely nothing keeping the soul and spirit of that person from Jesus Christ. The Scripture says in John 12:32, **"And I, if I be lifted up from the earth, will draw all *men* unto me."** There will be a force exerted upon that soul and spirit that draws them into the bosom of Jesus Christ. That is the pull from the "heavenly" we talked about earlier. That person is transported to the third heaven like a shot from a gun.

Here is the sad part of this treatise. When the unsaved person dies, the earthly cords are still connected. As soon as his soul and spirit are released from the decaying flesh, the earth begins to take that soul and spirit down. Gravity takes him to the center of the earth where there is no up or down, no east or west, no more time, and no way out. The angels escorted Lazarus to Paradise, but the rich man didn't need an escort. Gravity took him to hell. As long as an unsaved man is alive, his physical body keeps him from being pulled (by gravity) down into hell. It's similar to walking on deep snow with snow shoes – get rid of the snow shoes and you sink into the snow. When the Red Sea enclosed upon Pharaoh and his army, the Scripture says, **"Pharaoh's chariots and his host hath he cast into the sea: his chosen captains also are drowned in the Red sea. The depths have covered them: they sank into the bottom as a stone"** (Ex. 15:4-5). The disembodied soul and spirit would be just like Pharaoh in the Red Sea. It would sink to the bottom (center of earth) like a stone. The Scripture says in Prov. 30:15-16 **"...There are three *things that* are never satisfied, *yea,* four *things* say not, *It is* enough: The grave; and the barren womb; the earth *that* is not filled with water; and the fire *that* saith not, *It is* enough."** The fires of hell will never be quenched. Prov. 27:20 says, **"Hell and destruction are never full; so the eyes of man are never satisfied."** Hell is always looking for more inhabitants and it will never be full or satisfied. Isa. 5:14 – **"Therefore hell hath enlarged herself, and opened her mouth without measure: and their glory, and their multitude, and their pomp, and he that rejoiceth, shall descend into it."**

Thank God for Calvary and the atonement Christ made on the cross. The Psalmist said, **"For great *is* thy** mercy toward me: and thou hast delivered my soul from the lowest hell" (Psm. 86:13). 2 Pet. 3:9 – "The Lord is not slack concerning his promise, as some men count slackness; but is longsuffering to us-ward, not willing that any should perish, but that all should come to repentance." Now is the time to make things right with Jesus Christ if you don't know Him as your Savior. *You do not want to be released from your body without knowing Christ.* Come to Him now. The Bible says in Rom. 10:13, **"For whosoever shall call upon the name of the Lord shall be saved."** If you don't know Christ as Savior, please bow your head and ask Him to forgive you of your sin and save your soul right now.

CHAPTER FIFTEEN

THE NECESSITY OF CHRIST'S APPOINTMENT IN HELL

Introduction

THE WORD OF GOD CONTAINS MANY areas of concentration that should concern those of us who are part of the Body of Christ. Prophecy, typology, character studies, and eschatology are some chief areas of interest to many Christians when it comes to Bible study. However, there are certain fields of study of which every Christian should have a clear understanding. When we first get saved there should be an inborn interest in learning all about the Lord. Peter said in 1 Pet. 2:2, **"As newborn babes, desire the sincere milk of the word, that ye may grow thereby:"** The subject of Redemption is one area in which we all need to be grounded. What is the basis of our redemption? The history? The types? The Person? The details? And so forth. Jesus Christ's redemptive work on the cross, including the

216

shedding of His precious blood, His three days and nights in the heart of the earth, His resurrection, and His trip to the Heavenly Tabernacle (John 20:17 and Heb. 9:12-14) were enough to complete the eternal redemption of our souls. He took our sins with Him when He died. When He came up from the grave the sins were gone. What happened to them? Where are they? Will they ever come back? What did Christ do with them? The purpose of this paper is to answer these questions and shed light on a particular aspect of this whole redemptive process; specifically, The Necessity of Christ's Appointment in Hell.

Hell

When our Lord died on the cross He spent three days and three nights in the heart of the earth (Mat. 12:40). At that time "hell" consisted of at least two compartments. We learn from Luke 16 some details about those two sections of hell. One was called "Paradise" or "Abraham's Bosom" and the other was the "fire and torment" side of hell. There are those who believe that Christ only went to the Paradise side during his visit to the heart of the earth. It is the purpose of this paper to prove the great importance and necessity as well as the reality of His visit to *both* sections of hell.

The word for "hell" in the Scripture refers to "the grave" or the "place where the dead go." We learn from Scripture study that hell is divided into at least two parts (Luke 16). One side known as Paradise or Abraham's Bosom is where the Old Testament saints went when they died. Of course their bodies were in a grave corrupting and their spirit and soul went to this place. The unsaved went into the side of hell with fire, torments, and thirst. David prayed in Psm. 16:10, **"For thou wilt not leave my soul in hell; neither wilt thou suffer thine Holy One to see corruption."** The "hell" David spoke of was not the fire, torment, and tongue-gnawing pain side of hell, but rather Abraham's Bosom.

There is another section of hell found in 2 Pet. 2:4, **"For if God spared not the angels that sinned, but cast** *them* **down to hell, and delivered** *them* **into chains of darkness, to be reserved unto judgment;"** The Greek word for, "hell" in this verse is "tartaros," which means "the deepest abyss of hell." Everywhere else in the Old and New Testaments "hell" is translated from either "sheol," "hades," or "gehenna." 2 Pet. 2:4 is the only place where the word is translated from "tartarus." These angels that kept not their first estate were placed in a separate compartment of hell unlike the two sections mentioned in Luke 16.

The rationale for the "Paradise Only idea" came from the erroneous notion that Christ preached to the saints in Paradise for three days and did not need to preach to the occupants of the hell fire side because they couldn't be saved anyway. And since Christ didn't need preach there, there was no need for Him to go there.

In our argument that Christ did in fact go there, we will look at multiple passages of Scripture. We will look at typology, prophecy, parables, as well as the study of various subject matter having to do with Christ's activities for the three days and nights of His passion. We will show beyond any shadow of doubt that *Jesus Christ did indeed go into the fires of hell* during His time in the heart of the earth. We will show further, that if He did not go into the fires of hell, our redemption is not complete and His work was unfinished. Let me say before we get into the proof that Jesus Christ was victorious in His work on the cross. His redemption is complete and eternal.

Water

We read in Luke 16 that there is no water in hell. The

rich man requested that Lazarus **"dip the tip of his finger in water, and cool my tongue; for I am tormented in this flame"** (Luke 16:24). Joseph is the most complete type of Christ in Scripture. Joseph's brothers threw him into a pit until a company of Ishmeelites riding camels showed up on their way to Egypt. In the narrative we find in Gen. 37:24 the Holy Spirit includes a seemingly meaningless point regarding the lack of water in the pit. **"And they took him, and cast him into a pit: and the pit was empty, there was no water in it."** Samson was also a type of Christ. In Jud. 15:18 the Scripture says, **"And he was sore athirst, and called on the LORD, and said, Thou hast given this great deliverance into the hand of thy servant: and now shall I die for thirst, and fall into the hand of the uncircumcised?"** Psm. 69 is a Messianic Psalm and speaks of Christ suffering on the cross. In verse 21 we read, **"They gave me also gall for my meat; and in my thirst they gave me vinegar to drink."** Jeremiah was a type of Christ (Mat. 16:13-14). In Jer. 37-38 Jeremiah was sent to the land of Benjamin and ended up in prison. While in prison he was in two different compartments: the court of the prison and the dungeon. The dungeon was the lowest part and was filled with mire. Another characteristic about the dungeon was that "there was no water" there (38:6). In Christ's suffering on Calvary's cross He cried out, **"I thirst"** in John 19:28.

These are all references to a lack of water in the hell-fire side of the heart of the earth. We have types of Christ that are suffering in places where there is no water.

The Fire of the Offerings

From the beginning of the time when God dealt with man there have been burnt offerings for sin. In Genesis 4 we are told of Cain's and Abel's offerings. One was accepted and one rejected. The accepted offering from Abel was a firstling from his flock (4:4). While it does not say it was put on an altar and burned, the implication is present. That is the standard throughout the Old Testament. When the Lord commanded Abraham to take his son Isaac to the land of Moriah to offer him for a burnt offering in Gen. 22, he took three things: a knife, wood, and fire (22:6). The fire is, of course to *burn the offering*. This was a very clear picture of God the Father offering His Son as an offering for sin.

When God revealed Himself to Job in the presence of Eliphaz, Bildad, Zophar, and Elihu in Job 42:8 He said, **"Therefore take unto you now seven bullocks and seven rams, and go to my servant Job, and offer up for yourselves a burnt offering; and my servant Job shall pray for you:"** When Noah disembarked from the Ark, the first thing he did is found in Genesis 8:20, 21 – **"And Noah builded an altar unto the LORD; and took of every clean beast, and of every clean fowl, and offered burnt offerings on the altar. And the LORD smelled a sweet savour;"** The Lord would not have smelled the sweet savor if the offering had not gone into the fire of the altar. Then later God gave Moses the Law, which included all the burnt offerings: The Burnt Offering (Lev. 1), the Meat Offering (Lev. 2), the Peace Offering (Lev. 3), the Sin Offering (Lev. 4), and the trespass Offering (Lev. 5). All of these offerings went into the fire on the altar. The brazen altar was a picture of the eternal fires of hell. It was to burn continually and never go out (Lev. 6:13). The countless innocent animals whose innocent blood was shed were all pictures of a sinless and innocent Christ paying a sin debt for those who are guilty. If the animal's blood was shed, but it did not go into the fire the offering was incomplete and no redemption resulted. Did Jesus Christ visit the hell fire and brimstone section of hell during His three days and three nights? Absolutely!

Serpents and Worms

In Num. 21 we read about the serpent of brass that Moses made and put on a pole. The person bitten by a serpent only had to behold the serpent of brass and he lived. In John 3:14 we read, **"And as Moses lifted up the serpent in the wilderness, even so must the Son of man be lifted up:"** Here the Lord Jesus is likened to a serpent. In Psm. 22:6 (Messianic Psalm) the Scripture says, **"But I am a worm, and no man; a reproach of men, and despised of the people."** Here Christ likens Himself to a worm. These passages depict Jesus Christ when He became sin for mankind. Read and compare the following verses: Isa. 14:11 – **"Thy pomp is brought down to the grave, *and* the noise of thy viols: the worm is spread under thee, and the worms cover thee."** Isa. 66:24 – **"And they shall go forth, and look upon the carcases of the men that have transgressed against me: for their worm shall not die, neither shall their fire be quenched; and they shall be an abhorring unto all flesh."** Job 7:5 – **"My flesh is clothed with worms and clods of dust; my skin is broken, and become loathsome."** Job 21:26 – **"They shall lie down alike in the dust, and the worms shall cover them."** Mark 9:44, 46, 48 – **"Where their worm dieth not, and the fire is not quenched."**

When we read these verses we get a sense of what hell is like. These passages give us the picture that hell is like a big pile of maggots crawling all over each other and burning in a fire. If you didn't get that picture, you need to read them again carefully. When Christ became sin for us, He became a serpent and/or a worm and became part of this scene. Just to make sure we get the picture the Holy Spirit repeated the same verse three times (Mark 9:44, 46, 48).

Simon Peter wrote, **"Who his own self bare our sins in his own body on the tree, that we, being dead to**

sins, should live unto righteousness: by whose stripes ye were healed" (1 Pet. 2:24). Christ bore our sins in His own body. When His body died, it was placed in a tomb for three days and did not decay (corruption did not take place because Christ was sinless). What happened to those sins that He bore? The sins of mankind He took with Him into the heart of the earth where the fires of hell burn. Isaiah 53:10 says, **"Yet it pleased the LORD to bruise him; he hath put** *him* **to grief: when thou shalt make his soul an offering for sin, he shall see** *his* **seed, he shall prolong** *his* **days, and the pleasure of the LORD shall prosper in his hand."** Remember, the offering is not complete until it goes into the fire. When Christ was resurrected, He was no longer carrying those sins. The sins of the ages were "off-loaded" in the fires of hell.

Let's say that when you trusted Christ as your Savior you made a trade. He gave you a coat of righteousness to wear and you gave Him your coat of unrighteousness to wear. The theological term for this is imputation. When the Lord Jesus became our sin, He wore that sin like a coat of unrighteousness. When He went into the fires of hell as our sin offering, He left that coat there to burn for all eternity. Now let's look at some passages of Scripture that strangely support this concept: Remember Joseph is a strong type of Christ. When his brethren sold him for twenty pieces of silver he was wearing a coat of many colors (Gen. 37:3). When they threw him into the pit (with no water) *they took his coat away from him.* Later Joseph worked for Potiphar and became his household overseer. His master's wife tried to seduce him and in order to get away, he had *to leave his garment there* (Gen. 39). In Mark's gospel there is an unknown young man (some think it was Mark) who followed Jesus. In chapter 14 when Christ as abducted by the mob a strange occurrence takes place: **"And they all forsook him, and fled. And there followed him a certain young man, having a linen cloth cast about** *his* **naked** *body***; and the young men laid hold** on him: And he left the linen cloth, and fled from them naked" (14:50-52). The young man in his haste to escape, *left his garment* with his pursuers. When Christ was crucified the Roman soldiers *took His garments*, "Then the soldiers, when they had crucified Jesus, took his garments..." (John 19:23). In Lev. 13 we are given many details about leprosy. There are specific instructions for a garment that is suspected to contain the dreaded disease. If leprosy is found in the garment (leprosy is a type of sin) it is to be *cast into the fire*. "And if it appear still in the garment, either in the warp, or in the woof, or in any thing of skin; it *is* a spreading *plague*: thou shalt burn that wherein the plague *is* with fire" (Lev. 13:57). This concept is supported when we get to the New Testament in Jude 1:23, "And others save with fear, pulling *them* out of the fire; hating even the garment spotted by the flesh." When we get to Daniel 3 we find a remarkable passage which factors into this discussion: Shadrach, Meshach, and Abednego were condemned to go into the fiery furnace. They were bound when they went into the fire (Dan. 3:24). Nebuchadnezzar witnessed four men walking in the midst of the fire (vs. 25) "and the form of the fourth is like the Son of God." When they came out of the fire they were not burned, yet the ropes that bound them were burned off. Think about this in light of the facts given above. Jesus Christ already had "furnace experience" prior to Calvary. Additionally, He has the power to determine what gets burned and what doesn't get touched in the conflagration. The ropes were consumed in the fire, but not the flesh of the men who were bound!

Finally, we have a passage tucked away in Job that brings all this together. Among other things, Job is a picture of someone suffering unjustly: "And now my soul is poured out upon me; the days of affliction have taken hold upon me. My bones are pierced in me in the night season: and my sinews take no rest. By the great force *of my disease* is my garment changed: it bindeth me about as the collar of my coat. He hath cast me into the mire, and I am become like dust and ashes. I cry unto thee, and thou dost not hear me: I stand up, and thou regardest me *not*. Thou art become cruel to me: with thy strong hand thou opposest thyself against me" (Job 30:16-31). In this passage we find a picture of Christ on the cross suffering:

His soul is "poured out" (Isa. 53:12). His "bones are pierced," not broken (John 19:36). *His "garment" has "changed."* His own garments were taken by the soldiers and now He wears a garment associated with disease and sin (Lev. 13). Regarding this garment, **"it bindeth me about as the collar of my coat."** Shadrach, Meshach, and Abednego were bound and cast into the fiery furnace, **"Then these men were bound in their coats... and were cast into the midst of the burning fiery furnace"** (Dan. 3:21). While in the fire, the ropes burned, but not their flesh.

To summarize, when Jesus Christ died on the cross and His soul and spirit went down into the heart of the earth, He "wore" a garment much like the leprous garment mentioned in Lev. 13:57 above. That garment represented all the sin of mankind. He went directly into the fires of hell to make the once and for all payment for sin (Rom. 6:23). He left that garment of sin there where it burns today. If He did not go into the fires of the damned, then what did He do with that garment representing our sin? He did not bring it back in His resurrection. There is only one place He could have taken it.

Christ's Cup in the Garden

On the night in which He was betrayed, our Lord prayed in the garden. All four gospels record this event, giving it great significance. Prior to His prayer was the Last Supper. The careful reader will note that Christ did not eat or drink anything because He was fasting. He divided the contents of His cup among the twelve Mat. 26:27-29, Mark 14:22-23, Luke 22:17-18. Christ uses His cup as an object lesson for His disciples in Luke 22:20, **"Likewise also the cup after supper, saying, This cup *is* the new testament in my blood, which is shed for you."** The next cup mentioned is a figurative cup that was the subject of Christ's prayer in the Garden of Gethsemane. That same cup is mentioned in all four gospels, again very significant. Mat. 26:39 – **"And he went a little further, and fell on his face, and prayed, saying, O my Father, if it be possible, let this cup pass from me: nevertheless not as I will, but as thou *wilt*."** Luke 22:42 – **"Saying, Father, if thou be willing, remove this cup from me: nevertheless not my will, but thine, be done."** Mark 14:36 – **"And he said, Abba, Father, all things *are* possible unto thee; take away this cup from me: nevertheless not what I will, but what thou wilt."** John 18:11 **"Then said Jesus unto Peter, Put up thy sword into the sheath: the cup which my Father hath given me, shall I not drink it?"**

This cup that the Father gave to His beloved Son was a source of great consternation for the Lord Jesus. Christ prayed three times that it might pass from Him and added each time, **"nevertheless not as I will, but as thou wilt."** All along He knew He would "drink" the contents of that cup, but He wasn't looking forward to it. Why? What did the cup represent?

Some believe the cup represented His death by crucifixion, which was a very painful way to die. That might be true if Christ were a mortal man. Whatever the cup represented, it wasn't merely a painful death. Christ came to die a painful death. From a child He knew what His mission was. Luke 2:49 – **"And he said unto them, How is it that ye sought me? wist ye not that I must be about my Father's business?"**

No, this cup was something much more significant than death. This cup affected the Lord enough to cause Him to "sweat great drops of blood." This cup was the subject of the Messianic Psalm 22, when Christ cried out, **"My God, my God, why hast thou forsaken me? Why art thou so far from helping me, and from the words of my roaring? O my God, I cry in the daytime, but thou hearest not; and in the night season, and am not silent...But I am a worm, and no man; a reproach of men, and despised of the people."** This cup represented the point when Jesus Christ became sin ("I am a worm") and entered into the torments of hell. God the Father had to forsake Him and turn His back on His beloved Son during this time. There had never been a time when the Father's face was not toward His son until this time. In Prov. 8 there is a passage that gives us a glimpse of the eternal relationship between God the Father and God the Son: **"The LORD possessed me in the beginning of his way, before his works of old. I was set up from everlasting, from the beginning, or ever the earth was. When *there were* no depths, I was brought forth; when *there were* no fountains abounding with water. Before the mountains were settled, before the hills was I brought forth: While as yet he had not made the earth, nor the fields, nor the highest part of the dust of the world. When he prepared the heavens, I *was* there: when he set a compass upon the face of the depth: When he established the clouds above: when he strengthened the fountains of the deep: When he gave to the sea his decree, that the waters should not pass his commandment: when he appointed the foundations of the earth: Then I was by him, *as* one brought up *with him*: and I was daily *his* delight, rejoicing always before him; Rejoicing in the habitable part of his earth; and my delights *were* with the sons of men"** (Prov. 8:22-31).

For the first time in all eternity there would be an interruption in the relationship between the Father and Son of the Godhead. But His prayer ended with, **"not my will, but thine, be done."** There is nowhere that Christ could have gone other than the fires and torments of hell that would have brought about such a reaction upon the Son of God.

The Sting of Death

Paul wrote, **"O death, where is thy sting? O grave, where is thy victory? The sting of death is sin; and the strength of sin is the law. But thanks be to God, which giveth us the victory through our Lord Jesus Christ"** (1 Cor. 15:55-57). The "sting of death is sin," Paul points out. In Rom. 6:23 he says more about this death, **"For the wages of sin *is* death; but the gift of God *is* eternal life through Jesus Christ our Lord."** The death that Paul speaks of isn't the simple death of the flesh at the end of life. It is the "second death," which is the opposite of "eternal life through Jesus Christ." Rev. 20:14 – **"And death and hell were cast into the lake of fire. This is the second death."**

When Jesus Christ entered into the fire-and-torments-side of hell and resurrected Himself with a Glorified Body, He conquered death and hell, removing its sting forever. If He had only gone into the Paradise side of hell this would never have happened.

Another Dungeon

Earlier we made reference to the dungeon in the "Water" segment of this paper. There is another dungeon mentioned in Scripture that should be mentioned in this study. The book of Lamentations is (among other things) a picture of the sufferings of hell. We read: **"They have cut off my life in the dungeon, and cast a stone upon me.**

Waters flowed over mine head; *then* **I said, I am cut off. I called upon thy name, O LORD, out of the low dungeon"** (Lam. 3:53-55). This passage smacks of Jonah 2 and Psm. 69. Both of these Scripture references have to do with the suffering of the Savior. It should be noted here that Christ did suffer on the cross before He went into the heart of the earth. However He was not finished with His suffering. The worst of it came when He entered into the fires of hell and torments as depicted by the references given above.

"They have cut off my life in the dungeon, and cast a stone upon me," (Lam 3:53). Here again is the dungeon that typifies the suffering or hell-fire side of the heart of the earth (Jer. 38). **"They have cut off my life"** indicates death. **"Waters flowed over mine head,"** is part of this eternal suffering found in the two passages given. Psm. 69:1-3 − **"Save me, O God; for the waters are come in unto** *my* **soul. I sink in deep mire, where** *there is* **no standing: I am come into deep waters, where the floods overflow me. I am weary of my crying: my throat is dried: mine eyes fail while I wait for my God." Verse 15 says, "Let not the waterflood overflow me, neither let the deep swallow me up, and let not the pit shut her mouth upon me."**

The **"waters flowed over mine head"** in Lam. 3 also speaks of Jonah. In Mat. 12:40 Christ compared His three day-three night experience *after* His death on the cross of Calvary experience with the prophet Jonah in the belly of the whale. **"For as Jonas was three days and three nights in the whale's belly; so shall the Son of man be three days and three nights in the heart of the earth."** If He had gone only to Paradise His sufferings would have been over. But they were not over. He entered into the fire and torments side of hell in order to complete His Father's business (Luke 2:49).

Jonah wrote, **"Then Jonah prayed unto the LORD his God out of the fish's belly, And said, I cried by reason of mine affliction unto the LORD, and he heard me; out of the belly of hell cried I, *and* thou heardest my voice. For thou hadst cast me into the deep, in the midst of the seas; and the floods compassed me about: all thy billows and thy waves passed over me"** (Jonah 2:1-3). Christ suffers the torments of hell in these verses. **"The waters compassed me about, *even* to the soul: the depth closed me round about, the weeds were wrapped about my head. I went down to the bottoms of the mountains; the earth with her bars *was* about me for ever:"** (2:5-6). **"Even to the soul"** (regarding His suffering) in verse 5: Christ's body was in the tomb up on the surface of the earth at this time. **"The earth with her bars was about me forever"** – the "bars" in this verse speak of imprisonment with no escape. Jesus Christ spoke to Simon Peter in Mat. 16:18 and gave us additional information about hell when He said, **"And I say also unto thee, That thou art Peter, and upon this rock I will build my church; and the *gates of hell* shall not prevail against it."** So hell has bars and gates as do most prisons, but Christ was in possession of the keys of hell and death according to Rev. 1:1.

If Christ did only visit Paradise and not the hell fire section of hell, then His comparison with Himself to Jonah's three days and nights in the belly of the whale makes no sense. There definitely was no suffering going on in Abraham's Bosom (Luke16).

Summary

There is more Scripture to support the fact that Christ did indeed enter into the fire and torments side of hell during His time in the heart of the earth. We have covered more than enough passages to eliminate any question to the fact.

Paul wrote, **"For he hath made him *to be* sin for us, who knew no sin; that we might be made the righteousness of God in him"** (2 Cor. 5:21). When Jesus Christ died on the cross (at approximately 3 PM on Wednesday of Passion Week) His Soul and Spirit left His body and allowed gravity to take Him directly to the fires of hell. While there He preached condemnation to the damned, **"By which also he went and preached unto the spirits in prison; Which sometime were disobedient, when once the longsuffering of God waited in the days of Noah, while the ark was a preparing, wherein few, that is, eight souls were saved by water"** (1 Pet. 3:19-20). Afterwards, He unlocked the gates with His keys, let Himself out, and then locked the gate once again (Rev. 1:18). Then Christ bridged "the great gulf" that separated Paradise from the hell and torments side. While in Abraham's Bosom AKA Paradise, He preached deliverance (Luke 4:18) to the Old Testament saints, **"For this cause was the gospel preached also to them that are dead, that they might be judged according to men in the flesh, but live according to God in the spirit"** (1 Pet. 4:6). After this, Christ used His keys again and unlocked the door to Abraham's Bosom and led the occupants of Paradise from the heart of the earth to Glory (2 Cor. 12:4) where it is today. Eph. 4:8-10 says, **"Wherefore he saith, When he ascended up on high, he led captivity captive, and gave gifts unto men. (Now that he ascended, what is it but that he also descended first into the lower parts of the earth? He that descended is the same also that ascended up far above all heavens, that he might fill all things.)"** Paul wrote, **"We are confident, *I say*, and willing rather to be absent from the body, and to be present with the Lord"** (2 Cor. 5:8). **"The grace of our Lord Jesus Christ *be* with you all. Amen"** (Rev. 22:21).

CHAPTER SIXTEEN

MARRIAGE DIVORCE AND SCRIPTURE

Introduction

ONE OF THE MOST CONTROVERSIAL subjects alive among God's people today is the subject of marriage, divorce, and remarriage. The confusing thing is that for each opposing position there are Bible verses to support their claims to truth. So what makes this treatise different? Please keep reading.

The important thing to remember as we begin this study is a dispensational truth. We live in the dispensation of grace and not Old Testament Mosaic law. We were born *after* the resurrection of Jesus Christ. The veil was torn in twain when Christ came up from the grave. I do not require a priest to intercede for me before God. I can come boldly before the throne of grace and have an audience with the Son of God Himself. I am writing this paper for those who have trusted Jesus Christ as Savior. If you are that person your sins are gone. They are forgiven. Your sins were placed on Jesus Christ on the cross. In return, He gave you His righteousness (Rom. 3). The burden and guilt of sin are both gone. Picture this as a transaction between you and the Savior. You gave Him the filthy and vile coat of sin that you wore. He took His coat of righteousness and gave it to you. He put on your garment of sin and you donned His coat of righteousness. You will wear that coat forever. Even though we drop the ball and sin we still wear that coat of righteousness.

Jesus said, **"Come unto me, all *ye* that labour and are heavy laden, and I will give you rest..."** (Mat. 11:28). There are still people out there preaching the "Good Works Gospel" rather than Paul's Gospel of the Grace of God.

Simply put, this works Gospel binds the Christian under heavy burdens and grievous to be borne as did the scribes and Pharisees, mentioned in Mat. 23:4. One of the main tools of the preacher of works-rather-than-grace is guilt. The church member is shamed for not attending all the services or not doing this or that. If a woman comes to church wearing slacks instead of a dress, then she simply "doesn't love the Lord like we do" – shame on her. You must be baptized by a certain preacher in a particular fashion or you are not really saved. You must attend church on a certain day of the week or you may or may not utilize musical instruments in church. If a young man or woman is unfortunate enough to experience a divorce early in his or her life, he or she must remain single and celibate for the remainder of their life if they want to please the Lord. If you don't live a good clean life you lose your salvation. Do this, don't do that, works, works, works, it's all up to you, not Jesus. Length of hair, dress codes, rules, regulations, etc. This is not the Gospel of the Grace of God. Paul wrote to the churches of Galatia to remind them they are free from the law, in Christ. After salvation they went back to the rules and regulations of Moses. **In Christ, you are free from bondage!** You can lay those heavy burdens down at the feet of Jesus. He wants them. Give them to Him and enjoy His freedom. You don't have to feel guilty about whatever it is you've been made to feel guilty about.

The reader should understand that so much of this type of twisted theology is inculcated into the writings of many who address the subject of marriage, divorce, and remarriage. If you are saved by the Grace of God, you are free in Christ. The Lord is not the author of a life of misery and strife.

Notwithstanding in or out of God's plan, things don't always work out the way people hope and couples end up in the divorce court. Sadly, the Body of Christ is not without its share of divorce. This is not a happy time for these people. If there was ever a time a Christian needed a friend it's during a divorce. Yet, in many of our churches these people are looked down on by others and singled out for the silent treatment. While this is not the purpose of this paper, I will take the time to encourage Christians to support your brothers and sisters in Christ who are going through a divorce. It is an extremely difficult time in their lives and they need the love and support of the Body of Christ.

The title of this paper is Marriage, Divorce, and Scripture. I want to first address a worldly definition of marriage before we define what the Scriptural says about it. Divorce and remarriage are the same in either realm. The hurt and disappointment of divorce are also the same. Again, the ideal is for a couple to get married and stay married to each other for the long term. Since we live in a cursed world of sin and Satan never takes a day off, about half of all marriages end up in the divorce court.

Legal Definition of Marriage

In our modern society and within the laws of the

land, a "marriage" is a legal ceremony. This is the way it is throughout most of the world today. A man and a woman fall in love, a date is set, plans are made, rings are purchased, application for license is submitted, arrangements are made for one or more cakes, photographs, live music, tuxedos and gowns, food, invitations, the proper venue, and so on. Finally the date arrives and the event takes place. An officiate of some sort, whether a judge, justice of the peace, minister, priest, ship's captain, or whatever conducts a ceremony in which the engaged couple exchanges vows and rings. The officiate pronounces them husband and wife and a legal document is signed and witnessed so everything is legal and proper. From that point on the couple is married in the eyes of the world.

During the marriage ceremony the man and woman vow faithfulness to each other "till death do we part." The man and woman are entering wedlock for the remainder of their lives by taking an oath and making holy vows. The ideal situation is for these two to stay in love with each other until death parts them.

The Christian is under an obligation to abide by the laws of the land according to Rom. 13:1-7 just as any other citizen. Therefore in order to be legally married, a Christian couple should follow the laws of the land to be properly married. And why not? It is a time of celebration, joy, and fulfillment. God's people have an advantage that the unsaved don't. A Christian is the temple of the Holy Spirit. As a child of God we have access to power that the world knows nothing about. But in spite of all this problems can arise and a happy home can end up on the rocks. Later on in this paper we will talk more about the vows mentioned in the Legal definition of marriage.

Scriptural Marriage

We looked at the legal definition of marriage, now let us consider what the Bible says about marriage. We need to plainly understand the difference between the two. They are not the same.

Definitions – The first thing we need to do is define exactly what we are talking about. We need some benchmarks and solid ground on which to stand. We now enter the realm of semantics. Words and meanings of words change over time. As stated in the front of this paper we use the Authorized Version for all Scripture reference. The King James translators did their work in the 1600's, which is well over 400 years ago. Some word meanings change over the course of time. In 1600 AD the word "gay" meant something altogether different than what it means today. So when we use words like "marriage" and "divorce" which come from a text that is over 400 years old, we should make certain that we understand exactly what the translators (and the Holy Spirit) were talking about.

Marry/Marriage – The law of first mention in Scripture is usually a trustworthy method of determining a word's meaning. The first mention of "marry" is found in Gen. 38:8, **"And Judah said unto Onan, Go in unto thy brother's wife, and marry her, and raise up seed to thy brother."** By reading the passage it should be obvious what the word means. There was no ceremony with candles, flowers, photos, cakes, rings, tuxedos, food, etc. Onan was instructed by his father to "marry" his brother's widow. That meant Onan was to become sexually intimate with her and raise up seed for his deceased brother. She would, from then on, be his "wife." Therefore the definition of "marriage" in the Bible is a man and a woman joining flesh with flesh. This simple definition follows suite from Genesis to Revelation.

Another example of Bible marriage is found in Deut.

235

21:10-13: " **When thou goest forth to war against thine enemies, and the LORD thy God hath delivered them into thine hands, and thou hast taken them captive, And seest among the captives a beautiful woman, and hast a desire unto her, that thou wouldest have her to thy wife; Then thou shalt bring her home to thine house; and she shall shave her head, and pare her nails; And she shall put the raiment of her captivity from off her, and shall remain in thine house, and bewail her father and her mother a full month: and after that thou shalt go in unto her, and be her husband, and she shall be thy wife.**" In this passage it is when the man goes "in unto her" that he becomes her husband and she becomes his wife. Again, it is the physical union of flesh joining flesh that constitutes a Bible marriage.

Another example of Bible marriage is found in Gen. 24 when Abraham's servant brought Rebekah to Isaac. "**For she** *had* **said unto the servant, What man** *is* **this that walketh in the field to meet us? And the servant** *had* **said, It** *is* **my master: therefore she took a vail, and covered herself. And the servant told Isaac all things that he had done. And Isaac brought her into his mother Sarah's tent, and took Rebekah, and she became his wife; and he loved her: and Isaac was comforted after his mother's** *death*.**" (Gen 24:65-67). There is no marriage ceremony in the text. Isaac simply took Rebekah into his mother's tent and the two became one flesh – husband and wife.

There are marriage feasts found in Scripture since it is a time of great celebration. In Mat. 22 we read the parable about a certain king which invited people to come to the "marriage" of his son. This was a feast celebrating the marriage event. The actual "marriage" (flesh joining flesh) took place in private. This same rule applies to John 2 when the Lord Jesus and His disciples were called to the marriage.

This was a feast to celebrate the couple who are going to marry. The actual marriage took place privately in the bedroom when they jointed flesh with flesh. It is common in our day and time to see "unwed" couples living with each other and then at a later time get "married" in a ceremony with an officiate, family and friends, wedding rings, etc. As far as God and His word are concerned, they were "married" the first time they joined each other in sexual intimacy. They were married "legally" when they exchanged vows with a legal officiate.

Luke 17:27 - **"They did eat, they drank, they married wives, they were given in marriage, until the day that Noe entered into the ark, and the flood came, and destroyed them all."** I heard a preacher expound on this text on the radio and he said, "They ate they drank, they conducted weddings..." No, a "wedding" is a ceremony where presumably a virgin couple exchanges marriage vows. That isn't what takes place in this text. The context of the passage is one where there is no regard for God just as in Noah's day. This was a situation of revelry (Gen. 6:5, Ex. 32, Jer. 25:27, Dan. 5:4, 23) "eat, drink, and be sexually intimate with anyone and everyone," just as it will be prior to the Lord's return.

Additional support for this definition is found in Heb. 13:4, **"Marriage is honourable in all, and the bed undefiled: but whoremongers and adulterers God will judge."** Marriage has to do with the bed. In today's vernacular and understanding the verse should read, "Marriage is honorable in all and the *wedding chapel* undefiled..." But according to Scripture a marriage takes place in the bed.

Wedding – This word is used seven times in Scripture each of which refers to a marriage feast. These seven passages are found in Mat. 22, Luke 12, and Luke 14. The Law of First Mention also applies in this word definition.

The context of each passage shows a marriage feast and may or may not include a ceremony of sorts. Again, the actual "marriage" takes place before or after the marriage feast and only involves the husband and wife in private.

Wife - The first use of the word is Gen. 2:24, **"Therefore shall a man leave his father and his mother, and shall cleave unto his wife: and they shall be one flesh."** The first mention defines it again as having to do with flesh joining flesh. The next verse says, **"And they were both naked, the man and his wife, and were not ashamed."** When you find the word "wife" in Scripture, it has to do with a female sex partner. When we get to Genesis 16:3 we find a man who has two "wives." In the case of each wife, he joins flesh with flesh. **"And Sarai Abram's wife took Hagar her maid the Egyptian, after Abram had dwelt ten years in the land of Canaan, and gave her to her husband Abram to be his wife."** Sarah did not organize a wedding ceremony where vows and rings were exchanged. Remember, a Bible marriage is defined as a man and a woman who become sexually intimate or "one flesh."

Husband – This is the word used for the male partner in the intimate relationship we have spoken of thus far in this study. 1 Cor. 7:2 – **"Nevertheless, to avoid fornication, let every man have his own wife, and let every woman have her own husband."**

Divorcement – The first mention of divorcement is Deut. 24:1 – **"When a man hath taken a wife, and married her, and it come to pass that she find no favour in his eyes, because he hath found some uncleanness in her: then let him write her a bill of divorcement, and give it in her hand, and send her out of his house."** This term has to do with a wife no longer being sexually intimate with a particular husband. If a woman is "divorced" from a husband, she is no longer having sex with him and a "bill of divorcement" has been executed. A "bill of divorcement" is mentioned four times, Deut. 24:1, 3, Isa. 50:1, and Mk 10:4 and refers to a written document stating that a woman has officially been "put away" from her husband and they are no longer intimate. And, if they are no longer sexually intimate and a bill of divorcement has been issued, they are *no longer married.*

Put Away – The phrase, "put away" also has the same meaning as divorce. Mat. 5:31 – **"It hath been said, Whosoever shall put away his wife, let him give her a writing of divorcement."** If a man decides to "put away" his wife, he no longer wants sexual intimacy with her. If this happens he is admonished to give her a bill of divorcement so she will not become an adulteress.

Antitypes

Marriage and sexual intimacy constitute a "type" in Scripture. The "antitype" comes later. There are two antitypes to marriage and sexual intimacy in the Bible. In some cases marriage is a type of the relationship between God the Father and Israel. The reason the near kinsman in Ruth 4:6 could not redeem Ruth's inheritance was because he represented God the Father and His relationship with Israel. Israel is God's inheritance: Psm. 28:9, 33:12, 37:18, 68:9, 74:2, 78:62, 94:14, et al. Israel is said to be a wife that is "put away" from God in Isa. 50:1, **"Thus saith the LORD, Where is the bill of your mother's divorcement, whom I have put away? or which of my creditors is it to whom I have sold you? Behold, for your iniquities have ye sold yourselves, and for your transgressions is your mother put away."** Isa. 54:5 – **"For thy Maker is thine husband; the LORD of hosts is his name; and thy Redeemer the Holy One of Israel..."** See also Jer. 3:1 and 31:32. The Book of Hosea is a picture of the relationship between God the Father and Israel. She has committed spiritual adultery with her idolatry and has been given a bill of divorcement by God. Hos. 2:2 – **"Plead with your mother, plead: for she is <u>not my wife, neither am I her husband</u>: let her therefore put away her whoredoms out of her sight, and her adulteries from between her breasts..."** The intimacy is gone for the present, but it will return at the Second Advent (Hos. 2:14-23). This passage shows that when a bill of divorcement has been executed there is no longer a marriage. There are those who believe and preach that if a couple have been legally divorced they are still married. In the passage sited above which is God the Father Himself speaking about His former wife (who is divorced), **"... she is not my wife, neither am I her husband."** Keep this in mind because later in this paper this comes up again with respect to qualifications for bishop and deacon. Again, if there is a writing of divorcement, the two parties are *no longer married.*

The other antitype is of course Jesus Christ and the Church (Rev. 19). Paul calls this a mystery in Eph. 5:29-33 – **"For no man ever yet hated his own flesh; but nourisheth and cherisheth it, even as the Lord the church: For we are members of his body, of his flesh, and of his bones. For this cause shall a man leave his father and mother, and shall be joined unto his wife, and they two shall be one flesh. This is a great mystery: but I speak concerning Christ and the church. Nevertheless let every one of you in particular so love his wife even as himself; and the wife see that she reverence her husband."**

One Flesh

The intimacy spoken of in Gen. 2:24 previously quoted, **"...and they shall be one flesh"** is a picture of our relationship with Jesus Christ. Paul said, **"Know ye not that your bodies are the members of Christ? Shall I then take** the members of Christ, and make them the members of an harlot? God forbid. What? Know ye not that he which is joined to an harlot is one body? For two, saith he, shall be one flesh" (1 Cor. 6:15-16). Here again, flesh joining flesh in sexual intercourse constitutes a marriage. In verse 16 above Paul refers to Gen. 2:24, **"Therefore shall a man leave his father and his mother, and shall cleave unto his wife: and they shall be one flesh."** Therefore if a man has sex with a woman they become "one flesh" and they are married in the Bible sense.

Illustration: If a married man goes out of town to a business convention, has too many drinks and has sex with a strange woman, he has become an adulterous polygamist with two wives. Further, if a married man looks at a woman and lusts after her, he has just become one flesh with her, which constitutes a marriage. He has also become an adulterous polygamist with two wives. **"But I say unto you, That whosoever looketh on a woman to lust after her hath committed adultery with her already in his heart"** (Mat. 5:28). According to Jesus Christ, lusting after a woman constitutes a marriage in the Biblical sense of the word.

Misunderstanding

Now that we have a Biblical understanding of what marriage, adultery, and divorce are, let's take a look at some of the popular passages of Scripture used to support the erroneous concepts foisted upon Christian congregations in our modern age.

Mat. 19:9 – **"And I say unto you, Whosoever shall put away his wife, except it be for fornication, and shall marry another, committeth adultery: and whoso marrieth her which is put away doth commit adultery."** This is one of the most misinterpreted verses in Scripture. Let's take a closer look:

First of all this passage is directed at Jews living under the Mosaic Law during the Tribulation and not specifically for Christians. However, with respect to marriage and divorce the truths of these passages still hold true. So, for the sake of correct exegesis and semantics, we'll continue. **"Except it be for fornication,"** Fornication is one of the grounds for divorce according to Mat. 5:32 and Mat. 19:9. If you put away your wife for reasons other than adultery, or in other words, if you stop having sex with her and begin having sex with some other woman ("and shall marry another"), you are committing adultery. No bill of divorcement has been issued. He's "stepping out on her" and the Bible calls it adultery. **"And whoso marrieth her which is put away doth commit adultery."** By not giving her a bill of divorcement after she's been put away, the husband causes her to commit adultery when she finds another man. In plainer words, the bill of divorcement officially terminates the marriage and the two are no longer married. Let me put this another way: If she receives the bill of divorcement, *she is no longer his wife.* Therefore the woman (single and unmarried) can marry someone else legally. See also Deut. 24:1, 3, Isa. 50:1, Mat. 5:31, Mark 10:2-6. The bill of divorcement is her legal ticket for remarriage.

The popular **incorrect** interpretation of this passage (in modern terms) is the following: If you get a divorce and remarry, you are an adulterer. If you marry a divorced woman, you are an adulterer. If you marry a divorced woman, you cause her to be an adulterer. It should also be noted here that this passage (Mat. 19:9) is one of the proof texts against the erroneous teaching that fornication is committed only by single, rather than married people. According to the Bible definition of marriage, if you fornicate, you are in the "marriage act." Fornication is committed by sinners whether they wear a wedding band or not.

Mark 10:11 – **"And he saith unto them, Whosoever**

shall put away his wife, and marry another, committeth adultery against her." This verse is a variation of Mat. 5:32 and 19:9. **"Whosoever shall put away his wife..."** Here, the man no longer wants to have sexual relations with the woman and "puts her away." If he gives her a bill of divorcement they both can go their separate ways and remarry without committing adultery. If he doesn't give her the bill of divorcement and has sex with another woman, he is committing adultery. If she has sex with another man without her bill of divorcement she is committing adultery as well. Remember, the bill of divorcement terminates the marriage. The common misinterpretation says that if either the man or woman gets remarried after a divorce they are committing adultery. The common misinterpretation states further that if the man remarries and the ex-wife is still alive, that he has "two living wives." Here, the reader needs to read again what God the Father said about this in Hos. 2:2.

1 Cor. 7:39 – **"The wife is bound by the law as long as her husband liveth; but if her husband be dead, she is at liberty to be married to whom she will; only in the Lord."** This passage was written to Christians by the Apostle Paul and says essentially the same thing we read back in Matthew. In this verse we read about a "wife" and a "husband." We have learned from Scripture that they are husband and wife because they are sexually intimate with each other. If the husband dies, she is free to "marry" another man. However, she is to marry "only in the Lord." That is, he must know Christ as Savior (2 Cor. 6:14).

During the days King David fled from his son, Absalom he left ten women (his concubines or wives) to look after his house. During David's absence Absalom took Ahithophel's advice and went in unto these women. The Bible says in 2 Sam. 16:22, **"So they spread Absalom a tent upon the top of the house; and Absalom went in unto his father's concubines in the sight of all Israel."** When David returned to Jerusalem after Absalom's death, **"And**

David came to his house at Jerusalem; and the king took
the ten women *his* concubines, whom he had left to keep
the house, and put them in ward, and fed them, but
went not in unto them. So they were shut up unto the
day of their death, living in widowhood." (2 Sam. 20:3).
Since these women had been defiled by his son, David put
the women away. The Bible refers to their situation as
"widowhood." Therefore, these women were no longer
married. The last man they had sex with was dead.

Grounds for Divorce

Scripture allows for divorce. Mat. 5:32 and 19:9 tell us
that if a spouse commits adultery, then the other can
scripturally put the other away. A written bill of divorcement
must follow to make it official so legal remarriage can take
place. Another reason is abandonment. Paul says in 1 Cor.
7:15, **"But if the unbelieving depart, let him depart. A
brother or a sister is not under bondage in such cases:
but God hath called us to peace."** Here, if an unsaved
spouse goes away and abandons the other marriage partner,
then that person is "not under bondage." Or in plainer words
they are not under the Mosaic Law and are free to remarry.

The Scripture says in Deut. 24:1-2 – **"When a man
hath taken a wife, and married her, and it come to pass
that she find no favour in his eyes, because he hath
found some uncleanness in her: then let him write her a
bill of divorcement, and give it in her hand, and send her
out of his house. And when she is departed out of his
house, she may go and be another man's wife."** Here,
under Mosaic Law the husband was allowed to put away his
wife because of "uncleanness," which in Numbers 5 turns out
to be adultery.

There is yet another legal reason for a divorce to take
place. This is found in Ex. 21:10-11 and as to do with an

abusive situation. **"If he take him another wife; her food, her raiment, and her duty of marriage, shall he not diminish. And if he do not these three unto her, then shall she go out free without money."** This is Mosaic Law, nevertheless it is Scriptural for our age. If the husband takes another wife (polygamy and adultery) he is to continue to supply the first wife with food, raiment, and "duty of marriage" (sexual intimacy). If he does not, she is free to leave.

There are some things that bridge the ecclesiastical Law/Grace division. Because certain laws fall under the heading of Old Testament Law they are not abrogated simply because we live in the age of Grace. If we are speaking of salvation of the soul, yes, things have changed. If we are speaking of murder, rape, abusive acts against mankind, adultery, etc. the law still stands. If a wife is the target of physical or emotional abuse from a husband as in Ex. 21 above, she has grounds for divorce. If a spouse has been unfaithful sexually, there are grounds for divorce. If these things can be worked out for good and a divorce can be avoided, then that is the best way to proceed. However that is not always the case and divorce is better than a life of physical and emotional abuse.

1 Corinthians 7

We can learn much from Paul about marriage in this chapter. However, for the purpose of this paper we will only concern ourselves with the passages that deal with divorce and remarriage. Paul encourages the Christian couple to stay together and work things out if there are problems, **"Art thou bound unto a wife? Seek not to be loosed"** (1 Cor. 7:27). Then he asks the question, **"Art thou loosed from a wife?"** Obviously, this is addressed to someone who was married but now is **"loosed from a wife"** or in other words, divorced. The answer is given for us, **"seek not a wife"** (1 Cor. 7:27). Then in verse 28 comes the disjunctive conjunction, "But…" Here's what follows: **"and if thou marry, thou hast not sinned…"** According to Paul if a man is divorced (loosed from a wife) he is encouraged not to get remarried, BUT if he does marry, **he has not sinned**. Since he *has not sinned*, then it means that remarrying after a divorce is not sin. It also means that the woman he married is his *only wife*. Additionally, if he is "loosed from a wife," it means that *she is no longer his wife*. If Paul and the Holy Spirit (ultimate Author of the text) say the man has not sinned, why do some of the brethren insist that he has?

John 4:5-26

In John 4 we find Jesus Christ sitting on a well waiting for a particular sinner to show up. The woman shows up and within a few verses she and the Lord are discussing the very topic of this treatise. In order for the woman to be saved, Jesus knew He had to deal with her sin. He went right to the heart of the matter by telling her to **"Go, call thy husband."** By using the word "husband" the Lord obviously meant her legitimate spouse, with whom she was sexually intimate. The woman knows that there is no one that fits this description, she only has men who pay for her services and replies, **"I have no husband."** Christ confirms her honesty by saying, **"Thou hast well said, I have no husband:"** (In these verses the subjects illustrate two different meanings for "husband." The first is a legitimate "husband" or spouse and the second is the male "customer" of a harlot. Both involve sexual intimacy.) Then Christ says, **"For thou hast had five husbands; and he whom thou now hast is not thy husband:"** In other words, "You have had five customers and the one you have now isn't really your husband, but just another customer." The Lord Jesus and the woman clearly understood what a husband was by the Bible text. The text in

John 4:5-26 is completely incomprehensible using the common modern-day meaning of the word, "husband." However, it is clear as a bell when we understand the Biblical meanings of these words.

Qualifications for Bishop and Deacon

Here again we come to a subject that is controversial is some circles. The meaning is clear if one understands the Bible meaning of marriage, divorce, and remarriage. The qualifications for bishop (pastor) are covered in the first seven verses of 1 Tim. 3 and deacon qualifications following in verses 8-13. We will limit our discussion to verses to that have to do with the wife of the bishop or deacon. However, it should be noted that there are 17 qualifications for bishop and 12 for deacon. Additionally we will note that the information we will cover on the wife is only one of these multiple qualifications, yet at times it gets most of the attention.

1 Tim. 3:2 – **"A bishop then must be blameless, the husband of one wife, vigilant, sober, of good behaviour, given to hospitality, apt to teach;"** One of the qualifications is that he be **"the husband of one wife."** To the chagrin of some females, a woman (according to Paul's epistle) is not qualified. Verse 12 covers the same issue for deacons. With what we have already learned in our study of Bible etymology this simple phrase should not present a problem. It simply means that the candidate for the office has only one wife and she is the one with whom he is sexually intimate. If a candidate has more than one wife they are disqualified.

Just prior to the Children of Israel entering the Promised Land, Moses spoke to them regarding rules for their future kings. He warned in Deut. 17:17, **"Neither shall he multiply wives to himself, that his heart turn not** away..." The King was not to have multiple wives because this would turn his heart away from God. Solomon was the proof: **"For it came to pass, when Solomon was old, that his wives turned away his heart after other gods: and his heart was not perfect with the LORD his God, as was the heart of David his father"** (1 Kings 11:4). The lesson which Paul understood and incorporated into the qualifications for pastor and deacon *had nothing to do with divorce or remarriage*. It had to do with the spiritual well-being of the men who held these high offices in the local church.

Let's look at some Bible characters who would have been Scripturally disqualified for the office of bishop or deacon (had they lived in this dispensation): Abraham had several wives (Gen. 16 and Gen. 25:6). Jacob had four wives (Gen. 30). Gideon had "many" wives (Jud. 8:30). Elkanah had two wives (1 Sam. 1:2). David had multiple wives (2 Sam. 5:13). Solomon had a thousand wives (1 King 11:3). In 1 Timothy 3 Paul is making a point that a polygamist (anyone with more than one wife) does not qualify for bishop or deacon.

The common erroneous interpretation says that if a man has been through a divorce and is remarried (in the modern vernacular) and his previous wife is still living, then he has "more than one wife." He is thus disqualified for the office. This is a misunderstanding of the passage covered previously. Mat. 19:9 – **"And I say unto you, Whosoever shall put away his wife, except it be for fornication, and shall marry another, committeth adultery: and whoso marrieth her which is put away doth commit adultery."** This is simply a matter of understanding Bible definitions for marriage terms and applying them properly. We have already correctly exposited these passages above. Paul says nothing at all in the passage about a divorced candidate for the office. It is clear from his writings in 1 Cor. 7 that he understands the very truths we present in this paper.

248

It should also be noted that the passages sited from Matthew and Mark (as we pointed out) are given to Jews under Mosaic Law. The Christian is not under Mosaic Law. The sins and mistakes of his past are not only forgiven, but they are forgotten (1 John 1:9). It is from Paul's writings that the Christian gets his doctrine and Paul uses the same terms as are found in Matthew and Mark (with the same meanings).

There is yet another weighty point that should be taken into consideration. We would be remiss if we did not mention the fact that God the Father has put away His "wife," Israel and is at this time divorced. **"Thus saith the LORD, Where is the bill of your mother's divorcement, whom I have put away? or which of my creditors is it to whom I have sold you? Behold, for your iniquities have ye sold yourselves, and for your transgressions is your mother put away"** (Isa. 50:1). **"For thy Maker is thine husband; the LORD of hosts is his name; and thy Redeemer the Holy One of Israel; The God of the whole earth shall he be called. For the LORD hath called thee as a woman forsaken and grieved in spirit, and a wife of youth, when thou wast refused, saith thy God"** (Isa. 54:5-6). **"They say, If a man put away his wife, and she go from him, and become another man's, shall he return unto her again? shall not that land be greatly polluted? but thou hast played the harlot with many lovers; yet return again to me, saith the LORD"** (Jer. 3:1). **"Surely as a wife treacherously departeth from her husband, so have ye dealt treacherously with me, O house of Israel, saith the LORD** (Jer. 3:20). **"Not according to the covenant that I made with their fathers in the day that I took them by the hand to bring them out of the land of Egypt; which my covenant they brake, although I was an husband unto them, saith the LORD:"** (Jer. 31:32).

Remember the passage where Christ said, **"That whosoever looketh on a woman to lust after her hath committed adultery with her already in his heart."** (Mat.

5:28). We pointed out that lust constitutes "becoming one flesh" with the woman according to Jesus Christ. Is it possible for a married man who pastors a church to have never one time ever lusted after a woman (and thus by his own definition disqualified himself from his position)? I cannot answer that. But I do know that the Grace of God covers a multitude of sin. I know that the common misunderstanding of this issue unduly discriminates against some Christians who want to serve the Lord.

Let's look at a hypothetical situation: A married man is called to preach early in his life. Later he takes the job as pastor of a local church. At some point his wife decides she does not want to be a pastor's wife and she leaves him and files for divorce. The deacons of his church ask for his resignation since he no longer qualifies as a pastor. What does he do? God called him into the pastorate. Now he has to quit his job. Did God change His mind? The Bible says in Romans 11:29, **"For the gifts and calling of God are without repentance."** What's the answer for this pastor? The man's wife abandoned him and according to 1 Cor. 7:15 and that constitutes Biblical grounds for divorce. Scripturally, the pastor does not have to resign and can continue doing what God called him to do.

Vows

I mentioned earlier in this paper that we would return and discuss vows again. A vow or an oath is a pledge or a promise to do something. In a marriage ceremony vows or oaths are made between two people. The Bible makes it plain that a vow or oath must be kept if it is uttered. The Scripture says in Num. 30:2, **"If a man vow a vow unto the LORD, or swear an oath to bind his soul with a bond; he shall not break his word, he shall do according to all that proceedeth out of his mouth."** When you get married you vow to your beloved to remain faithful until death. Therefore according to the word of God we are to "do according to all that proceedeth" out of our mouths. The verse from Numbers says "he shall not break his word." We are to follow up on what we say we will do. The message is clear – you cannot go back on an oath.

In Josh. 2 the two spies that Joshua sent into Jericho took an oath to save Rahab and her family from destruction if she would keep her mouth shut about their presence and help them make good their escape. Josh. 2:14 **"And the men answered her, Our life for yours, if ye utter not this our business. And it shall be, when the LORD hath given us the land, that we will deal kindly and truly with thee."** Josh. 2:17 **"And the men said unto her, We *will be* blameless of this thine oath which thou hast made us swear."** Even the heathen King Herod kept the oath he made to Herodias' daughter when she requested the head of John the Baptist in Mat. 14.

Another horrible oath made in the Scripture is found in Judges 11. Jephthah was Israel's ninth Judge and delivered Israel from the Ammonites. The Bible says in Judges 11:30-32, **"And Jephthah vowed a vow unto the LORD, and said, If thou shalt without fail deliver the children of Ammon into mine hands, Then it shall be, that whatsoever cometh forth of the doors of my house to meet me, when I return in peace from the children of Ammon, shall surely be the LORD'S, and I will offer it up for a burnt offering. So Jephthah passed over unto the children of Ammon to fight against them; and the LORD delivered them into his hands."** The student of Scripture might wonder what would possess a man to make such a terrible vow. Nevertheless the vow was made and God granted the victory as given in verse 32. In verse 34 we read that upon his return from the victory his beloved daughter came out of the house to meet him. The man obviously was distraught (vs. 35), but a vow is a vow. He told his daughter,

"I have opened my mouth unto the LORD, and I cannot go back."

Many have taken up the pen to write about this great event and explained that Jephthah did not offer his daughter up as a burnt offering. The Bible plainly says in Judges 11:39, **"And it came to pass at the end of two months, that she returned unto her father, who did with her *according* to his vow which he had vowed: and she knew no man. "** Yes, Jephthah offered his own daughter as a burnt offering. God has never required human sacrifices. He once told Abraham to offer his son Isaac in Gen. 22, but never intended to allow him to carry out the deed. This was a test to see if Abraham would trust the Lord with his son.

Jephthah offered a foolish vow and he was correct in saying he cannot go back on his word to the Lord. But at the same time God is merciful and longsuffering and understands how sinners can utter irrational promises with the best of intentions. Had Jephthah been more familiar with Moses' writings he might have been aware of Lev. 5, where we find a clause about making an oath to do something that he can't do. The instructions are given for what he needs to do for a trespass offering to the Lord. As the Scripture says, it is a sin to vow a vow and not keep it, but thank God He makes provision when we fail to keep His commandments. Jephthah could have refused to offer up his daughter as a burnt offering to the Lord and brought a trespass offering to the priest to offer before God.

Most marriages can be saved from the divorce court. There are Christian counselors available to help families stay together. Again, this paper was not written to encourage divorce. If at all possible God wants us to ride out the storm and stay together. The Apostle Paul has written much for the family and home life. He gives us the tools we need to fight Satan's onslaught against the Christian home. At the same time however the statistics still show about half of the homes don't make it. We want to provide encouragement to these people that God is not all through with you. There is life after divorce. There is hope. There is forgiveness. In many cases Christians get divorced without a Scripturally valid reason. Abandonment, unfaithfulness, and physical and emotional abuse are grounds for divorce and remarriage. Sometimes a divorce can be a sin. Other times it may not necessarily be a sin.

I had a counseling client who told me about a twenty-year period that he was out of fellowship with the Lord. He said that the Lord kept calling for him but he would not return to the fold. Finally the last of few years of that period, the Lord "turned up the heat." During that time the man went through a series of tragic events including a business failure, bankruptcy, and divorce. The man experienced a great spiritual revival after all the drama. This man loves the Lord and is active in his local church. He told me about reading through the Scripture and coming to 1 Cor. 7:27-28: **"Art thou bound unto a wife? seek not to be loosed. Art thou loosed from a wife? seek not a wife. But and if thou marry, thou hast not sinned; and if a virgin marry, she hath not sinned. Nevertheless such shall have trouble in the flesh: but I spare you."** The man said he remarried because he read this passage. It was for him. "Art thou loosed from a wife?" Yes, he was loosed from a wife. Paul says, "seek not a wife. But and if thou marry, thou hast not sinned;" I couldn't disagree with him. That's exactly what the passage says. He also quoted verse 2 of the same chapter, **"Nevertheless, *to avoid* fornication, let every man have his own wife, and let every woman have her own husband."**

This man told me he had no Scriptural grounds for his divorce. He should not have gone through the divorce – it was all his fault. After several years of single life he eventually remarried. He and his wife are happily married and are both proactive servants of the Lord. I asked him how many living wives he had. He looked at me strangely and said, "Just one."

This booklet is for people like this man. No one is without sin. Nobody bats a thousand. All have sinned and come short. Once you put your trust in the shed blood of Jesus Christ every sin you ever committed is under the blood, forgiven, and forgotten by God Almighty – including a divorce with questionable Scriptural grounds. When someone tries to exclude you from serving God in any way (pastor, deacon, etc.) because of being divorced and remarried, they have no Scriptural grounds for their position. We have shown in this paper the correct Bible interpretation of the proper passages. It is a matter of believing God or not believing Him. The goodness and grace of God is sufficient to cover our past mistakes and trespasses. The idea that the Blood of Christ can take care of all our sins EXCEPT divorce is an affront to God's redemptive plan. May the Lord give us His grace and mercy to walk in His service in the days to come.

ABOUT THE AUTHOR

Charlie Edwards received Christ as Savior in 1975 in Lakeland, Florida at the age of 24. His first year as a Christian he read through the Bible once. His second year of salvation he read it through twice and three times in his third year. Since then he has maintained a ravenous appetite for reading God's word.

He moved to Chattanooga, Tennessee in 1978 and earned a bachelor's degree at Tennessee Temple University while working as a broadcast engineer and radio announcer. Since then he earned a Master of Theology, Doctor of Theology, and most recently a Doctor of Philosophy degree in Clinical Christian Counseling. He and his wife Gloria are both Licensed Clinical Pastoral Counselors. He is the President and co-founder of Chattanooga Academy of Christian Counseling, which is a part of Edwards Ministries, Inc.

His first writing project was entitled "The Preacher's Radio Ministry Handbook" and was published in 1983. His first novel, "Caribbean Sentinel," was published by Tate Publishing in 2012. He also wrote a book for Pastors, Worship Leaders, and laymen sound technicians entitled, "Church PA System Handbook."

Currently Dr. Edwards is working on the sequel to the first novel and volume two of Bible White Papers. Also in the works is a re-write of his doctoral dissertation, which will be entitled, "Israel, God's Peculiar Treasure." He is a musician and vocalist and ministers regularly to senior saints in area assisted living facilities.

www.ingramcontent.com/pod-product-compliance
Lightning Source LLC
LaVergne TN
LVHW051113080426
835510LV00018B/2022